PUZZLES
&
PARADOXES

Fascinating Excursions in
Recreational Mathematics

T. H. O'Beirne

DOVER PUBLICATIONS, INC.
Mineola, New York

Bibliographical Note

This Dover edition, first published in 1984 and reissued in 2017, is an unabridged and unaltered republication of the work first published by Oxford University Press, New York and London, in 1965, under the title *Puzzles and Paradoxes*.

Library of Congress Cataloging-in-Publication Data

O'Beirne, T. H.
  Puzzles and Paradoxes.
  Reprint. Originally published: London ; New York : Oxford University Press, 1965.
  Bibliography: p.
  Includes index.
  1. Mathematical recreations. I. Title.
  QA95.02   1984   793.7'4   83-20548
  ISBN-13: 978-0-486-24613-0
  ISBN-10: 0-486-24613-2

Manufactured in the United States by LSC Communications
24613202   2017
www.doverpublications.com

THIS BOOK
IS DEDICATED
TO MY WIFE:

SINE QUA—NON!

Acknowledgement

This is a rearranged and amplified collection of some of the articles of a series with the same title which appeared from January 1961 to February 1962 in the periodical *New Scientist*.

Editorial permission to use this title and material is gratefully acknowledged.

Preface

For the purposes of this book, a PUZZLE will mean any problem whose method of solution is not—we will hope—immediate or obvious: and a PARADOX will mean something whose truth and explanation can ordinarily be established only in the face of some initial sales resistance.

On this basis we seek to consider a variety of topics in recreational mathematics, and to make these attractive and comprehensible without requiring mathematical knowledge appreciably beyond school certificate level. (We may have occasional asides for the more expert—but we expect others to skip these without undue sense of loss.)

An arbitrary multiplication of complications is not the best recipe for a puzzle, as we see it: puzzles and their solutions should rather derive a maximum of effect from an economy of means. Both can then have an aesthetic element—charm, elegance, beauty—which we wish to make apparent; but some of this is absent when solutions give no suggestion of how they could originally have been obtained.

This book does not have a miscellany of problems in one section, with their answers in another: each section deals with a collection of problems of related type, which we discuss in open association with solutions which can be seen to arise directly from a natural analysis. We do this designedly; for we consider the explanations to be as important as the solutions—if not more so. In this way we can proceed by easy stages to more difficult questions which are awkward to handle otherwise; and readers may then find more assistance towards solving other problems.

Some of our topics—ferry problems, counterfeit coins, problems in pouring liquids—will be familiar to many. It may be well to assure the more experienced that we have included much original material, and much not readily available elsewhere. This applies also when we deal with linear arrangements of coloured cubes and with games which are played with heaps of objects or with counters.

Paradoxes (in the strict sense) are rarer than puzzles. We hope that the 25-point geometry will qualify under this heading. In similar vein we have considered the mathematics and astronomy involved in the varying date of Easter (for which we give a simple method of calculation which has not been previously published); and we have reprinted our discussion of the paradox of the unexpected examination.

Preface

To some, we know, the idea that recreations can be mathematical —or mathematics a recreation—may itself seem the supreme puzzle or paradox: we might hope to make a few converts even among these. In many of our topics, the mathematics as such is relatively slight— the real need is more for the careful logical reasoning which some readers may already enjoy when reading detective novels.

Two sections include some detective work of our own. In one case we believe we have exposed a most successful scientific hoax; and in another we have followed a trail 1,500 years back—and half-way round the world—from what at first sight seemed to be a trivial and ephemeral scrap of paper.

In this last pursuit, we found that the annotation *Laetitiae causa*— 'FOR YOUR ENJOYMENT'—was thought appropriate for a collection of mathematical recreations made many centuries ago. This can also indicate our true intent in what now lies before you.

T. H. O'B.

Glasgow, 1965.

Contents

Contents

Contents

PUZZLES
&
PARADOXES

1 *One More River to Cross*

Transport problems and imperial exercises

The first problems we shall discuss are based on difficulties which can arise when travellers have to cross rivers in small rowing-boats. Some of the difficulties derive merely from the limitations of carrying capacity, part of which must continually be reserved for a traveller who will be passenger, crew, and prime mover, all in one: in some cases the problem is further complicated by actual or potential antagonisms between different travellers. Problems of this type may well have once been matters of real practical concern. Similar questions of a more complicated nature can nowadays provide employment for specialists in logistics and operational research.

About 1,000 years ago, some of these questions were offered as problems for sharpening the wits of the young, or as diversions for their presumably more acute elders: probably they circulated by word of mouth for some time before that. Since then they have passed into popular tradition, and intermittently they emerge into print, in a variety of places—unaltered, or trivially rejuvenated—with little to show how old they actually are.

We start with one of the best-known problems of this type, which we can state in the words of Charles Hutton, LL.D., F.R.S., Professor of Mathematics in the Royal Military Academy, Woolwich, who in 1803 included it in the first of his four volumes of *Recreations in Mathematics and Natural Philosophy*:

> Three jealous husbands with their wives having to cross a river at a ferry, find a boat without a boatman; but the boat is so small that it can contain no more than two of them at once. How can these six persons cross the river so that none of the women shall be left in company with any of the men, unless when her husband is present?

This is a translation from the *Problèmes plaisants et délectables* of Claude-Gaspar Bachet, Sieur de Méziriac—a book first published at Lyons in 1612, and still in print today.

This problem may have been first recorded by one or other of two celebrated Englishmen. In one early source it is attributed—probably spuriously—to the Venerable Bede, in the ninth century A.D.: it also appears in a mixed collection of about fifty problems which are included (with more plausibility) in the *Works* of Alcuin of Northumbria, who sent 'some examples of subtlety in Arithmetic, for your enjoyment', to accompany his *Letter LXXXV* to his august pupil, the Emperor Charlemagne.

It is fair—and perhaps enough—to remark that in its original form our problem reflected the dangers and crudities of contemporary behaviour in a way which Bachet evidently thought unsuitable for the polite society of seventeenth-century France. Those who seek more details will find them in the Latin original.

Three men and a boat—not forgetting their wives

Even if no question of jealousy arose, a minimum of nine one-way crossings would be needed to transport six persons across: a back-and-forward trip can take no more than one person across, before the final crossing, since someone must go back with the boat. The jealousy of the husbands in fact involves the party in one additional trip in each direction.

This is fairly easy to establish, for if we rule out all the arrangements which violate imposed conditions, cancel previous progress or merely exchange one couple for another, we find that very little effective choice is left.

At the start, two must embark and one return. Two men cannot leave their wives with the third man, and no man can let his wife cross with another man. If a husband crosses with his wife, he cannot send her back alone to the other men. So a woman must be left on the far side while either her husband or another woman returns with the boat.

No progress is made if only one person now embarks. It is futile merely to visit the first woman, or bring her back, and equally futile for another woman to change places with her. Her husband could cross over, but could not send her back to the other men, and neither of the other men could be allowed to cross over to her.

Two men cannot embark, as one (at least) would be leaving his wife with the remaining man. So a second woman must be taken across, not by her husband, since he would meet the first woman without her husband on the far bank, but necessarily by the third woman; and one woman must return with the boat.

It is now useless for the third woman to cross alone, as she or another woman would have to return. Neither of the men alone, nor the third couple together, can cross to two unaccompanied women. It must be two men, and these the husbands of the two women on the farther bank.

The boat cannot be brought back by the two women, or by one woman, returning to the third man; nor by one man alone, who would leave his wife with another man on the far bank. If the men are not to return uselessly, the boat must be brought back by a married couple.

In this fashion we can go on and solve our problem. But there is a better way.

Half-way through the return crossing last mentioned there is one couple on either bank, and one in mid-stream. Suppose at this point they decided to abandon the whole project. The boat would turn and everything would be done in reverse, back to the beginning.

If, instead, they keep this reversal in mind, but go through its steps with the banks of the river exchanged, as well as the couples on them, the boat will in fact continue to the other side and finally all three couples will be transported to the farther bank.

This will take eleven one-way crossings in all: the five necessary before the symmetrical position arose, the one which produced the symmetrical situation when the boat was in the middle, and five more which are the reflections in space and time of the first five. The latter five cannot be replaced by anything better, since if they could, so could the first five; and we have seen this is impossible.

A solution can be shown diagrammatically as in Table 1a, where capital letters denote men, and corresponding lower-case letters their wives. There must be a minimum of three who can handle a boat, and if there are *only* three, these must be two women and the third woman's husband.

$A C a c$	$\rightarrow$	$B b$	$\rightarrow$	*None*
$A C a c$	$\leftarrow$	B	$\leftarrow$	b
$A B C$	$\rightarrow$	$a c$	$\rightarrow$	b
$A B C$	$\leftarrow$	a	$\leftarrow$	$b c$
$A a$	$\rightarrow$	$B C$	$\rightarrow$	$b c$
$A a$	$\leftarrow$	$B b$	$\leftarrow$	$C c$
$a b$	$\rightarrow$	$A B$	$\rightarrow$	$C c$
$a b$	$\leftarrow$	c	$\leftarrow$	$A B C$
b	$\rightarrow$	$a c$	$\rightarrow$	$A B C$
b	$\leftarrow$	B	$\leftarrow$	$A C a c$
None	$\rightarrow$	$B b$	$\rightarrow$	$A C a c$

TABLE 1*a*

Our solution, like Alcuin's, makes men row rather than women if a choice is possible, but his requires four persons able to row. As with many old problems, there is a traditional mnemonic for the solution, in Latin elegiac verse. Hutton gives this with an English rendering in which the solution is symmetric though that in the Latin is not, and both of these make women row unnecessarily.

With four couples (or more), the first four crossings are no different and leave two women on the far bank. Then either a third woman must

3

be taken across by a fourth who returns; or else the two husbands cross together to their wives, and one couple returns.

With three women (or more) alone on the far bank, no man, no couple, and no pair of men are allowed to cross. Women must transport women until an impasse arises when there are no more: all else will merely undo previous work.

With a couple alone on the far bank there is another impasse. Only a couple can embark, and only a couple can return. With only three couples, two men could cross and leave their wives entirely alone; now at least one strange man would remain with the forsaken wives. The problem with more than three couples is therefore insoluble.

The sixteenth-century Italian mathematician Tartaglia (so named from a speech defect) had the wrong view of this; it is better to remember his claim to be the first to solve a cubic equation.

It may be well to dispel some common misconceptions by emphasizing that the conditions are not merely that a wife must not be alone with another man; and that they do not imply that a husband will be content so long as all other husbands have their wives with them if they are with his wife when he is not present himself. These husbands are jealous in the worst sense of the word: they see their own presence as the *only* security against maltreatment or misbehaviour of their wives. More reasonable husbands would in fact have an easier passage.

When valets or cannibals are second-class passengers

Another traditional problem is almost—but not exactly—equivalent to that of the three jealous husbands with their wives. Again there are two classes of travellers, usually taken to be either three gentlemen each with his lackey or valet: or alternatively three missionaries or explorers accompanied by three cannibals or savages. Here, too, the boat can hold no more than two; and undesirable behaviour is now to be expected if passengers of the first class are ever in a minority to passengers of the second class, in any isolated assembly.

Very little goes wrong if we now assume that the husbands are like the gentlemen (or the missionaries or the explorers), and that the wives are like the valets (or the cannibals or the savages). A preponderance of wives in any company is unacceptable, for some wife must then be apart from her husband in the company of another man, or men: but the conditions of the new problem would permit husbands and wives to associate in equal numbers but not necessarily in married couples. This raises new possibilities.

Actually these involve less change than might be feared: the travelling arrangements are virtually unaffected. No type of journey which was allowed before is now prohibited; and only two types of journeys are freed from prohibition. In one of these, a couple in the boat are travelling between isolated couples on either bank, just as in the journey which forms the mid-point of the previous solution: but either two or all three of the couples concerned can now be unmarried. In the other type of journey an unmarried couple are in the boat, and all the others are on the same bank.

The first possibility provides an alternative way of making a crossing at the half-way stage, and the second possibility allows the wife who makes the first or last crossing to be ferried by any of the men—not by her husband only, or by one of the other wives. Apart from this, the optimum programme must proceed as before: the only difference is that interchange of husbands may take place, and similarly of wives, in ways which now are considered to be immaterial. If the husbands who treat their wives like this are then considered to be gentlemen, and not to be savages, we obtain the solutions of the other problems.

It is of some interest to consider what other possibilities are open to our travellers, in addition to crossing successfully together. There is one obvious impossibility: they cannot all be on one bank, separated from the boat. All other divisions which do not involve prohibited assemblies can be achieved, with one exception—wives or savages can not be abandoned on either bank without a boat: which seems only elementary justice.

Readers may now wish to consider how best to leave varied selections of personnel on either bank, with or without the boat. We shall return to these questions later.

Tribulations of a father of five

Our next problem is one which we composed for the purposes of a prize competition.

A father rowing a boat has to transport his five sons across a river, with a minimum number of one-way crossings, such that finally all the children have had an identical number of one-way trips. The boat will hold the father and not more than two children; no pair of children of immediately neighbouring ages can be left together in the absence of their father, or they will start a fight; but children more separated in age will content themselves with more peaceful occupations. Only the father is allowed to row; and he may or may not be able to stop fights in the boat.

Here is the prize-winning solution which came from Mr. A. J. Casson, then in the Sixth Form, Latymer Upper School.

'Let the sons be labelled A, B, C, D, E in descending order of age, and let the starting-point and destination be referred to as the first bank and second bank respectively.

'The first move must be to take *B* and *D* to the second bank. For, if *B* is not taken, *A* and *C* must both be taken to prevent them from fighting *B*, leaving *D* and *E* together. Similarly, *D* must be taken on the first trip. The last move in any solution must be to bring *B* and *D* to join their brothers on the second bank, for similar reasons. Therefore *B* and *D* must make at least three crossings: the first trip to the second bank, a return crossing at some time, and the final trip, also to the second bank.

'If peace is to be preserved, this means that each son must make at least three crossings, so at least fifteen man-crossings must be made altogether, not counting those made by the father. Only two boys can be taken on each trip, so at least eight one-way crossings are required. Eight crossings would leave the boat on the first bank, so at least nine one-way journeys are in fact necessary.

'The table below [Table 1*b*] gives a solution in which nine crossings are made, three by each son, and it has been shown that the problem cannot be solved with fewer crossings. Therefore this solution completes the manoeuvre in the minimum number of trips. It can be seen from the table that two rival brothers never cross the river together, so it does not matter if the father cannot manage the oars and his sons at the same time.

No. of Trip	First bank		Sons in Boat		Second bank
1	*A, C, E*	→	*B, D*	→	*None*
2	*A, C, E*	←	*B*	←	*D*
3	*B, E*	→	*A, C*	→	*D*
4	*B, E*	←	*A, D*	←	*C*
5	*B, D*	→	*A, E*	→	*C*
6	*B, D*	←	*C, E*	←	*A*
7	*B, D*	→	*C, E*	→	*A*
8	*B, D*	←	*None*	←	*A, C, E*
9	*None*	→	*B, D*	→	*A, C, E*

TABLE 1*b*

'It will now be shown that there are eight solutions. We have seen that fifteen man-crossings must be made in nine boatloads, and that on the penultimate move *A*, *C*, *E* must be on the second bank but the boat must be on the first bank. To achieve this the boat must be returned to the first bank on some trips without a full complement, and exactly three man-journeys must have been sacrificed in this way. But only three can be sacrificed if the problem is to be solved in the minimum number of moves. Therefore no solution can include a journey from the first to the second bank without two passengers on board.

'The first move is forced, as we have seen. *B* and *D* cannot return immediately, as this would restore the original position and *B* and *D* would now have to make five crossings altogether. Therefore either *B* or *D* returns, or the boat must return light. If *B* returns, the next move is forced, for *B* cannot move again until the final journey, so the only way to separate *A*, *B*, and *C* is to take *A* and *C* across.

'On the fourth move *C* and *D* must be separated. If *D* returns alone, *E* is the only one who can make the fifth crossing to the second bank. But we have seen that such a move is bound to fail. If *C* makes the fourth crossing alone, *C* and *E* must make the fifth trip. *C* cannot move again, having made three trips, therefore the sixth crossing must be made by *D*, possibly with *A* or *E*. But *B* and *D* cannot move until the ninth trip, therefore two boys cannot cross to the second bank on the seventh trip. Therefore this fourth move also fails. If *A* and *C* cross together, they must return on the fifth trip, completing their three crossings. Therefore *D* must make the next trip alone, which fails for the same reason as before.

'If *A* and *D* make the fourth crossing, the solution already given is obtained. *B* and *D* must stay on the first bank until the final trip, therefore the fifth move is forced. *A* has now completed his three crossings, so the sixth trip must be made by one or both of *C* and *E*. Whoever crosses must return immediately, therefore both *C* and *E* must take a joy-ride to the first bank and back. All those on the second bank have now made three crossings, so the boat must return light to pick up *B* and *D* and complete the operation.

'If, from the fourth move onwards, *A* and *C* are interchanged, a solution is obtained in which *C* and *D* make the fourth move, and the above reasoning shows that all subsequent moves are forced. However, the father would not like this method, since it requires him to watch *C* and *D* while rowing the boat.

'We could equally well have taken *A*, *B*, *C*, *D*, *E* to be in ascending order of age, and applied the same reasoning. This would have the effect of interchanging *A* with *E* and *B* with *D*, so all the solutions in which *D* makes the second journey can be obtained from those already given, by this substitution. Thus we have four solutions so far.

'There remains the possibility that the boat returns light on the second move. If this is the case, there must be a passenger on the eighth journey, since only three man-journeys can be wasted. Therefore all such solutions can be obtained from the four known ones by reversing the order of the moves and interchanging the river banks.

'Thus the father has a choice of eight methods of crossing the river. If he is not prepared to risk overturning the boat while stopping a fight, his choice is cut down to four methods.'

Some statistics and other diversions

The competition produced a variety of other solutions, both correct and incorrect. Figure 1*A* is a column graph of the frequency with which various minimum numbers of crossings were thought necessary; it may require a little explanation.

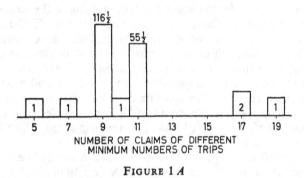

NUMBER OF CLAIMS OF DIFFERENT
MINIMUM NUMBERS OF TRIPS

FIGURE 1 *A*

One entrant—whose name might account for some unfamiliarity with English—solved the problem in five crossings, with one trip per boy. This followed with exact logic from a single wrong assumption: that 'next' oldest and 'next' youngest brothers have two of intermediate age between them! The seven-trip solution was from a father of five himself, who maintained that nothing could stop all squabbling, and the father might as well do as little rowing as would take them all across without an actual fight. The odd halves represent an entrant who sent an after-thought correcting his first entry: the unique even-number claim arose from not counting a trip with the boat empty.

One entrant prefaced a 'more impersonal analysis' by a vivid mono-logue:

'Come along, Brian and Derek, I'd better take you first—at least the others will keep the peace while you're away (1). Brian, you come back with me to keep an eye on Eric (2) and now I'll take Alan and Charles across (3). Charles, you stay here, I'll take Alan and Derek back with me (4). Alan, lift Eric over the mud and stop him crawling overboard during this trip (5). Now all I've got to do is to fetch Brian and Derek. Eric, what are you crying about now? But why must you all want the same number of trips when Daddy's tired? Oh, all right—I'll give you and Charles an extra ride there and back (6, 7). Now I will go over (8) and fetch Brian and Derek (9).'

This identifies a minimum-trip solution. Another entrant gave a similar solution in verse, from which we quoted eight lines:

> All sons can't be moved with only one ride,
> While two bring them back to their starting side.
> Three rides are the least which will meet the case.
> So fifteen passengers Dad has to face.
>
> As his boat is small, he takes only two;
> Eight trips are the least he is able to do.
> But to land them all on the other shore,
> An odd number, nine, he will need, or more.

We thought these lines would interest an entrant who betrayed some niggling doubt: 'Two is impossible of solution (I hope!) but three trips for each boy . . . seems possible'; likewise another who took eleven lines and two sets of alternatives to complete an otherwise correct solution by showing why eight moves would not do!

Boats and wolves and cabbages

The competition problem was a natural extension of another one which accompanies the problem of the jealous husbands in the collection attributed to Alcuin, and elsewhere.

In its traditional form, this other problem involves a traveller with a wolf (or dog), a goat and a basket of cabbages. He can take only one of the three into a boat with him at any one time. If left alone, the wolf will eat the goat, or the goat the cabbages: but the wolf is strictly non-vegetarian. The traveller is to cross a river with animal and vegetable possessions still intact.

His problem is then equivalent to that of a father with *three* sons, of whom the eldest and youngest form the only peaceful couple in his absence, if he can take no more than *one* son with him in the boat, and does all the rowing himself.

The sons can be made to correspond to the wolf, the goat, and the cabbages, in order either of increasing or of diminishing ages. It is sufficient to denote the sons by numerals 1, 2, 3 and to assume that a pair whose numerals differ only by 1 may not be left together without their parent. Any solution expressed in terms of the numerals is then capable of two alternative interpretations, and any solution remains a solution if we interchange the numerals 1 and 3 throughout, leaving 2 unaltered.

A solution also remains a solution if the passenger lists for successive voyages are taken in an exactly reversed order, for this too will transport the whole party from one bank to the other with all conditions respected. In both this case and the last, the resulting solutions may or may not be different from the one from which they were derived: this depends on whether certain forms of symmetry are absent or present in the solutions concerned.

The traditional problem (or its equivalent for the three sons) can fairly readily be solved by straightforward reasoning only; but it can conveniently be used to illustrate a method which is of still greater service in the five-son problem which is our ultimate objective.

We first consider all the different sets of passengers who may be in the boat: for each of these sets we then note the corresponding absentees, and determine to what extent their mutual antagonisms restrict the ways in which they may be divided into parties on opposite banks, if the boat is to make an allowable crossing with the set of passengers first considered.

We need not take explicit account of the father, as he is always in the boat. We shall denote the sons by numerals, in age order, and we can use 0 to indicate the absence of all the sons either from the boat or from one of the banks. If any sons are together, we shall put their numerals together without separating commas, and we shall use a dash to indicate a division between sets located on opposite banks.

In the three-son problem there are then four possible passenger lists: 0, 1, 2, or 3. For 0, the others must be divided 13—2; for 1 the division must be 2—3, and for 3 it must be 1—2. Only for 2 is there an alternative; the others may then be split either 1—3 or 0—13.

We can now determine who must be together with their father at the opposite ends of any crossing: we have only to attach the symbols of the passengers to the symbols on *both* sides of the dashes, in the symbols expressing allowable modes of division of the others. The *repeated* symbols then indicate the passenger list for a voyage specified by a new symbol.

For the three-son problem, the possible voyages in the order considered above are then denoted by the symbols 13—2, 12—13, 13—23, 12—23, 2—123: these denote voyages such that if the father is on one bank together with sons whose numerals are *either* to the left *or* to the right of the dash, in one of these symbols, he can make a trip after which he will find himself on the *other* bank with sons whose numerals are those on the *other* side of the dash, in the same symbol; and symbols common to both sides indicate which son (if any) must accompany him on his trip.

Different possible voyages may still involve identical parties at one extremity of each; the next step is to use the symbols to construct a connected network where each set of sons who may be temporary companions to their father ashore is represented inside a circle, two circles being joined by a junction line if and only if there is a permissible voyage which can change the father's companions from the one set of sons to the other set. Letter references can be given to the circles, and passenger lists can be indicated on the junction lines concerned.

Figure 1*B* shows this done for the three-son problem. We note that the father starts with companions 123, and travels to a different bank with every voyage; he must finish with the whole party on the other bank, so he must make an *odd* number of voyages, and again have companions 123 at the finish. This means we have to find a route from *M* back to *M* which passes over an odd number of junction lines.

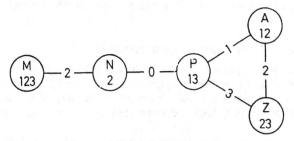

FIGURE 1 *B*

Lines traversed in both directions do nothing to help (or hinder) us in this aim: the essential requirement is to make a circuit, somewhere, over an odd number of lines. Here there is only one possible circuit of this type.

The minimum effort thus requires seven one-way trips, corresponding to a path over seven lines from *M* back to *M*—two to reach the triangular circuit, three to traverse it, and two more to return to the starting-point. Such a path is specified by the route *MNPAZPNM*: the sets of companions change in a succession 123—2—13—12—23—13—2—123, and the passengers on successive voyages are 2, 0, 1, 2, 3, 0, 2. Taking the circuit in the other direction is equivalent to taking the voyages in a reversed order, and either change is equivalent to reversing the correspondence between symbols and ages.

$$
\begin{array}{ccccc}
13 & \rightarrow & 2 & \rightarrow & 0 \\
13 & \leftarrow & 0 & \leftarrow & 2 \\
3 & \rightarrow & 1 & \rightarrow & 2 \\
3 & \leftarrow & 2 & \leftarrow & 1 \\
2 & \rightarrow & 3 & \rightarrow & 1 \\
2 & \leftarrow & 0 & \leftarrow & 13 \\
0 & \rightarrow & 2 & \rightarrow & 13 \\
\end{array}
$$

TABLE 1 *c*

There are thus only two different minimum-effort solutions. These are given by Table 1*c*, either read normally, or else from the bottom to the top with all arrows reversed. All other solutions involve waste effort by retracing steps or by adding unnecessary double circuits of the triangle, over and above the single circuit which is both necessary and sufficient.

In the minimum solution, the son 2 crosses three times, and his brothers only once each. If the children demand equal treatment which we can assume to be superfluous in the traditional problem, the most economical procedure is to give each of 1 and 3 a triple crossing, with an otherwise unnecessary back-and-forward trip, when the time comes for them to be passengers. This then requires eleven one-way crossings in all.

How father can make his connexions

We can now apply a similar procedure to the five-son problem. Here there are sixteen possible passenger lists—0, five singles and ten pairs. This leads to thirteen possible sets of sons who may be companions to their father ashore: these are connected by twenty-eight permissible voyages.

With a little ingenuity—and attention to the symmetry deriving from possible age-reversal—these can be combined into a connected network as in Figure 1C, where dotted lines have been used to distinguish

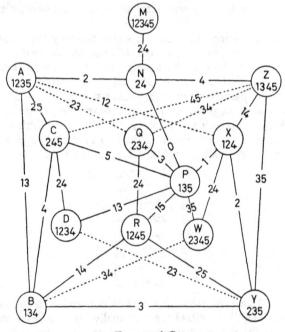

FIGURE 1 C

voyages with antagonistic passengers. Here, too, a solution must correspond to a route from M back to M over an *odd* number of junction lines. The next junction point to either end must be N, and the one next to this must be one of A, P, or Z.

We next note that if all are to cross, not only the father (and the boat) must make an odd number of one-way trips, but also each individual son must make an odd number of one-way trips. We can then use the diagram to find how to give them the impartial treatment which alone will content them.

The first and last trips must in both cases transport the same passengers—2 and 4—who are thus guaranteed three trips at least. The best hope for an impartial solution is to achieve this with only three trips for every son, with a total of fifteen individual passages in all.

The figure shows that the first two one-way trips and the last two, taken together, must provide either four, five, or six of the necessary fifteen passages. The best hope is that a solution exists for a case where the number is five or six, with the other ten or nine provided in five more one-way crossings. So we look to see if there is an impartial solution involving only nine one-way trips in all.

Two steps from either end must find us at one of the points A, P, or Z, and our impartial solution must involve a five-step connexion of two of these points.

The alternative of connecting one with itself can be dismissed: if this were A (or Z), four passages would already be booked for the son 2 (or 4); if it were P, only four passages in all would be provided by the two first and two last voyages together, and it would be impossible to provide another eleven in only five trips with a limit of two passengers per trip.

If the two points are A and Z, both 2 and 4 are already guaranteed their three passages, and they cannot be passengers again. This forces the route from A to Z through the points B and Y, giving three passages to 3, but only one each to 1 and 5; and neither of the latter can be given more, by giving them a triple instead of a single trip, without giving 3 an excess. We here have a seven-trip non-impartial solution which cannot be extended to the impartial solution which we want.

The only hope is now the case of A and P (or the case of P and Z, which is identical after age reversal). When A is included, three trips are already booked for 2, so he cannot be a passenger again; and 4 is already committed to two trips, so he can have only one more. Only five passages are provided here by the first two and last two one-way trips jointly. The five-step join of A and P must therefore involve two passengers on every trip.

This forces the continuation from A to be either $ABRP$ or $ABWP$, closing on P in only three steps. We thus obtain two more seven-trip non-impartial solutions, given by the routes *MNABRPNM* and *MNABWPNM*.

When we examine these to see how the individual passages are distributed, we find that all sons have three passages except 3 and 5 in the first case, and 1 and 5 in the second; those excepted have only one, so far.

Fortunately, one of the two possible trips with passengers 3 and 5 involves at one end a set of companions who are already assembled at one stage of the non-impartial solution, in the first case, and the same is true of the unique trip with passengers 1 and 5, in the second case.

By replacing *P* by *PWP* in the first case, and by *PRP* in the second, we can then satisfy all the conditions for a nine-trip impartial solution. This means that at a suitable time two sons are taken forward and back across the river, in an otherwise unnecessary trip which achieves the impartial distribution demanded.

The second case involves the dotted join *BW*, and a trip where the passengers are 3 and 4; this solution is available only if discipline can be maintained in the boat.

If we assume this is impossible, our problem has four solutions only (instead of eight). These four are essentially equivalent, being the one shown in Table 1*d*, together with three others derived from this by reversal of voyage order, or age order, or both.

135	→	24	→	0
135	←	2	←	4
25	→	13	→	4
25	←	14	←	3
24	→	15	→	3
24	←	35	←	1
24	→	35	→	1
24	←	0	←	135
0	→	24	→	135

TABLE 1*d*

In the course of our work we incidentally found three (non-impartial) solutions in seven trips. No solution is possible in fewer than seven trips, since Figure 1*C* has no three-step circuit in which *N* is included. It is not unduly difficult to use the figure to show that there are in all forty different seven-trip solutions, of which twenty-four involve no danger of trouble in the boat.

Table 1*d* is equivalent to Table 1*b*, with an alteration of notation; and much of our argument repeats what was given in Mr. Casson's solution.

Odd paths for missionaries

We can employ a diagram of similar type in the problem of the three missionaries and the three cannibals. Here we can use a symbol like pq/rs to denote that p missionaries and q cannibals are on one bank, and r missionaries and s cannibals on the other. We then must have $p+r = q+s = 3$, for numbers satisfying $p \geqslant q$ unless $p = 0$, and $r \geqslant s$ unless $r = 0$. There are then only five allowable divisions, of the types 33/00, 32/01, 31/02, 30/03, and 22/11. (Note that a division 11/22 means the same as a division 22/11, for instance.)

We next can attach a symbol $\ddagger$ to one pair or the other, to indicate which party has possession of the boat. This leads to ten arrangements which are admissible: but with 33/00$\ddagger$ all transportation is impossible, and with $\ddagger$30/03 it is suicidal. The eight remaining possibilities are interconnected as in Figure 1D, where passengers are indicated for each voyage in the same manner as for parties on either bank—first a number of missionaries, then a number of cannibals.

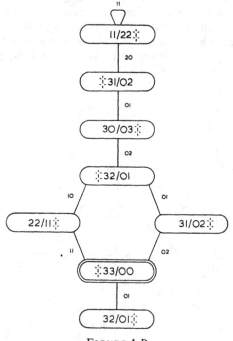

FIGURE 1 D

The important feature here is the small loop which connects the symbol 11/22$\ddagger$ with itself, at the top. This gives the only way of introducing the odd number which is required. We must make an eleven-step trip from ‡33/00 back to itself, including the loop, for an optimum solution. There are alternative ways of arranging the first two trips, and the last two.

A diagram of precisely similar structure applies to the three jealous husbands with their wives, if we assume that a symbol 11 always refers to a married couple.

From our diagram we can readily solve a variety of other problems. The most awkward problem is to leave a single cannibal behind, with a boat: for all must cross first, and then send him back. If a married couple are to stay behind and have the use of the boat, this requires only one trip fewer than the complete crossing.

On and on, up and up . . .

To proceed further in similar fashion, we must increase the capacity of the boat. In Figure 1*E* we show the diagram for four pairs, for a boat which can hold three passengers but no more. Double lines indicate trips where the boat has a full load. A circuit with an odd number of steps cannot be secured without using the path represented by the horizontal double line at the top of the diagram, and a minimum of nine trips is required if all are to cross. No solution here can have symmetry about a half-way point.

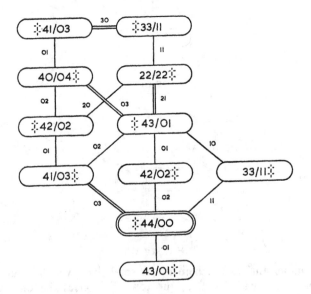

FIGURE 1 *E*

Table 1*e* exhibits a particular solution which meets the added complications of pairing husbands and wives. There are other solutions of this type: we choose the one which should take least time, assuming that all passengers row and that the boat goes faster for an increased number rowing.

$$
\begin{array}{rcl}
A\,B\,C\,D\,d & \rightarrow\ a\,b\,c & \rightarrow\ None \\
A\,B\,C\,D\,d & \leftarrow\ b\,c & \leftarrow\ a \\
A\,B\,C\,D & \rightarrow\ b\,c\,d & \rightarrow\ a \\
A\,B\,C\,D & \leftarrow\ d & \leftarrow\ a\,b\,c \\
D\,d & \rightarrow\ A\,B\,C & \rightarrow\ a\,b\,c \\
D\,d & \leftarrow\ C\,c & \leftarrow\ A\,B\,a\,b \\
d & \rightarrow\ C\,D\,c & \rightarrow\ A\,B\,a\,b \\
d & \leftarrow\ b\,c & \leftarrow\ A\,B\,C\,D\,a \\
None & \rightarrow\ b\,c\,d & \rightarrow\ A\,B\,C\,D\,a
\end{array}
$$

TABLE 1 e

Figure 1*F* deals with five couples, again with room for no more than three passengers in the boat. Circuits with an odd number of steps must here include the loop at the top of the figure, and the **complete**

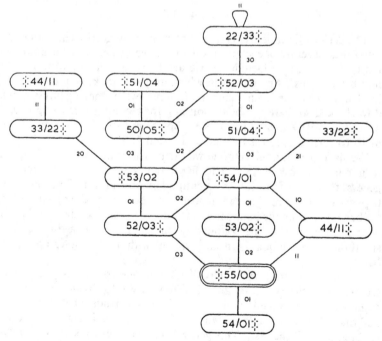

FIGURE 1 F

crossing requires a minimum of eleven trips. Dudeney considered this case for husbands and wives, introducing the sacrifice of chivalry to speed, to provide faster trips with larger crews. In Table 1*f* we give a solution which meets conjugal difficulties. There are alternatives to either side of the mid-way point, and symmetric solutions are possible here: we give an asymmetric solution which indicates the alternatives. One alternative—but not the other—would allow *all* the wives to abandon their husbands simultaneously!

$A\,B\,C\,D\,E\,d\,e$	$\rightarrow$	$a\,b\,c$	$\rightarrow$	*None*
$A\,B\,C\,D\,E\,d\,e$	$\leftarrow$	$b\,c$	$\leftarrow$	a
$A\,B\,C\,D\,E\,e$	$\rightarrow$	$b\,c\,d$	$\rightarrow$	a
$A\,B\,C\,D\,E\,e$	$\leftarrow$	d	$\leftarrow$	$a\,b\,c$
$D\,E\,d\,e$	$\rightarrow$	$A\,B\,C$	$\rightarrow$	$a\,b\,c$
$D\,E\,d\,e$	$\leftarrow$	$C\,c$	$\leftarrow$	$A\,B\,a\,b$
$c\,d\,e$	$\rightarrow$	$C\,D\,E$	$\rightarrow$	$A\,B\,a\,b$
$c\,d\,e$	$\leftarrow$	$a\,b$	$\leftarrow$	$A\,B\,C\,D$
$d\,e$	$\rightarrow$	$a\,b\,c$	$\rightarrow$	$A\,B\,C\,D$
$d\,e$	$\leftarrow$	c	$\leftarrow$	$A\,B\,C\,D\,E\,a\,b$
None	$\rightarrow$	$c\,d\,e$	$\rightarrow$	$A\,B\,C\,D\,E\,a\,b$

TABLE 1*f*

The design of our figures is such that each one-way trip will change the horizontal level by one step, up or down, everywhere but for a unique path which must be included if we are to have a circuit with an odd number of steps. Any circuit in which all paths make unit changes of level must have an even number of steps—what goes up must come down!—and so there can be no solution for a complete crossing unless we can arrange either to introduce a horizontal step (as in Figure 1*E*), or to traverse a loop (as in Figures 1*D* and 1*F*).

We have seen that eleven one-way trips will transport three couples in a boat for two persons, and five couples in a boat for three: in general they will suffice for $2n-1$ couples in a boat for n. Four one-way trips with women rowing can deposit n unaccompanied women on the far bank and bring the boat back; one more trip can take their husbands over to them; and if one couple now embarks, there is a symmetrical situation when the boat is in mid-stream, with $n-1$ couples on either bank.

Nine one-way trips will suffice if there is one couple less. The first six are as in the last case, and this now serves to divide the couples equally on the two banks: all the remaining husbands must then cross, and one of them can take his wife, if he likes; one wife can then return to fetch over all the rest. This generalizes the nine-trip solution which we found for the four couples.

We feel that readers can now handle—and even invent—ferry problems for themselves. Those who wish a simple task can consider how a regiment of soldiers can cross a river with the help of two small boys, assuming there is a boat which can take two boys or one man, but no more. Those who are more ambitious can consider benefits which can be derived from the presence of one or more islands in mid-stream—especially if the travellers are polygamists, or engaged couples who have to show respect for propriety by not being alone together.

A map is a help, if you can find one

A diagram of the type we have considered can be of use in many other types of problem also, of which some will occur later in this book. We can consider many puzzles to be the equivalent of planning a route through a sequence of points which are interconnected by various paths; and our task can be the easier if we can find and make use of an appropriate map. With our ferry problems, any path can be traversed in either direction: in some other applications we may have to consider one-way paths. In practical traffic problems, and in other equivalent problems, we may require to introduce a distance or a capacity associated with each path.

An important branch of modern mathematics is concerned with the general properties of diagrams of these types. (In this context they are termed 'graphs'—a usage quite distinct from the more usual reference to curves drawn on squared paper.) From recreational beginnings, as here, this has grown to a point where it now has important practical applications in fields as diverse as quantum mechanics and business management.

2 *False Coins and Trial Balances*

A man of principle, and some others

Good specimens of coins of identical design are perhaps as nearly indistinguishable objects as any which we ordinarily handle. False coins are met less often: but gold coins have been clipped, in times past, and coiners have included lighter metals in them in excess proportion; silver coins have similarly had the heavier admixture of lead, or the lighter admixture of tin, to reduce costs of unofficial reproduction. Practical difficulties usually prevent an ideal combination of light and heavy alloy, so it is reasonable to assume that counterfeit productions will betray themselves by a difference of weight.

A related problem is believed once to have had the attention of Archimedes: we hope we can discuss others here with no danger that readers will leap from their baths to run through the streets with a cry of 'Eureka'. (We later refer to a periodical of this title, but it is more readily obtained by postal subscription.)

False coins in two World Wars

We shall consider a series of problems which have become increasingly sophisticated in type in recent years. In a problem which apparently dates from the First World War, two weighings on a beam balance without weights were to find whether eight coins were all good, or whether there was a unique bad coin among them, on the assumption that any bad coin would necessarily be deficient in weight. The modern phase begins with the consideration of a similar problem which allows three weighings for twelve coins, when a bad coin may be either light or heavy. This variant seems to have arisen during the Second World War: the first published account which we know is one by Howard Grossman in 1945.

It has been alleged that this latter problem diverted so much war-time scientific effort that there was serious consideration of a proposal to inflict compensating damage by dropping it in enemy territory. Since then, so much else has been published on this topic that an addition requires some justification: we hope to give a treatment which is more comprehensive than some others, with some original features; and we shall go on to consider some related problems which have only recently appeared.

A solution of the first problem is relatively simple. The eight coins are divided into a pair and two groups of three: the two groups of three are then weighed against each other. If they balance, this will prove six coins to be good, and leave the pair as the only two which are suspect: these two can then be weighed against each other to see whether one is lighter than the other, or not—and if so, which. If the two groups of three do not balance, there must then be a bad coin among the three in the lighter group: weighing any two of these three against each other will then show which—if either—is light, or whether the light one is the third one of the three.

In this solution, the result of the first weighing is made to discriminate between different ways of making the second weighing; but this is not necessary. We can label the coins *A, B, C, D, E, F, G, H* and decide that in all circumstances we shall first weigh *A, B, C* against *F, G, H* and then weigh *A, D, F* against *C, E, H*. Whatever happens in the first weighing, there will be two known coins in each pan at the second weighing which have been freed from suspicion; it would make no difference if these four were removed, and this would produce the solution which we first gave.

For twelve coins with three weighings, when the bad coin—if any— may be either light or heavy, we again can have solutions of two types, as in our first problem. We can arrange to note previous results, and weigh diminishing numbers of coins in later weighings—the more easily to pick out and remove the bad coin, perhaps; or we can prescribe all weighings in advance, the better to delegate the work to a less intelligent operator, who will report his findings for interpretation by a superior. There are merits either way—so we shall give a solution of each type: but we wish to dispose of a related matter, first.

Tempting, but wrong . . .

An idea which may at first present itself in the second problem is that with three possible results in each of three weighings—a balance, or an unbalance either way—we have twenty-seven possibilities overall; so we might hope to associate these with twenty-seven other possibilities, involving thirteen coins, instead of twelve: namely that all are good, and that each in turn can have either type of defect.

It is of some interest to show why this will not work. The reason is that the two later weighings cannot jointly discriminate among more than nine cases which are still at issue: but no way of arranging the first weighing can avoid the possibility that at least ten cases may remain. If we weigh five coins against five, with three coins off the scales, an unbalance will leave five coins suspect for one defect and the other five for the other defect; with four coins against four, with five off, a balance will leave five coins suspect for both defects, with a further possibility that all are in fact good: all other divisions are still more unfavourable.

Similar arguments apply to larger numbers of coins, when there are more than three weighings. We must start by putting doubtful coins into both pans in equal numbers, and if they do not balance, an even number of cases will remain to be examined: the remaining weighings provide for discriminating a number of cases which is a power of 3, and therefore odd; resolving this difficulty is impossible if there are no possibilities to spare.

Putting twelve coins through a sieve

In Table 2*a* we give a solution of the first type, where weighings are not prescribed in advance, but results of earlier weighings are used to reduce the number of coins weighed later, to single out the false coin—if any—at the end. The table gives the weighing directions and has full interpretation instructions, to discriminate among twelve coins in three weighings.

The treatment after initial balance is taken from a solution which has been specified diagrammatically by H. Steinhaus in the English-language edition of *Mathematical Snapshots*. (In his Polish edition he has given one of the other type.) The treatment after initial unbalance follows a general treatment of both types of solution—for all numbers of coins—given in 1947 by C. A. B. Smith.

False coins and the Cartesian Method

To find a solution with weighings prescribed in advance, for twelve coins and three weighings, we can proceed as follows.

If we use symbols *L*, *R*, *O* to denote respectively that the left or right pan descended, or that there was a balance, in some particular weighing, there are twenty-seven different arrangements available for results corresponding to different possibilities. There must always be equal numbers of coins in the two pans, so that a balance can show that all the weighed coins are good, with an unbalance indicating that there is a bad coin among those being weighed: and the case *OOO* must be reserved for the case where all coins are good.

Twelve coins each liable to have either type of error correspond to twenty-four further possibilities, so there are two arrangements to spare. Two are obviously specialized, and thus form a natural choice for the rejections: those with all three results the same, *LLL* or *RRR*. We decide to forgo these; and this then prohibits us from putting any coin in the same pan in all three weighings.

IF TWELVE COINS ARE ALL GOOD, OR CAN HAVE ONE HEAVIER OR LIGHTER THAN THE OTHERS:

(A): Weigh four coins against four coins, with four coins off the scales.

UNBALANCE proves that the four unweighed coins are good, and rules out one type of error for each of the others; those in the descending pan are now suspect for overweight only, and those in the ascending pan for underweight only: and one of them *must* be a bad coin. *Proceed to (B1).*

BALANCE proves that all the eight weighed coins are good: the four unweighed coins are still suspect for both types of error, but *may* all be good. *Proceed to (B2).*

(B1): After UNBALANCE in (A), place two overweight suspects and one underweight suspect in each pan, leaving two underweight suspects off the scales.

UNBALANCE reduces the doubtful coins to the two overweight suspects from the descending pan, together with the underweight suspect from the ascending pan; and one of these three must be a bad coin. *Proceed to (C1).*

BALANCE reduces the doubtful coins to the two unweighed underweight suspects, one of which must be a bad coin. *Proceed to (C2).*

(B2): After a BALANCE in (A), weigh three doubtful coins against three of the proved good coins, leaving one doubtful coin off the scales.

UNBALANCE reduces the doubtful coins to three which are now suspect for only one of the types of error—overweight if they descended, underweight if they ascended: and one of these is definitely a bad coin. *Proceed to (C3).*

BALANCE proves all coins good except the unweighed doubtful coin: this may have either type of error, or none. *Proceed to (C4).*

(C1): After UNBALANCE in (B1), weigh the two remaining overweight suspects against each other.

UNBALANCE identifies a heavy coin in the descending pan.

BALANCE identifies the unweighed underweight suspect as a light coin.

(C2): After a BALANCE in (B1), weigh the two remaining underweight suspects against each other.

UNBALANCE identifies a light coin in the ascending pan.

BALANCE is here *impossible.*

(C3): After UNBALANCE in (B2), weigh two suspects against each other, leaving one suspect off the scales.

UNBALANCE identifies the bad coin, since the type of error is known.

BALANCE proves the third suspect to have the known type of error.

(C4): After a BALANCE in (B2), weigh the sole remaining doubtful coin against a proved good coin.

UNBALANCE proves the doubtful coin is bad, and identifies its type of error.

BALANCE proves that all coins were in fact good coins.

TABLE 2 *a*

Every coin must be weighed at least once: but coins can in fact be weighed once, or twice, or three times. If a coin is weighed three times, it must be twice in one pan, and once in the other, since *LLL* and *RRR* are ruled out. If a coin is weighed twice, it may be twice in the same pan, or else in different pans on the two occasions.

Suppose we divide the coins into four sets of three: *A*, *B*, *C*; *D*, *E*, *F*; *G*, *H*, *K*; *X*, *Y*, *Z*. Consider the scheme of Table 2*b* and interpret it thus: the numbers are to indicate how many of the coins in the set corresponding to each row will be in the location corresponding to each column, in every one of the weighings. It will be seen that the arrangement makes the total numbers of coins equal for both the pans, in all three weighings.

	Off scales	*Left pan*	*Right pan*
A B C	0	1	2
D E F	1	2	0
G H K	2	0	1
X Y Z	1	1	1

TABLE 2*b*

In each of the first three rows the number 1 appears once only: the coin in the location corresponding to the column where the 1 appears is to be the first, second, or third in the set, in the first, second, and third weighings, respectively. In the case of the fourth set, we arrange to make the coins *X*, *Y*, *Z* proceed in cyclic order through the positions 'off scales', 'left pan', 'right pan', with the first, second, and third coins *off the scales*, in the first, second, and third weighings respectively. This leads to directions as in Table 2*c*.

	With these coins off the scales	*put these in the left pan*	*and these in the right pan*
I	*D H K X*	*A E F Z*	*B C G Y*
II	*E K G Y*	*B F D X*	*C A H Z*
III	*F G H Z*	*C D E Y*	*A B K X*

TABLE 2*c*

After this we can interpret our results as follows, in terms of the rows of our earlier table:

If there is no balance in any weighing, the bad coin was weighed three times, and must be from the set corresponding to the *first* row. There must either be two *L*'s and one *R*, or two *R*'s and one *L* (since *LLL* and *RRR* are impossible). In the first event there is a *light* coin, in the

24

second there is a *heavy* coin. The coin is *A*, *B*, or *C* according as the odd result was in the first, second, or third weighing.

With only one balance, and the other two results the same, the bad coin was weighed twice and was in the same pan in both weighings, so it must be from the set in the *second* row. With two *L*'s it is *heavy*, with two *R*'s it is *light*. The coin is *D*, *E*, or *F* according as the odd result was in the first, second, or third weighing.

With two balances and only one unbalance, the bad coin was weighed only once, and must be from the set in the *third* row. With one *L* it is *light*, with one *R* it is *heavy*. The coin is *G*, *H*, or *K* according as the odd result was in the first, second, or third weighing.

With one balance, and the other two results different, the bad coin was weighed twice, in different pans, and must be from the set in the *fourth* row. For results *OLR*, *ROL*, or *LRO*—in cyclic order *O*, *L*, *R*—the bad coin is *heavy*: for results *ORL*, *LOR*, *RLO* (in the opposite cyclic order) it is *light*. The coin is *X*, *Y*, or *Z* according as the *balance* occurred in the first, second, or third weighing.

With a balance in every weighing, all twelve of the coins are in fact good coins.

Solutions have been published which are equivalent to this (possibly after interchange of the pans for one or more weighings, or reversal of cyclic order for *X*, *Y*, *Z*): some of these have word-mnemonics for the labels and weighings; readers may like to try this as a change from anagrams.

The Cambridge undergraduate mathematical journal *Eureka* of 1950 included a solution of this type, in verse form, attributed to one Blanche Descartes. The mnemonic part is contained here in the lines:

> F. set the coins out in a row
> And chalked on each a letter so
> To form the words:
>
> F. AM NOT LICKED
>
> (An idea in his brain had clicked).
> And now his mother he'll enjoin:
>
> MA! DO   LIKE
> ME, TO   FIND
> FAKE   COIN!

This may be seen to be equivalent to our solution encoded by a code which a cryptographer would write

A	B	C	D	E	F	G	H	K	X	Y	Z
O	I	E	F	A	D	L	T	C	N	K	M'

after which the pans are reversed for the second weighing only.

Readers curious to know who F was, and why he should instruct his mother in the procedure, are referred to the original for an explanation; this is included in the poem, as also is the proof, from which we quote:

> No two agree in their effect,
> As is by pen and patience checked.
> For instance, should the dud be L
> And heavy, here's the way to tell:
> First weighing, down the right must come;
> The others—equilibrium!

Our treatment as in Tables 2*b* and 2*c* in fact owes much to a study of this Cartesian System!

Three weapons against the coiner

We shall now give more general consideration to the difficulties which can be encountered by someone who has cause to suspect the possible presence of one false coin in an apparently uniform collection: and we shall assume he has to work with weighing apparatus under conditions which are sufficient—but no more than sufficient—to provide answers to the questions which we shall ask. We shall assume that all coins may in fact be good, but that it is impossible that two or more may be bad: likewise that a counterfeit will have a weight which is appreciably different from the weight of a true coin, but that we have no means of knowing whether it will be lighter or heavier.

Three different forms of problem readily suggest themselves. With a beam balance, but no weights, we can detect differences of weight, even if we can make no actual weighings: so we can here ask how to detect if a counterfeit is present; if so, how to identify it; and how to tell whether it is light or heavy. With a beam balance and a set of weights, we can make weighings with coins in both pans, if we like: with a spring balance (or weighing machine) we can weigh collections of coins, but we cannot measure a difference of weight by one weighing alone. If actual weighings are possible, we can demand to know the weight of a true coin, and whether a counterfeit is present: and if so, we can ask for both the identity and the weight of the counterfeit to be determined. In all the three cases, we shall be interested to know the maximum number of coins for which these questions can be answered, after various numbers of weighings.

About false coins, in double-column

We first take the case of the equal-arm beam balance without weights, and consider how to find an efficient procedure for successively reducing the numbers of suspect coins, until finally we either find one with a known type of defect, or else prove all of the coins to be good. The important considerations here are as follows.

All coins can be proved to be good only if we can have a balance in every weighing: so we must always weigh equal numbers of coins against each other. A balance in any weighing proves only that all the coins then on the scales are good; it gives no new information about coins which then are elsewhere. When there can be only one bad coin, an unbalance proves that the bad coin is then somewhere on the scales: but all coins absent from the scales are then proved to be good, and each weighed coin is thereafter suspect for only one type of defect—overweight if it was in the descending pan, and underweight if it was in the ascending pan.

Coins which have been proved good can be of future interest only as makeweights, but they can be very important in this capacity. There is no difficulty in temporarily demoting a known good coin, to make up numbers in a set of suspects—this means only that thereafter we agree to suspect one further coin unnecessarily (and unjustifiably), before all unjustified suspicions are removed at the end. We then have a method of providing equal numbers for both pans when we should otherwise have an odd number to weigh; and it can also provide a means of introducing greater simplicity and uniformity in a series of weighing specifications.

We can now start at the end, working backwards; and for each weighing we consider two cases: there may have been a balanced result in every earlier weighing, in which event we shall know that some coins are good, while all others are still suspect for both types of defect; or there may have been an unbalance in at least one earlier weighing, after which there will be coins suspect for either defect singly, or no longer suspect, but none remaining suspect for both.

If the scales have been balanced in all earlier weighings, we cannot afford to have more than one suspect remaining, by the last weighing: the unique suspect may then prove to have either defect, or none, and we must have a good coin to weigh it against, to solve the problem.

If an earlier unbalance has occurred, we can afford to have three suspects at the final weighing. At least two coins must inevitably be suspect for the same defect (since only two types of unilateral defect are possible): if these coins are weighed against each other, lack of balance will acquit one and condemn the other, according to the way in which the unbalance occurs; a balance will acquit both and prove the third to be defective as suspected.

If it is to allow either form of last weighing as a sequel, indifferently, the second-last weighing must be certain to produce no more than one bilateral suspect, or alternatively no more than three unilateral suspects: and we now have to distinguish cases for the second-last weighing.

If all suspects are then unilateral (in view of an earlier unbalance) we can afford to have nine of them: for we can pair off suspects of similar types, to weigh three against three, disregarding a final three; and only three unilateral suspects will remain—possibly of different types, and possibly some from each pan—no matter whether there is a balance, or an unbalance of either type.

If the suspects are bilateral at the second-last weighing (for lack of an earlier unbalance), we can then have no more than four. For we can allow only one suspect to be off the scales, in case they balance; and no more than three to be on the scales, in case they do not: and to have the full benefit of three, we must also have at least one good coin which we can use as a makeweight in one of the pans.

Similar arguments then show that the next earlier weighing could have no more than twenty-seven unilateral suspects, to be weighed nine against nine, with nine off the scales: or else no more than thirteen bilateral suspects—when four could be left unweighed, while five were weighed against four and a known good coin.

Proceeding in this way we obtain a scheme as in Table 2*d*. In one column we indicate that a single good coin is additionally required, for bilateral suspects: on the right we see that unilateral suspects can be handled in groups by numbers which are powers of 3; on the left we see how bilateral suspects can be handled in groups whose numbers involve halving a corresponding power of 3, and then rounding the odd half upwards for some purposes and downwards for others.

WITH BILATERAL SUSPECTS			WITH UNILATERAL SUSPECTS		
Do not weigh:	*Weigh these*	*against these*	*Do not weigh:*	*Weigh these*	*against these*
0	0 + 1	1	1	1	1
1	1 + 1	2	3	3	3
4	4 + 1	5	9	9	9
13	13 + 1	14	27	27	27
40	40 + 1	41	81	81	81

TABLE 2 *d*

This scheme can be continued backwards indefinitely: but we have still to consider how we can enter it at the first weighing, when all coins are bilateral suspects, and no coin is known to be good. Absence of the good coin then requires a compensating reduction of one coin in the other pan: we can therefore provide for 3, 12, 39, 120, ... coins in 2, 3, 4, 5, ... weighings, or indeed for $\frac{1}{2}(3^r-3)$ coins in r weighings.

Our procedure requires that we enter the left-hand table, and keep going directly upwards on the left as long as balanced weighings still continue; at the first unbalance we move across and then keep going upwards on the right: if there is unbalance at the first weighing, we preserve the simplicity of the scheme by deciding to treat one good coin as a supernumerary suspect.

If we start with other numbers of coins than the critical or maximal numbers 3, 12, 39, 120, ..., we need only divide them into two equal groups and a remainder, for the first weighing, such that no group is larger than the corresponding group in the critical case: by casting unjust suspicion on an appropriate number of coins thereafter, we can then continue in the way indicated by the table.

If we know that one good coin is available, we can increase our critical numbers by 1, in an obvious fashion; we can do likewise if we have a balance with unequal arms, such that it will show a balance notwithstanding the absence of the good coin from the first weighing—for we can use good coins as makeweights, to ensure that we always weigh unchanged numbers thereafter: but these must be regarded as inelegant expedients introduced only to evade natural restrictions!

When all suspicions point the same way

If only unilateral suspects are in question, we can use the right-hand scheme as it stands, if it is known that there is a bad coin present: if all coins may be good, we must have one coin fewer, and we reduce the unweighed coins by 1 at the start. A similar deficiency will remain, and will be treated similarly, so long as balanced conditions continue in all weighings: the first unbalance will remove it, and make the table directly applicable; if no weighings prove to be unbalanced, no coin will remain unweighed at the end, and all coins will be proved to be good.

If all coins may be good, we can deal with $3^r - 1$ coins in r weighings (our problem from the First World War is the case of $r = 2$): once again, unjust suspicion is recommended as the simplest basis for handling non-critical numbers.

Three weighty trifles

In the next problems which we shall discuss, the key to success lies in extracting the maximum benefit from three apparently trivial but actually fundamental considerations. These can be summarized: coins which are invariably together cannot be distinguished from one another; if two coins always affect weighings in exactly opposite ways, excess in one will be indistinguishable from defect in the other; finally, if a bad coin is never weighed, there can be nothing to show whether it is light or heavy.

This leads us now to ask: within these limitations, how many different ways *are* there of affecting weighings, using different coins differently, over a series of weighings? At this point we can profitably digress for a little, to consider two weighing problems of an altogether different nature.

Scales of other types, and how to use them

Suppose that we have a series of weights 1, 2, 4, 8, ..., where every later weight is double its predecessor: and that we want to know how many different weighings we can make with the first r of these weights, if weights must be put only in one pan of a balance, with the load in the other pan.

The answer to this question takes a slightly simpler form if we assume that putting no weights on the scale is to be considered as the weighing of a zero load. We then note that every weight weighs one unit more than the sum of all weights smaller than itself; if two collections of weights differ, the largest weight which is present in the one but not in the other cannot be replaced by any collection of smaller weights: so different collections will always weigh different amounts.

Each weight—independently—can be either in the weighing pan (and in the collection), or not in the pan (and missing from the collection); and our convention for a zero weighing allows all to be simultaneously absent. With this understanding, we can multiply factors 2, one for each weight, and deduce that r weights will allow the use of 2^r different collections.

If we now consider any particular collection, we can take the weights in increasing order of size, and proceed from right to left writing a 0 if the weight is absent, and a 1 if it is present: in this way we obtain a specification 1 1 0 1 for a collection (1, 4, 8), for instance. We then have what we may regard as a number in the scale of 2—the *binary* scale—using digits 0 and 1 with place-values of 1, 2, 4, ... from right to left (in place of digits 0, 1, 2, ..., 9 with place-values 1, 10, 100, ..., as in our usual scale of 10).

By expressing a number in the scale of 2, we can determine a unique collection of weights for making the corresponding weighing. (If we wish, we can add initial digits 0, in positions of higher place value further to the left, to indicate that some larger weights are absent from some given collection: *left-hand* zeros will make no difference, just as with numbers in our more usual scale of 10.) If we can have r weights in all, this will give one of the members of a set of 2^r numbers (from 0 by unit steps to 2^r-1) which specify all the different patterns which can arise when each of r choices can independently be taken in either of two possible ways.

In this way we would write $13 = 8+4+1$ and derive 1 1 0 1: or having 1 1 0 1 we would form $8+4+1$ and derive 13. For larger numbers we can obtain successive binary digits, in order from right to left, by noting remainders for successive divisions by 2, as in Table 2e.

```
2 | 13          3 | 29          3 | 29
2 | 6 + 1       3 | 10 + 1̄      3 | 9 + 2
2 | 3 + 0       3 | 3 + 1       3 | 3 + 0
2 | 1 + 1       3 | 1 + 0       3 | 1 + 0
    0 + 1           0 + 1           0 + 1

  TABLE 2e        TABLE 2f        TABLE 2g
```

If, instead, we had a series of weights 1, 3, 9, 27, ..., where every weight was three times the preceding weight, we could proceed as follows, if we had liberty to place weights in either of the pans at will.

Taking each weight in ascending order of size, we could consider whether it was in the pan with the load, off the scales, or in the pan opposite to the load; and proceeding from right to left we could write digits -1, 0, or $+1$ (more conveniently, $\bar{1}$, 0, or 1) in the corresponding cases. If weights 27 and 3 could balance against the load and a weight 1, with the weight 9 off the scales, we would then obtain 1 0 1 $\bar{1}$, for instance: the load would then have a weight $27 + 3 - 1 = 29$, and we could regard 1 0 1 $\bar{1}$ as a number in the scale of 3—the *ternary* scale—which used digits $\bar{1}$, 0, 1 instead of the perhaps more to be expected 0, 1, 2.

For larger numbers we can obtain these digits $\bar{1}$, 0, or 1, in order from right to left, if we note remainders of minimum numerical value—positive or negative—for successive divisions by 3; and digits 0, 1, 2 would arise similarly if we took the more usual positive remainders: Tables 2f and 2g show the working in the two cases. Conversion from one form to the other only requires noting that $2 = 3 - 1$, $6 = 9 - 3$, and similarly, in a simple form of 'borrowing' or 'carrying' procedure.

If, however, we assume there are no *negative* weighings, the largest weight used must be in the opposite pan from the load; so the non-zero digit of highest place-value must be a 1, not a $\bar{1}$. In all, there will be 3^r possibilities, if any of r weights may independently have any one of three locations (either pan, or off the scales): when we single out the zero weighing, the others then fall into pairs whose non-zero digits are exactly opposite; and for each pair we have positive and negative weighings of equal amounts. There then are $\frac{1}{2}(3^r + 1)$ ways of weighing from 0 by units to $\frac{1}{2}(3^r - 1)$; and we obtain a similar number of patterns of sets of r digits, such that each pattern identifies a weighing procedure and associates with it some number in the series 0, 1, 2, 3, ...

The binary and ternary systems which we have just discussed are of some interest in their own right; and when weights are expensive—as with high-class standards—the use of binary or ternary series can even make for economy and efficiency in practical affairs. In other contexts, a binary series is appropriate when all the combinations must be of an additive type; the ternary series requires the possibility of subtractive combinations as well. For instance, bases with thicknesses in a binary series would be an efficient means of giving an object uniformly spaced vertical displacements: bases with thicknesses in a ternary series could similarly provide relative displacements for two objects. Sets of wedges or of thin lenses are other cases which will permit both additive and subtractive combinations.

Here, however, our application is the following: by referring to our previous examples, readers will see how we can use binary numbers to identify distinct weighing procedures for different coins which may be either on or off the pan of a spring balance (or weighing machine) in different weighings; and likewise how we can use ternary numbers with digits $\bar{1}$, 0, and 1 to do the same when coins may be in either pan of a beam balance.

With the spring balance, for instance, the number 13 in its binary form 1 1 0 1 could identify a coin together with a weighing procedure which requires this coin to be among those weighed in the first, third, and fourth weighings, associated with place-values 1, 4, and 8—but not in the second weighing associated with place-value 2, nor in a fifth or later weighing, if there are to be any. Similarly, a number 29 in its ternary form 1 0 1 $\bar{1}$ could indicate a coin together with a weighing procedure which put it in one of the pans in a first weighing on a beam balance, but in the opposite pan in a second weighing and in a fourth, while leaving it off the scales in a third weighing (and any other).

Equipped with this terminology, we can give further consideration to false-coin problems of the three types which we have mentioned earlier. We shall now find it more convenient to make an obviously permissible alteration: *from now on, place-values will be associated with weighings in a precisely opposite order; and successive weighings will involve successive digits in the order in which digits are usually read, from left to right.*

3 New Weighs with False Coins

When you have nothing to weigh

When we discussed binary and ternary series of weights, it made for simpler forms of statement when we decided to include a zero weighing as one of the possibilities to be considered: a similar device provides the best way of dealing with the case where no coin is counterfeit, in coin-weighing problems.

We assign the symbol 0 to a notional coin which we will associate with the actual set, and this symbol will then indicate that the notional coin is never concerned in any weighing. This can allow us to say that some general procedure will identify a counterfeit by number, without devoting space to provide for an exceptional case: for should the number turn out to be 0, the interpretation that only the notional coin is defective will imply that all the actual coins are good.

(Devices such as this are common everywhere in mathematics: similar considerations explain why 1 is not considered as a prime number, and why parallel lines are said to meet at a point at infinity. They make life much easier for mathematicians; but they can be a fruitful source of misunderstanding if they are first encountered by others without proper explanation.)

Programmes and how they are numbered

If we wish to prescribe all weighings in advance, when we have an equal-arm balance but no weights, we now have a concise means of simultaneously labelling the coins and providing weighing programmes for them. Our three basic requirements then demand that no two coins have weighing programmes with the same symbol (and associated number); nor with exact correspondence of digits 1 and $\bar{1}$ (giving numbers which differ only in sign); and that the zero programme (which leaves a coin totally unweighed) must be reserved for the notional coin, to cover the case where all coins are good.

We can now associate the positive digits 1 with one pan, and the negative digits $\bar{1}$ with the other, and there is now no need to avoid negative numbers: in fact we shall require some, as there is still one further requirement to meet—we must have equal numbers of coins in both pans, at every weighing.

How to make exceptions

We can take no more than one weighing programme from each associated pair: but we cannot take one weighing programme from every pair and still have equal numbers for every weighing. The number of pairs is $\frac{1}{2}(3^r-1)$, or $1+3+9+...+3^{r-1}$, if there are to be r weighings: and we can write symbols for all the positive numbers by columns, with corresponding digits in successive rows, as we have done for the case $r = 3$ in Table 3a. We then see how they fall into groups according to their non-zero digits of highest place-value, and in each of these groups the remaining places will include digits 1 and $\bar{1}$ in equal numbers: but since the number in each group is a power of 3, and therefore odd, the total number of non-zero digits is therefore odd, in every row.

13	12	11	10	9	8	7	6	5	4	3	2	1
1	1	1	1	1	1	1	1	1	0	0	0	0
1	1	1	0	0	0	−1	−1	−1	1	1	1	0
1	0	−1	1	0	−1	1	0	−1	1	0	−1	1

TABLE 3 *a*

The best we can hope to do is to omit one weighing programme (which must have either a 1 or a $\bar{1}$ in every digit position), and then find a way of changing signs for some of the rest, in such a way that finally each row has equal numbers of digits 1 and $\bar{1}$. The easiest way is to start by taking all odd numbers with a negative sign, and all even numbers with a positive sign: once this is done, each row (or place-value) has a surplus of only a single digit 1 or $\bar{1}$, with signs alternating in successive rows, and the number to be omitted is then obvious. In this way we find that from the set of numbers from 0 up to 1, 4, 13, 40, ..., for cases where there will be 1, 2, 3, 4, ... weighings, we have only to omit the single number 1, 2, 7, 20, ... in the respective cases, to have our problem solved, for 0, 3, 12, 39, ... coins, by a weighing programme of precisely the type we want.

The nature of these numbers becomes still more obvious if we give them their ternary representations: if there are to be r weighings, the programme of highest number has symbol 1 1 ... 1, the omitted number has digits 1 $\bar{1}$ 1 $\bar{1}$ ... in strict alternation, and the allowable number of coins is 1 1 ... 1 0, where there are r digits in each number. (In effect, we remove the middle column of our series of columns, if we assume that the column of zeros can here be included or omitted—whichever will produce a unique central column.) The omitted number is $\frac{1}{4}(3^r+1)$ if r is odd, and $\frac{1}{4}(3^r-1)$ if r is even: we can write it as $\frac{1}{4}[3^r-(-1)^r]$, to cover both cases.

Another way—due to Howard Grossman—allows coins to be given successive numbers with no omissions: all steps are exactly as before, except that signs for all numbers in the series 1, 4, 13, 40, ... are taken with an exact reversal of the rule which applies to the others; these are the numbers 1, $1+3$, $1+3+9$, $1+3+9+27$, ... whose ternary forms have nothing but digits 1. We add a further contribution of our own: if r leaves a remainder 0 or 1 (not 2 or 3) when divided by 4, we can replace the multiple exceptions by a single exception. For $r = 4$, this is the number *ten*, with ternary symbol 1 0 1; for $r = 5$, it is the number *thirty*, with ternary symbol 1 0 1 0: for larger numbers there would be one complete group of ternary symbols 1 0 1 0, or several such groups, further to the left.

A foolscap sheet to cover 120 coins

We made use of this last result in a solution for 120 coins—with five weighings prescribed in advance—which we give in Table 3*b*. This was originally produced for non-mathematicians, on a single typewritten foolscap sheet.

In all cases, a solution with prescribed weighings is essentially unique: any differences can be attributed to permutations of coins, possibly with interchanges of pans in individual weighings.

In these problems for the beam balance without weights, we lose nothing by requiring that all weighings are to be prescribed in advance: we can handle the same number of coins in a given number of weighings whether or not we are allowed to specify later operations in terms of earlier results.

You can do more if your balance has weights

We can now consider a different type of problem for the equal-arm beam balance. We provide the weights which we withheld before: in return, we want to know the actual weight of a good coin, and of any false coin—in addition to finding out whether all coins are good, or one bad, and if so, which. To begin with, we shall assume that there are thirteen coins, and three weighings allowed; and we shall require all weighings to be prescribed in advance.

Much of our previous work will apply here also: only thirteen pairs of weighing programmes are possible when a coin is to be weighed at least once in the course of three weighings; our three basic principles again show that we must take one and only one from each pair, for the actual coins—and leave a zero programme for a notional additional coin.

The next task is to determine which sign to choose for each of the

FIVE WEIGHINGS FOR ONE POSSIBLE DEFECTIVE COIN
(LIGHT OR HEAVY) IN A SET OF 120

	Leave these coins off the scales					Put these in the left-hand pan					Put these in the right-hand pan				
	1	2	3	4	5	41	43	45	47	49	42	44	46	48	50
	6	7	8	9	10	51	53	55	57	59	52	54	56	58	60
	11	12	13	14	15	61	63	65	67	69	62	64	66	68	70
(I)	16	17	18	19	20	71	73	75	77	79	72	74	76	78	80
	21	22	23	24	25	81	83	85	87	89	82	84	86	88	90
	26	27	28	29	30	91	93	95	97	99	92	94	96	98	100
	31	32	33	34	35	101	103	105	107	109	102	104	106	108	110
	36	37	38	39	40	111	113	115	117	119	112	114	116	118	120
	1	2	3	4	5	15	17	19	21	23	14	16	18	20	22
	6	7	8	9	10	25	27	29	30	31	24	26	28	32	34
	11	12	13	68	69	33	35	37	39	42	36	38	40	41	43
(II)	70	71	72	73	74	44	46	48	50	52	45	47	49	51	53
	75	76	77	78	79	54	56	58	60	62	55	57	59	61	63
	80	81	82	83	84	64	66	95	97	99	65	67	96	98	100
	85	86	87	88	89	101	103	105	107	109	102	104	106	108	110
	90	91	92	93	94	111	113	115	117	119	112	114	116	118	120
	1	2	3	4	23	5	7	9	11	13	6	8	10	12	15
	24	25	26	27	28	14	16	18	20	22	17	19	21	32	34
	29	30	31	50	51	33	35	37	39	42	36	38	40	41	43
(III)	52	53	54	55	56	44	46	48	59	61	45	47	49	60	62
	57	58	77	78	79	63	65	67	68	70	64	66	69	71	73
	80	81	82	83	84	72	74	76	87	89	75	86	88	90	92
	85	104	105	106	107	91	93	96	98	100	94	95	97	99	101
	108	109	110	111	112	102	113	115	117	119	103	114	116	118	120
	1	8	9	10	17	3	6	11	13	14	2	4	5	7	12
	18	19	26	27	28	16	21	24	29	30	15	20	22	23	25
	35	36	37	44	45	31	32	34	39	42	33	38	40	41	43
(IV)	46	53	54	55	62	47	49	50	52	57	48	51	56	58	59
	63	64	71	72	73	60	65	67	68	70	61	66	69	74	76
	80	81	82	89	90	75	78	83	85	86	77	79	84	87	92
	91	98	99	100	107	88	93	96	101	103	94	95	97	102	105
	108	109	116	117	118	104	106	111	114	119	110	112	113	115	120
	3	6	9	12	15	1	2	7	8	13	4	5	10	11	16
	18	21	24	27	30	14	19	20	25	26	17	22	23	28	29
	33	36	39	42	45	31	32	37	38	43	34	35	40	41	46
(V)	48	51	54	57	60	44	49	50	55	56	47	52	53	58	59
	63	66	69	72	75	61	62	67	68	73	64	65	70	71	76
	78	81	84	87	90	74	79	80	85	86	77	82	83	88	89
	93	96	99	102	105	91	92	97	98	103	94	95	100	101	106
	108	111	114	117	120	104	109	110	115	116	107	112	113	118	119

TABLE 3*b*

For explanation of table see p. 37 opposite.

pairs; but this time we have a simpler answer—we can take positive signs in every case.

We show this in Table 3c. In the first row, each of the numbers 13, 12, ..., 1, 0 gives a label for a particular coin. Below each number we give the successive digits of its ternary representation, using digits 1, 0, $\bar{1}$; the rows designated (A), (B), (C) relate to the ternary powers 9, 3, 1 which we associate with the first, second, and third weighings respectively.

Coin number

	13	12	11	10	9	8	7	6	5	4	3	2	1	0	
(9)	1	1	1	1	1	1	1	1	1	0	0	0	0	0	(A)
(3)	1	1	1	0	0	0	$\bar{1}$	$\bar{1}$	$\bar{1}$	1	1	1	0	0	(B)
(1)	1	0	$\bar{1}$	1	0	$\bar{1}$	1	0	$\bar{1}$	1	0	$\bar{1}$	1	0	(C)
(A−3B)	−2	−2	−2	1	1	1	4	4	4	−3	−3	−3	0	0	(X)
(B−3C)	−2	1	4	−3	0	3	−4	−1	2	−2	1	4	−3	0	(Y)
Ratio	1	−2	$-\frac{1}{2}$	$-\frac{1}{3}$	∞	$\frac{1}{3}$	−1	−4	2	$\frac{3}{2}$	−3	$-\frac{3}{4}$	0	?	X/Y

T ABLE 3 *c*

This scheme can then be interpreted as the directions for a set of weighing programmes:

FIRST WEIGHING:

> *put no coins in the left pan, and coins (5, 6, 7, 8, 9, 10, 11, 12, 13) in the right pan;*

SECOND WEIGHING:

> *put coins (5, 6, 7) in the left pan, and coins (2, 3, 4, 11, 12, 13) in the right pan;*

T ABLE 3 *b (cont.)*

Imagine an auxiliary set of scales with weights 81, 27, 9, 3, 1 which are to be associated with the successive weighings I, II, III, IV, V. If there is an *unbalance* in any weighing, place the associated weight on the auxiliary scales on the side which *descended* in the actual weighing; if there is a *balance*, leave the associated weight *off* the auxiliary scales. As all five weighings are taken into account, keep replacing the weights on the auxiliary scales by a *single* weight which produces an equivalent weighing. The final weight obtained after the five weighings will give the number of the defective coin. With no defective coin, there will be five balances and no weights on the auxiliary scales.

The defective coin is *heavy* if finally there is an odd-numbered weight in the left-hand pan, or an even-numbered weight in the right-hand pan. It is *light* if finally there is an even-numbered weight in the left-hand pan, or an odd-numbered weight in the right-hand pan. There is one exception only to this: *the coin numbered 30 has the opposite type of defect to that given by the general rule.*

THIRD WEIGHING:

> *put coins* (2, 5, 8, 11) *in the left pan, and coins* (1, 4, 7, 10, 13) *in the right pan.*

We now assume that A, B, C are the weights needed—in the left pan—to establish a balance. (Values will be negative if the odd coin differs sufficiently to require weights actually to be placed in the right pan.)

If in fact there is *no* odd coin, the ratios $A:B:C$ will be as $9:3:1$ and the weight of a single coin will be easily determined. In other cases our first task is to establish which coin is the odd coin; and we must find a way which does this independently of variations in the weight of a true coin, and in the difference of weight for a false coin. We can do this by an appropriate procedure based on differences and ratios.

Suppose that the weight of a good coin is W and that the weight of a false coin is $W+w$: the difference in weight for a false coin is then w, which may be negative; and a false coin may be regarded as a good coin plus an extra piece which is of weight w.

If we now form the two combinations $A-3B$ and $B-3C$, using the results A, B, C of our three weighings, the weight W of a good coin will disappear from these expressions, and our two values will give multiples of the difference w by the factors which are found in Table $3c$ in the lines labelled $(A-3B)$ and $(B-3C)$, under the symbol of the coin concerned. The ratio of $(A-3B)$ to $(B-3C)$ is then the ratio of the two multipliers concerned, independently of the value of w: and each such ratio unambiguously identifies one particular coin, as only certain ratios are possible, and there are no duplications among them.

Assume now that we have made weighings in terms of our given scheme, and have determined actual values of A, B, C. If we have $A-3B = B-3C = 0$, we know we have no false coin, and the weight of a good coin is then $W = A/9 = B/3 = C$. In other cases there is only one column of the table which will show multipliers in the same ratio as the values of $(A-3B)$ and $(B-3C)$; this column lets us identify the coin, and by dividing either value by the corresponding multiplier we obtain the value w of the excess weight of the false coin.

Knowing the weighing programmes, we can apply a correction to find what weights would have been obtained if instead of the false coin we had in fact had a good one: the weight of a good coin, W, now follows exactly as in the case where all coins were in fact good, and by forming $W+w$ we then find the weight of the false coin.

Evaluation of the ratio is of course possible only if the denominator $B-3C$ is non-zero: but if either the numerator or the denominator would be zero, identification of the coin and of an error-multiple can take place at an earlier stage. In the table, symbols ? and ∞ have been used to indicate ratios where the denominator would be zero, with numerators zero and non-zero, in the respective cases.

All other solutions are necessarily equivalent to this, within trivial variations. In other cases we may proceed similarly with altered labels for the coins, possibly interchanging pans or taking the weighings in a different order; but we cannot keep the discriminating ratios all distinct if we select alternatives from the thirteen pairs of opposite programmes in any way which would make the magnitudes of the weighings have ratios other than $9:3:1$ in the case where all coins are good. We could base other identification procedures on ratios of other combinations of A, B, C; but these would require to be suitable functions of our combinations $(A-3B)$ and $(B-3C)$. No alternative seems likely to give much advantage over the solution we have just described.

Our procedure will in fact deal with positive or negative weights of any magnitude, however large: but if we can be given an assurance that no coin will have a negative weight, and that a false coin will not weigh more than twice as much as a good coin, we need not then be told the order of the weighings, but only the set of results for the three weighings.

The point here is that if these restrictions apply, the true order cannot well be concealed, since we then must have $A > B > C$ except in some cases where the odd coin has weight zero, or twice that of a true coin. Even in these extreme cases we can still succeed: the critical cases are weighings with the ratios $8:2:2$, $9:2:2$, or $10:2:2$; but each of these still admits of only one interpretation—we must have 11 a weightless coin, 2 a weightless coin, or 7 a double-weight coin, in the respective cases.

We can obtain a graphical representation of our procedure if we take a basic equilateral triangle and assume that a set of weighings (A, B, C) is represented by the point whose perpendicular distances from the sides are in the ratio of $A:B:C$. Weighings for cases where each possible false coin was *infinitely* heavy would then be represented for the different coins by points labelled as in Figure 3A. The points for the coins 1, 3, 9 are the vertices of the basic triangle; for 12, 10, 4, they are the mid-points of sides; for 13, 11, 7, 5, they are the in-centre and the three ex-centres: and for 6, 8, 2, they are the points 'at infinity' on the sides (and on all lines parallel to them) which we indicate at the outer limits of the figure. If now a point 0 represents the case of *no* false coin, the point for a false coin of *finite* weight must lie somewhere on the straight line which joins the point 0 to the point labelled with the symbol for the coin concerned.

The weighing procedure must therefore be chosen to give separate joins between the point 0 and each of the other thirteen points, as in our figure. Only the point 0 is changed if we select weighing procedures differently, one each from our thirteen possible pairs: and unless we have net overbalances of one, three, and nine coins in the different weighings of our selected programme, the point 0 will lie on the join of some other points, which will represent coins whose errors cannot then be distinguished from each other.

We can prove this last result if we determine the conditions which will make the point 0 collinear with some two of the other points. The point 0 must be interior to the basic triangle, since its three co-ordinates are all positive: to escape unwanted collinearities, it must have no two

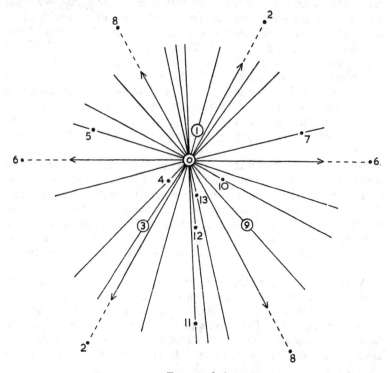

FIGURE 3 *A*

co-ordinates equal, and no co-ordinate can be equal to the sum—or, equivalently, the difference—of the other two; the mean (or semi-sum) of the other two is prohibited also, and so is their semi-difference.

Co-ordinates for the point 0 have to be obtained by summing across rows of a table which can differ from Table 3a only by sign-changes for individual columns; so all three co-ordinates must here be odd numbers. To satisfy these conditions, and avoid unwanted collinearities, the set of co-ordinates can then only be some permutation of (1, 3, 9): all other possibilities are either unsuitable or unobtainable. Different permutations can arise from appropriate reversals of signs for sets of columns; but these amount only to the trivial variations which were mentioned earlier.

How to exercise discrimination

In a problem of this type, a single weighing gives no satisfactory criterion for choosing between alternative procedures: it could do this only if we were to put equal numbers of coins in the two pans, when we would obtain no quantitative information if all coins were good; and this involves a degree of inefficiency which we cannot here afford.

After two weighings, however, we can make a distinction between two cases: the ratio of the two previous weighings may be consistent with the assumption that all coins are good, or it may not be; and if a true ratio is found for *unequal* weighings, every coin weighed in either weighing must be good. (With equal weighings, a bad coin might be affecting both identically.)

To take advantage of this, we cannot allow more than one coin to escape the first two weighings: for if these show a true ratio, the bad coin has not yet been found, and must still be weighed; so we can allow no dubiety about which one it is. Coins to be included in the first two weighings must have programme numbers from 2 to 13, if the coins are all to be distinguishable after the third weighing; and the unweighed coin must have the programme number 1.

Discrimination possibilities do not let us handle any more coins; and they can contribute little to simplifying our earlier procedure. We can make the first two weighings as before; and if these show a true ratio, we know the weight of a true coin, deduce that the unweighed coin is the only suspect, and find its weight in a final weighing: this is the only simplification. If the first two weighings show a false ratio, this indeed proves the unweighed coin to be good: but we still must include it in the final weighing; for otherwise we would be unable to discriminate between coins with the weighing programmes 12, 9, 6, 3.

False coins in ever-increasing numbers

After all this, it is pleasant to find that we can handle the maximum number of coins in a similar fashion, with little extra complication, when we have greater numbers of weighings: in all cases, we could indeed prescribe all weighings in advance, by taking positive numbers from all the available pairs of programmes; but there is a simpler way.

In the ternary scale, the number of programme-pairs for r weighings is a number with r digits all of which are 1: to pass from one such number to its successor, we can either add a new power of 3, or we can triple the given number and add 1 to the result. The second method can provide the basis of a simpler scheme for using extra weighings; we show how to use this if two extra weighings are possible.

We then can deal with 121 coins, which we divide into thirteen groups of nine accompanied by a unique group of three and a unique single coin: and in the first three weighings we use the procedure of our last solution, treating groups of nine as if they were single coins. We may find that a group of nine has a bad coin, and if so we shall know the weight of a true group, of the false group, and so of the false coin itself. We then have only to isolate the coin; and we can dispense with further use of the weights: unilateral suspects and numbers of weighings available are related as in a problem we have already considered. If instead we find that all the groups of nine are proved to be good, we shall know the weight of a good coin: we can then weigh the group of three. This will tell us whether we have to discriminate within this group, in the final weighing, or to continue with an examination of the unique single coin.

A three-weigh split of six coins

Much of our previous procedure still applies if the beam balance and weights are replaced by a spring balance, or weighing machine: equivalently we might have to make weighings on a beam balance, but with coins all in one pan, and weights all in another.

With three weighings we now can have only eight different weighing programmes, including the zero programme: all digits must now be either 1 or 0. The seven programmes available for actual coins are as in Table 3d; and once again we shall start by requiring all weighings to be specified in advance.

7	6	5	4	3	2	1
1	1	1	1	0	0	0
1	1	0	0	1	1	0
1	0	1	0	1	0	1

TABLE 3d

Co-ordinates for a suitable point 0 in a triangular diagram are again required: these must be summations across rows, and sign-changes are no longer possible. Collinearity with pairs of points corresponding to pairs of columns of the table has again to be avoided: we can look for this either directly in the diagram, or implicitly, by examining whether we can succeed in finding a discrimination procedure similar to that of Table 3c.

Our first discovery is that we cannot use all seven programmes; we would have co-ordinates (4, 4, 4) for the point 0, and this would then coincide with the point 7, at the centroid of the triangle: so we must content ourselves with discriminating among fewer coins.

We next find that we can succeed no better with six programmes; whichever programme we endeavour to omit, undesired collinearity will remain. (We can permute the weighings, if necessary: so we need consider only three typical cases, omitting a coin which would be weighed once, twice, or three times.)

However, we can indeed succeed in discriminating among five coins, with weighings prescribed in advance. Apart from permutations of weighings, there are only two distinct ways of doing this: we can omit the coin which would be weighed three times, and one of the coins which would be weighed once, to give a scheme as in Table 3e; or we can omit two programmes such that the pair of associated coins would be absent in one weighing, divided in another and together in the third, to give a scheme as in Table 3f.

1	1	1	0	0	(A)
1	0	0	1	1	(B)
0	1	0	1	0	(C)
−2	1	−2	3	0	$3C-2A = X$
−2	3	0	1	−2	$3C-2B = Y$
1	$\frac{1}{3}$	∞	3	0	X/Y

TABLE 3 e

1	1	1	1	0	(A)
1	1	0	0	1	(B)
1	0	1	0	0	(C)
3	−3	3	−3	0	$6C-3A = X$
1	1	−3	−3	4	$4B-3A = Y$
3	−3	−1	1	0	X/Y

TABLE 3 f

One question remains—if weighings need not be prescribed before-hand, can we do any better: and this is a case where we can, indeed. For if we adopt the scheme of Table 3f, five coins have been weighed at least once, when the second weighing is complete: if the first and second results were in the ratio of 4 to 3, this would prove all five coins were good, and give the true weight; and at this point we could turn aside to weigh a sixth coin, which might be either good or bad. If the first weighings were not in the true ratio, we would know the sixth coin to be good, with the bad coin elsewhere; and we would continue exactly as in Table 3f, to find the bad coin, and its weight. (We cannot afford to include the sixth coin in the third weighing, when it is proved to be a good coin; if we did, the coins with programmes 7 and 4 would then become indistinguishable.)

A similar development is impossible with the scheme of Table 3*e*. Any pair of weighings here involves four coins only; or alternatively they weigh equal numbers of coins, and equal results could occur if a twice-weighed coin were bad, as well as when all coins were good.

A spring-balance extension

We can apply similar methods if we are allowed four weighings instead of three. If weighings are to be prescribed in advance, we have to make a selection from fifteen possible weighing programmes: sums of digits by rows will again give co-ordinates for a point 0, which this time we should have to consider in relation to a tetrahedron; and the resulting point would have to avoid collinearities with any pair of points whose co-ordinates corresponded to two of the chosen programmes.

It is probably easier to consider differences and ratios directly, for possible schemes; and we then find we cannot use all the programmes. We would then have equal totals for all weighings, when all coins are good: we cannot even allow three equal totals or two equal pairs. This difficulty arises because several lines of symmetry in the tetrahedron each contain three of the critical points: if we omit the programme for one of these points, we obtain a point 0 collinear with the others.

This prevents us from dealing with either fifteen or fourteen coins, with four prescribed weighings: but we can find three ways of dealing with thirteen coins; typically we may omit the programmes 7 and 3, or 7 and 1, or 3 and 1.

With four weighings, we can turn away to deal with one extra coin if all others are proved good in three weighings: or with three extra coins, if all others are proved good in two weighings; in this event we weigh one coin twice, and the others once each, in the last two weighings. We can in fact extend any of our thirteen-coin solutions to provide for fourteen coins, by using the latter alternative in an appropriate way; but fourteen coins are not the maximum possible: we can do still better.

A spring problem from Japan

Solving the problem for fifteen coins in four weighings was a question proposed by Kobon Fujimura in *Recreational Mathematics Magazine*: this led us to discover the solution which we publish here. There is scope for a little variation, in solutions; we have sought to give as simple a one as we can contrive.

Some of our previous discussion has indicated that four prescribed weighings will not suffice: and the rest is readily extended to show that we cannot separate fifteen coins into two groups, such that after the second or third weighings we can either continue with the whole of the first group, or move over to consider the second group alone, according to results of the earlier weighings.

Only one possibility remains: we may be able to make distinctions among the weighed coins of the first group, for separate treatments. We cannot have all coins weighed at least once, with distinguishable effects, in fewer than four weighings; so when we subdivide we will have another group of coins as yet unweighed: there must therefore be three distinct groups of coins involved, at least.

In fact we make two weighings, before we discriminate. The three groups of coins are those weighed in both these weighings, in one or other only, or in neither: the first two weighings involve equal numbers of coins, so that an equality of weighings leaves the twice-weighed group suspect, as well as the unweighed group, and proves all singly-weighed coins to be good; whereas an inequality leaves only the once-weighed coins suspect, and acquits both the other groups. Once we have found which of these alternatives applies, we concentrate on the group of remaining suspects.

In both cases, we have to make two more weighings, and then we use differences and ratios: two different groups each containing four suspects have to be weighed; and the secret of success is that in at least one of these weighings we *must* introduce one or more of the proved good coins, if ambiguity is to be avoided in the final ratios.

In our solution, we add two good coins in the third weighing only: this seems to give the simplest sets of numbers to handle. (The actual condition is that three numbers of coins—the number which is common to the first two weighings, and the numbers involved in the third and fourth weighings respectively—must all be different, and none must equal the sum of the others; this can in fact be secured in more ways than one, by adding proved good coins: but not otherwise.) In this fashion we obtain the solution which we give in Table 3g.

Coin number

UPPER SET	15	14	13	12	3	2	1	0	(SUSPECT IF $A = B$)	
LOWER SET	7	6	5	4	11	10	9	8	(SUSPECT IF $A \neq B$)	
(UPPER SET)	1	1	1	1	0	0	0	0	}	(A)
(LOWER SET)	0	0	0	0	1	1	1	1	}	
(BOTH SETS)	1	1	1	1	0	0	0	0	(+4)	(B)
(SUSPECT SET ONLY) {	1	1	0	0	1	1	0	0	(+2)	(C)
{	1	0	1	0	1	0	1	0	(+0)	(D)
(X)	−2	4	−6	0	−2	4	−6	0		4C−6D
(Y)	−1	1	−1	1	−2	0	−2	0		B−2D
X/Y	2	4	6	0	1	∞	3	?		RATIO

TABLE 3 *g*

In the table, the column headings are formed by two rows of numbers, associated in pairs which differ by 8: these numbers are used to label the coins, and their binary representations provide the weighing programmes; a symbol 0 is included for a notional coin, to cover the case where all coins are good. Not every coin will here complete its full weighing programme, however. It will do this only if it is still a suspect coin after the second weighing: and in other cases the remaining part of its programme will be abandoned.

For the first two weighings, the table provides the equivalent of the instructions:

FIRST WEIGHING:

weigh the set of coins (15, 14, 13, 12, 11, 10, 9, 8),

SECOND WEIGHING:

weigh the set of coins (15, 14, 13, 12, 7, 6, 5, 4),

with eight coins involved, in both cases. If we obtain weights A and B, respectively, a result with $A = B$ will indicate that the twice-weighed and unweighed coins jointly forming the upper set (15, 14, 13, 12, 3, 2, 1, 0) will remain the only suspects thereafter; a result with $A \neq B$ will imply that suspicion now rests only on the singly-weighed coins which form the lower set (7, 6, 5, 4, 11, 10, 9, 8).

In the third and fourth weighings, we use the binary representations to provide weighing programmes only if earlier weighings leave the coin suspect: in the third weighing, we add two proved good coins to provide makeweights; but in the fourth weighing we have four of the suspect coins, only.

If we find that the first two weighings give *identical* results, we can in this event continue according to instructions:

THIRD WEIGHING:

weigh the set of coins (15, 14, 9, 8, 3, 2),

FOURTH WEIGHING:

weigh the set of coins (15, 13, 3, 1),

where we have taken 9 and 8 as the makeweights.

When the first two weighings give *different* results, however, we can instead continue according to the instructions:

THIRD WEIGHING:

weigh the set of coins (14, 11, 10, 7, 6, 3),

FOURTH WEIGHING:

   weigh the set of coins (11, 9, 7, 5),

where the makeweights are taken as 14 and 3.

To interpret the results, we next concentrate on the results of the final three weighings. In each of these, we effectively have different selections of four coins, from a suspect set of eight, with a number of makeweights equal to four, two, and none, in the successive cases. We indicate this by symbols $(+4)$, $(+2)$, and $(+0)$, inserted in the table.

As before, we first take such multiples of the various weighings as would lead to identical results if all coins were good; and according to whichever coin—if any—is defective, we may or may not have similar multiples of the error included also: table entries give rows of error-multipliers for different cases.

The weight of a good coin then disappears when we take differences of these multiples of the weighing results; two independent differences suffice, and leave us with multiples only of the error. The ratio of these multiples does not then depend on the magnitude of the error, and is uniquely characteristic of a particular pair of coins.

The results of the first two weighings will enable us to discriminate between members in the final pair: if we had $A = B$, the bad coin will be identified by the symbol in the top row, at the head of the column; if we had $A \neq B$, we have to take the next lower symbol, in the second row of the table.

Once a unique ratio is available, we also know from what multiples of the error it was obtained; so we can obtain a value for the error. We can then apply corrections to the original weights, to deduce what they would have been had all coins been good: we can check that the corrected values are in the true ratios; and we can find the weight of a good coin. Since we already know the amount of the error, we then know the weight of a false coin. In effect we first proceed downwards in the table, keeping all columns in mind; afterwards we identify a relevant column, and we work backwards up the identified column.

The number of coins which we can handle in four weighings is thus fifteen, which has 1 1 1 1 for its binary form. This result can now be generalized: if $r \geqslant 4$, r weighings can deal with $2^r - 1$ coins—a number which has r binary digits each of which is a 1. To pass from each such number to its successor, we can add on a next higher power of 2; or we can double, and then add 1. The latter relation underlies a general procedure, which we can indicate briefly for sixty-three coins and six weighings.

We divide the sixty-three coins into fifteen sets of four, and three which form a unique pair and a unique single coin. In the first four weighings we treat the groups of four as our earlier solution would treat fifteen single coins; and if we prove that one group is faulty, we know enough to isolate the bad coin by applying a simple halving technique twice thereafter: for the result of weighing any two of the four will indicate whether we should next weigh one of them again, or one of the other two. If we prove that no group of four is faulty, we next weigh the pair: we then weigh one of the pair, if the pair is proved faulty; otherwise we weigh the last remaining coin.

4 *Jug and Bottle Department*

Trials and errors of pourers of fluids

Most readers will at some time have encountered problems in which a supply of fluid has to be partitioned into specified portions by making a succession of transfers each of which fills or empties one or other of several ungraduated measuring vessels. It has sometimes been said that these problems can be solved only by trial and error, and it can be argued that some of the methods we shall describe are still of this type: what matters is that they can substantially reduce the number of the trials (and the frequency of the errors).

Problems of this type can be traced back at least as far as Tartaglia, the Italian mathematician of the sixteenth century, who correctly solved cubic equations but went astray in extending Alcuin's ferry problem to more than three jealous couples. He gave two problems which continually reappear, in various places, with no essential change: with measures which respectively hold 3, 5, and 8 units, divide 8 units of fluid into two equal parts; with measures which respectively hold 5, 11, 13, and 24 units, divide 24 units of fluid into three equal parts.

We shall take the first of these as an actual example, and go on to show how to solve others of the same type as the second. We shall then be able to consider other problems where some fluid has to be consumed in the course of the pouring operations.

If you can't undo it, don't do it

Problems with three measures are not difficult to solve if you keep a clear head; for in fact there is very little choice, if you take care to avoid cancelling the effect of a step which you have just taken. At first we shall consider problems where every measure is either full or empty at the start, and where the total quantity of fluid thus determined is still held in the vessels at the end. Many problems are actually of this precise type; some others can be treated along similar lines, with minor variations.

We shall describe the state of a measure as *terminal* when the measure is either completely full or completely empty: this term is convenient, since at least one of the measures—sometimes one, sometimes another, in different steps—must be terminal after every pouring operation; this alone is what determines when pouring is to cease.

A further point is that a pouring operation is *reversible* only if one of the measures concerned is terminal at the start: irreversible operations have in fact to be avoided; their effect is to cancel progress which has already been made.

There are in fact three types of pouring operations which can be reversed. In any pouring operation, the quantity of fluid involved must be less than the joint capacity of the two measures concerned: but it may then exceed the individual capacity of either, of the smaller only, or of neither.

In the first case, different measures will be full at the start and at the finish; in the second case, the state of the smaller measure will change from full to empty, or from empty to full; in the third case, different measures will be empty at the start and at the finish. In all three cases, one measure is necessarily terminal at the start, and one at the finish: it may be the same one, or different ones, at the two ends.

Our earlier assumption implies that all three measures are terminal, at the start of the problem; we shall also suppose that only one is to be terminal at the finish. (If two are terminal at the finish, the problem is much simpler, as we shall see.) Suppose now that a problem of this type has been solved, and that we have the desired final distribution present in the measuring vessels: we can then work backwards, inquiring how it can have got there.

Consider any chain of successive pouring operations such that only one measure at a time is terminal when pouring starts or ceases. All steps here are necessarily reversible, and if no steps are retraced, the course of such a chain is uniquely prescribed, in either direction, as soon as any one of the steps is known: for two measures are involved in any individual pouring operation; one or other of these two must be terminal between successive steps; and with the type of chain assumed here, the unused third measure must be non-terminal during any pouring operation. Continuing a chain of this type—either forwards or backwards—then requires that the next step is a pouring operation involving the third measure together with that one of the others which is terminal at the end concerned: in other cases a step would be retraced, or else two terminal positions would arise in a non-reversible manner.

When only one measure is terminal in the *final* position, we have a choice of two alternatives according as we assume that one or other of the remaining measures was involved in the final pouring operation. We thus have two alternative ways to start a backward chain of moves, which we can continue automatically, pairing a terminal used measure with an unused third measure, for each next step.

This procedure can terminate only in one or other of two ways; either the chain will close cyclically by arriving back at its start, or else the time will come when two measures become terminal simultaneously: and if more than one measure is terminal at the start, the latter alternative *must* occur, if the problem is in fact solvable at all.

Once we thus obtain two terminal measures simultaneously, the backward chain forks into two branches: we then can involve either of the terminal measures with the third measure, in the next step, and we should require at least two measures to be terminal always from then on; any return to only a single terminal measure is then a retrograde step.

With all the possible alternatives, a stage must then come when we arrive at the starting position. The only problem then is to count steps, and decide which fork of which backward path gives the fewest operations. The shortest of the four alternative paths is then reversed to give the best solution of the original problem.

Dividing fluids with triangle-mesh nets

A graphical method given by Mr. M. C. K. Tweedie in 1939 will be found convenient for illustrating and applying this procedure; this method derives from the following considerations.

The contents of the three measures represent three variables whose sum is constant (a situation which arises also for percentages in colorimetry or ternary-alloy metallurgy): an appropriate procedure is to plot them as perpendicular distances from the sides of an equilateral triangle. These perpendiculars have a constant sum for all points, if distances measured from each side towards the opposite vertex are taken to be positive; each perpendicular multiplied by half the length of a side gives the area of one of three triangles whose areas add up to the area of the fundamental triangle.

Paper scaled with a network of equilateral triangles is commercially available, described as *isometric* paper. This is designed to facilitate a simple but effective type of pictorial representation which uses parallel projection in a direction equally inclined to the three mutually perpendicular directions of a fundamental cube. It can save much effort in drawing diagrams for pouring problems.

On this paper we can draw a triangle of such a size that it has as many graduations along each edge as there are units of measure in the total amount of fluid; perpendicular distances from the sides to a lattice point can then be determined by counting spaces between the ruled lines which are parallel to the side concerned. We associate one side with each measure, and draw a line parallel to this side at a (positive) distance corresponding to the full contents of this measure: points corresponding to possible contents for *all* the measures must then all lie on or between the two lines of every one of the three parallel pairs.

These points then all lie within a convex figure which must be bounded by four, five, or six of the lines; with only three boundaries, there would not be enough fluid to fill any measure, and its manner of division could not be altered otherwise than by uniting portions which were separate at the start. If initially all measures are terminal (but not all full, and not all empty!) the convex figure must have either four sides or else five sides. When at least one measure is terminal, the representative point will be a lattice point on the boundary of the convex figure; when two (or all three) are terminal, the point will be a vertex of the convex figure.

In any pouring operation with three measures, one measure retains its contents unchanged, and one of the other two assumes a terminal condition. This requires the representative point to move along a line of the diagram, parallel to the side associated with the measure whose contents are unchanged, until a point on the periphery is reached.

In any *reversible* path, if we have not arrived at a vertex, we must then take a new path which is reflected off the edge concerned, similarly to the path of a billiard ball, as Steinhaus has remarked; but if we arrive at a vertex, the billiard-ball analogy fails; we then must proceed round the periphery in one direction or the other. (Consideration of possible diagrams will show that the shortest path from one vertex to another is always round the periphery if all three measures are unequal: with two equal measures, this is still true of *equivalent* vertices if it is immaterial which equal measure holds either of their specified contents.)

We now have an appropriate procedure for the case where all measures are terminal at the start: our figures show it applied to an equal division of eight units of fluid using measures for 3, 5, and 8 units; the steps given in Figure 4*A* take one operation less than those of Figure 4*B* no matter whether the eight units of fluid are all in the 8-unit measure, or jointly in the 3-unit measure and the 5-unit measure, at the start.

From left to right in the reference symbols, the numerals relate to measures in order of increasing size, and they list the contents of the successive measures, taken in this order. The directions in the diagram which correspond to changes of contents for each separate measure can readily be appreciated by noting the varying breadths of the significant region measured transversely to the different sets of parallel graduation lines. Along any graduation line one numeral can be seen to be constant, and the two others to change oppositely, by unit amounts, in each step from one lattice point to the next.

There is another way of using this type of diagram. We can put the symbol 0 on the point representing the contents at the start; any point which can be reached from this point in one move is then marked 1, and any point which can be reached in one move from one or more of the points marked 1 is then marked 2 *if it does not already have a lower numeral*; we then add higher numerals in similar fashion.

If the problem is solvable, a numeral will finally be assigned to the point representing the contents wanted at the finish; this will give the minimum number of moves, and the appropriate route (or routes) can be back-tracked through whole-number symbols which decrease by

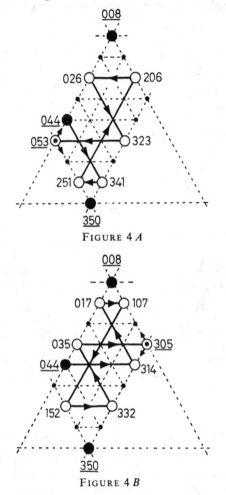

FIGURE 4 *A*

FIGURE 4 *B*

units. If the problem cannot be solved, a time will come when all the possible continuation points already have numerals assigned to them, while the point which corresponds to the desired distribution is still unmarked (and some other points likewise).

Figure 4C shows contents-symbols on the left, and sequence-symbols on the right, in corresponding positions, for the same problem as before:

the initial contents have been taken as 0 0 8; if they were 3 5 0, the only change would be an interchange of the symbols 0 and 2 on the two vertices where these appear.

This method leads readily to the shortest solution (or solutions); the previous method is more convenient if *all* solutions are required.

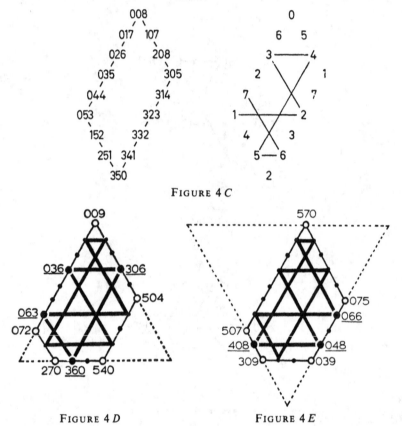

FIGURE 4 *C*

FIGURE 4 *D*   FIGURE 4 *E*

In Figure 4*D* we give an example of how we can show that some particular problem has no solution; the diagram considers the attempt to divide 9 units into 3-unit and 6-unit portions, using measures for 5, 7, and 9 units. With Figure 4*E* we show how any diagram can be used with two distinct interpretations. The lines corresponding to *empty* and *full* conditions can be interchanged for every measure, with appropriate relabelling of all the points. The diagram then relates to a pouring problem equivalent to immersing the containers—with the air they include—in a large volume of the fluid, and doing the same pouring operations as before, upside down, noting how this divides the air bubbles which are trapped in the different containers.

When we replace air by fluid, and vice versa, for a more conventional operation, we then obtain the solution of a pouring problem which we may term the *dual* of the original one. The total quantities of fluid separately involved in the original problem and in the dual problem must together amount to the whole joint capacity of all the measures.

In Figure 4*E* we have a figure which is identical to Figure 4*D*, apart from relabelling of the points: this new figure shows the impossibility of dividing 12 units either into halves, or into one-third and two-third portions, using 5-unit, 7-unit, and 9-unit measures as before.

A tetrahedron with every four containers

In our diagrams so far, each lattice point has represented a set of contents for all three measures, in terms of its perpendicular distances from the three sides of the basic triangle: one side was associated with each measure, and the three perpendiculars had a constant sum, corresponding to the constant total quantity of fluid involved. With four measures, we could use a regular tetrahedron as a basis, in analogous fashion: each of its triangular faces would then be divided as in the three-measure case, and parallel planes would replace parallel lines.

There would be a three-dimensional lattice whose points would be vertices of a space-filling of regular tetrahedra and octahedra: one of the four faces would be associated with each measure, and the perpendiculars to the four faces would here have a constant sum for all lattice points (each would be proportional to the volume of one of four tetrahedra, one based on each face, which summed to the volume of the basic tetrahedron).

Here too we should have to introduce additional boundaries to limit the region within which lattice points could represent actual contents of the measures; these would be faces parallel to those of the basic tetrahedron, at distances corresponding to the maximum content of the measure which was associated with each face concerned.

Once again we shall call measures *terminal* if they are completely full, or else completely empty; and one measure must be terminal after every pouring. Two measures now retain their contents unchanged when pouring takes place, and the representative point moves on a lattice line—the intersection of two planes, each parallel to a different face—until it reaches the boundary plane which corresponds to the measure which finally assumes a terminal state. (There are sets of lattice lines parallel to each of the six edges of the basic tetrahedron.)

We then have alternatives similar to the ones in the three-measure case: we can start with the initial state, and mark various points with

1, 2, 3, ..., successively, according to the minimum number of operations required to reach them, until we finally reach the point corresponding to the desired final state; or we can work back by reversible operations from the final state.

In the latter procedure, we must proceed along lattice lines through the interior of the basic tetrahedron, with a choice of *two* different continuations every time we hit a face, until the time comes when we hit an edge: then we should confine ourselves to continuations limited to the outer surface only, until we hit a vertex; finally we should proceed, along the edges, to other vertices, one of which will represent the initial state (we are again assuming that all measures are terminal initially). In the first steps of the backward path, we are compelled to proceed through the interior: but if we resume this when we could go on the faces, or avoid edge-paths when we could use them, the only result is to prolong our task unnecessarily.

Some readers may find it instructive to make a three-dimensional model: an easier way is to use isometric paper once more, to draw a representation of the outer surface. Convex and concave sets of faces can be shown separately, in parallel projection perpendicular to one of the basic faces: lattice lines for each face are given by rulings of the isometric paper, or lines perpendicular to these; a line of the second type is easily drawn through a collinear set of lattice points which are $\sqrt{3}$ graduation units apart. For the slant faces, one set of rulings is not used, and perpendiculars to these are used instead; these perpendiculars in fact give contour lines for the diagram, if it is considered as a map.

Perhaps the easiest way is to use this diagram to proceed forwards from the initial state until all points *situated on edges* have been labelled with the number of operations needed to reach them. For surface points which are *not* on the edges, we can then work backwards from the final state, keeping records in a numerical table: in each operation we note which two measures were involved; the one of these which becomes terminal as we go back must be used with one of the other two, in the next backward step. Orderly listing is desirable, to avoid double working when an identical set of contents is reached by two different paths.

Once two measures simultaneously become terminal, we know we have reached an edge, and we can transfer from the table to the diagram to see how many more moves will take us back to the start. We retain only the best alternative, and then continue the table until we can see that no continuation will improve upon what we already have.

Problems for secret agents and others

We will now apply these methods to a case where the contents of the four measures are respectively 2, 5, 7, and 12 units: we assume that the largest and smallest are empty, and the other two full; and that the problem is to divide the fluid into three equal parts. Similar methods can quite easily be applied in more complicated cases which would require more space than we can give them here.

Figures 4*F* and 4*G* exhibit the edge-labelling, continued up to all points which are three steps (or fewer) from the start. Sets of contents

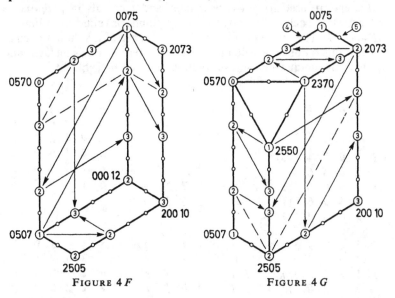

FIGURE 4*F* FIGURE 4*G*

are indicated appropriately for each vertex: for other edge-points, contents are readily found by noting that two of the four symbols remain constant, while two others change oppositely by unit steps, in proceeding along any edge. The points which are specially marked with symbols 4 and 5 are the points 0 1 7 4 and 1 0 7 4 respectively; we shall see that the latter is the first edge-point reached in back-tracking the optimum solution of Table 4*a*.

(0)	0	5	7	0	(1)
(1)	2	3	7	0	(2)
(2)	0	3	7	2	(3)
(3)	2	1	7	2	(4)
(4)	0	1	7	4	(5)
(5)	1	0	7	4	*i*
i	1	5	2	4	*c*
c	2	4	2	4	*a*
a	0	4	4	4	

TABLE 4*a*

Table 4*b* shows the back-tracking record. Heavy figures are used to indicate terminal measures; these *must* be used in the next backward step. Primed figures indicate measures which have just been used and must *not* immediately be used again; there will be two of these if the same set of contents is reached by two different paths. (Underlines can be used in manuscript working.)

Letters are used for cross-references, and numerals in parentheses refer to steps back to the start from edge points, as found from Figures 4*F* and 4*G*. The asterisk indicates the emergence of a solution in eight moves: this is not superseded by any better alternative arising later, and leads to the unique eight-move solution as given in Table 4*a*.

[0]

0	4	4	4	*a*

[1]

a	**2**	2′	4	4	*b*
a	**2**	4	2′	4	*c*
a	**2**	4	4	2′	*d*

[2]

b	**0**	2	4	6′	*e*
b	**0**	2	6′	4	*f*
c	**0**	4	2	6′	*g*
d	**0**	4	6′	2	*h*
c	1′	**5**	2	4	*i*
d	1′	**5**	4	2	*j*

[3]

i	1	**0**	**7**	4	(5)*
e	**2**	**0**	4	6	(6)
f	**2**	**0**	6	4	(6)
g	**2**	4	**0**	6	(7)
h	**2**	4	6	**0**	(7)
i	1	**0**	2	9′	*k*
j	1	**0**	4	7′	*l*
j	1	2′	**7**	2	*m*
eg	**2**	2′	2′	6	*n*
fh	**2**	2′	6	2′	*o*

[4]

o	1′	2	**7**	2	*m*
m	**2**	2	6′	2	*o*
k	**0**	1′	2	9	*p*
l	**0**	1′	4	7	*q*
n	**0**	2	2	8′	*r*
km	1	2′	**0**	9′	*s*
l	1	4′	**0**	7	*t*

[5]

t	1	4	**7**	**0**	(6)
r	**2**	**0**	2	8	(4)
p	**2**	1	**0**	9	(4)
r	**2**	2	**0**	8	(5)
s	**0**	2	1′	9	*u*
t	**0**	4	1′	7	*v*
pq	**2**	1	2′	7′	*w*
q	**2**	1	4	5′	*x*

[6]

u	**2**	**0**	1	9	(5)

TABLE 4*b*

A similar procedure will show that there would be four different eight-move solutions if the same quantity of fluid had started in the 12-oz. measure instead of jointly in the 5-oz. and 7-oz. measures.

Readers may now attack Tartaglia's second problem by the method we have just given; or they may prefer the following, which was another competition problem of our own composition:

Test-sample containers for a new rocket fuel are of three sizes, holding exactly 5, 8, or 13 fluid ounces respectively. Three secret agents have each stolen one full container, all of different sizes, but when they meet they find the smallest container has lost its stopper and all its contents.

They have only one other container, which was to have held all the stolen fluid; to guard against further accidents they decide to separate, each taking exactly one-third of the remaining fuel. All containers are opaque and ungraduated, and dip-sticks might contaminate the fluid: the only possibilities of measurement are by filling one container from another. How few pouring operations will suffice, and in how many ways can these be done?

We may note here that since the fourth container could contain all of the fluid which was originally stolen, it must therefore have been able to hold 26 oz. at least. With a total quantity of only 21 oz. of fluid to be divided, this container can never itself be used as a *measure*, since the total quantity of fluid is insufficient to fill it completely. There would be no difference in the solution—or in the essentials of our problem— if instead of this we had a 21-oz. measure, or any larger container.

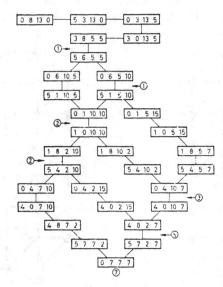

FIGURE 4 *H*

The problem cannot be solved with less than sixteen pouring steps, and there are seven different ways in which these can be performed. (We are here assuming, for instance, that 'fill *D* from *C* twice, using *A* as a measure' is to be regarded as *four* operations.) The seven solutions are shown, with their inter-relations, in Figure 4*H*: numerals in circles indicate how many alternative paths flow through each junction. The four numbers in each symbol, from left to right, give the contents of the 5-oz., 8-oz., and 13-oz. measures, respectively, followed by the contents of the fourth container. The loss of the stopper makes it unsafe to stop one move earlier, with one portion in two parts.

In the actual competition, some unsuccessful entries had diagrams which successfully listed several hundred solutions each with seventeen moves: the maximum here was 834; another had 733. But there are in fact still more; and we would not have demanded something like this, unless by error!

When one measure of fluid will suffice

Some other pouring problems can be treated as equivalent to those we have discussed, if we introduce a notional container which allows us to assume that the total volume of fluid remains constant. In some of these, we have to obtain various numbers of units using only two measures. The source of fluid may be a river which can act both as a source and as a sink: equivalently there may be a tap and a waste; or else a barrel which is not refilled, and a consumer who is.

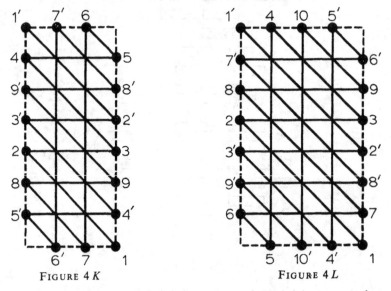

FIGURE 4 K   FIGURE 4 L

In these cases we can combine the source and the sink into a container whose capacity is immaterial: we assume it exceeds the joint capacity of the two measures. Our diagram then takes the form of a parallelogram divided into equilateral triangles, just as in Figures 4A and 4B, and if we like, we can distort this to a rectangular lattice formed from squares which are divided in one of the diagonal directions.

Figures 4K and 4L respectively show this for measures for 3 units and 7 units, and for measures for 4 units and 7 units. The contents of measures are here given by rectangular co-ordinates of the lattice points: plain numerals indicate the sequence of successive contents if a start is made by filling the smaller measure; numerals with dashes apply similarly if the larger measure is the first to be filled.

In Table 4c we list successive contents for measures for 4 units and 7 units. As can be deduced from Figure 4L, these include all the different whole-number contents for either measure, both when the other measure is full and when it is empty (not with *both* full), in sequence all the way down either of the divisions, then across and up the other.

0	0	0	0
4	0	0	7
0	4	4	3
4	4	0	3
1	7	3	0
1	0	3	7
0	1	4	6
4	1	0	6
0	5	4	2
4	5	0	2
2	7	2	0

TABLE 4 c

(To be read down either division, across, and up the other.)

In Figure 4L the changing state of the measures corresponds to a path which can be drawn to join the bottom right and top left corners of the figure: this path provides all the internal straight lines, and can be drawn without lifting pen from paper between one end and the other. (A similar result will always hold when the two measure-numbers—as here—have no common factor: if need be, we should work in terms of a larger unit of volume so that this will apply.)

By these means we can readily determine how best to convert one pair of contents into another, or how best to obtain some specified number of units. In the latter case we must begin at one end of the line, with one measure full, and the other empty; and by examining the diagram it is easy to determine which is the better end to choose in any given case. (If the measure numbers are A and B, the path joins $2A+2B-2$ points, and so has $2A+2B-3$ steps; since this last number is odd, the two choices must involve different numbers of pouring operations.)

The diagram shows other features which are characteristic of any solution: all the lines in any parallel set—horizontal, vertical, or diagonal—are traversed in the same direction, in each case; and every alternate step involves a diagonal line. This means that no measure is ever filled from the source unless it is completely empty, and no measure is ever poured into the sink unless it is completely full: and these last procedures involve different measures, throughout the course of any single solution. Proceeding in one direction, we in effect keep refilling the smaller measure and pouring it into the larger, interrupting this only to empty the larger at the instant it becomes full, before transferring a surplus which would otherwise overflow: in the other direction we similarly use the larger as a means of repeatedly filling the smaller. Since each alternate step of the path is a diagonal one, each alternate move is a transfer between the measures (the same way round in all cases): between these transfers, there is either the refilling of an empty supplier, or the emptying of a full receiver.

One-way traffic from a barrel

In some other problems of this type, the aim is to finish with neither container full, but with each container holding a specified amount—for instance, one unit in each. If the total fluid which is required amounts to the fill of one of the measures, we can proceed as we have just discussed. In other cases the source must either be one whose contents we know, or else one into which we can return some of the fluid: in either case we can conveniently assume that the source is a barrel.

When the total fluid which is finally to remain in the measures is different from the capacity of either of them, the last operation must be an emptying of the barrel into one of the measures, and the barrel must then contain the right amount and no more. So all the original excess content of the barrel must have been otherwise disposed of, as the operation proceeded: and we shall next consider how much this must have involved.

In the first instance we shall assume that we cannot pour back into the barrel: one consequence of this will be that the barrel can never be emptied otherwise than by the last operation. Here we can begin by ignoring the contents of the barrel, and at first merely assume that they are sufficient for any call which is made upon them: we then can consider the original source and the extraneous destination of the fluid to be compounded into a single notional container, just as we should do if our fluid came from and was returned to a river.

We then can use a diagram as in the previous problem, to determine how we can most quickly give one of the containers its final contents and have the other one empty: and in either case we can then work backwards and obtain a minimum possible content for the barrel. Since only one of the measures is ever emptied into the sink (or equivalent), the minimum contents are equal to a multiple of the contents of this measure, plus the final amounts for the two measures: the appropriate multiple is given by the number of lines—either horizontal, or vertical—which are traversed in an appropriate direction in the path concerned.

If two measures for amounts A and B are respectively to contain contents a and b at the end, we draw a diagram to determine how we can get from the point $(0, 0)$ to the points $(a, 0)$ and $(0, b)$; this involves proceeding along a side, either to $(A, 0)$ or to $(0, B)$, then turning on to a diagonal line, and never afterwards moving on a boundary line. These two paths give rise to four cases to consider when a and b are unequal, but only to two if a and b are equal: for in the latter case there can be no need to pour from one container to the other before emptying the barrel. In addition to the number of steps in the path, we need an extra operation to empty the barrel into a measure, at the end.

We can then take note of the fillings which are required, and work backwards to determine the number of moves and minimum content of the barrel, for the alternative routes. Apart from the minimum amount, the barrel may have excess contents which are multiples of the capacity of either measure: each such multiple can be run to waste at the cost of two operations—one to fill a measure from the source and one to empty it to the sink—either initially, or at any later stage when the measure concerned is empty.

0	0	9
4	0	5
0	4	5
4	4	1
1	7	1
1	0	1
1	1	0

TABLE 4*d*

0	0	22
0	7	15
4	3	15
0	3	15
3	0	15
3	7	8
4	6	8
0	6	8
4	2	8

0	2	8
2	0	8
2	7	1
4	5	1
0	5	1
4	1	1
0	1	1
1	1	0

TABLE 4*e*

As an example, we take the case of measures for 4 units and for 7 units; we can here refer to Figure 4L and Table 4c. In one direction we have a path from $(0, 0)$ which reaches $(1, 0)$ before $(0, 1)$, in five steps; in the other there is a fifteen-step path which reaches $(0, 1)$ before $(1, 0)$. We can list the corresponding sequences of contents in two columns, in each case; and if we adjoin a unit entry in the lowest position of a third column, we can complete this column by working backwards and upwards. We thus obtain solutions as in Tables 4*d* and 4*e*: the final emptying of the barrel requires one more move, and the supply of a concluding entry $(1, 1, 0)$, in both cases.

63

Apart from this, all we can do is to empty out full measures which we have filled from the barrel. Pursuing this further, we would find that there are solutions only if the initial contents are 9, 13, 16, 17, or 20 units, or any larger number of units; and that 22 units and 26 units are the only cases for which the longer way round is the shorter way home.

Barrels with unknown contents

Sometimes similar problems are proposed with the initial contents of the barrel only approximately known. Here we must be able to empty the barrel at some intermediate stage, and to continue with a measured quantity of fluid which is then held jointly in the two measures. This will require the subsequent use of a third container which can first receive and then supply fluids; this can be the empty barrel, or anything of adequate capacity, for we shall not require to use this container as a measure.

However, it is still possible that some more fluid may subsequently be run off to waste (or equivalently): so we still must have a sink, and take note of its contents, if we are to be able to regard the total fluid as constant after the first emptying of the barrel.

This means that we have to consider a four-container problem, but one which is less complicated than a general four-measure problem: for we here have one container—the sink—which only receives fluid, and never provides any. The total fluid in the other three containers will here remain constant, except when a contribution is made to the sink, when this total must decrease. As a result of this, we can discuss any problem of this type in terms of a sequence of three-measure problems, in each of which the same three measures are involved, but with a different total quantity of fluid in each case.

We can conveniently assume that we have a tetrahedral diagram where vertical heights indicate contents of the sink: we then can move only in horizontal planes at heights which correspond to particular contents of the sink, apart from ascending the slant faces parallel to one or other of their edges, to pass from a lower horizontal plane to a higher. We can study this in terms of triangular-mesh diagrams for the horizontal sections concerned; and these can here be given a very compact form which readily allows us to make a transfer from one to another, when we ascend to a higher plane.

Once again we start from an assumed solution and work backwards. We first draw a diagram which deals with the total quantity which is jointly in the measures at the end, when a solution is obtained. This will involve an equilateral triangle whose size is determined by the total amount of fluid finally required, and a region whose points can correspond to various possible distributions of this amount of fluid. The region will be the whole triangle, a quadrilateral part or a pentagonal part, according as the total quantity of fluid is sufficient to fill neither measure, one only, or both.

In this diagram we first mark the point corresponding to a solution, and we then insert all the paths which involve this point: we thus obtain the possible earlier positions which have an unaltered quantity of fluid jointly in the measures and in the barrel. Distances measured away from a horizontal baseline can represent contents of the barrel (which must finally be zero), and distances from the slant sides will then represent contents of the measures. On each of the slant sides of the basic triangle, we then obtain one or more associated points which specify sets of contents from which the final result can be attained. For each of these, one measure will be empty; and we next have to consider the possibility that it was previously full, before being emptied into the sink.

We then prolong the horizontal baseline in both directions and extend the slant sides upwards: in each case we need do this only so far as gives a line whose length corresponds to the joint content of the two measures, when we consider one side of the original triangle to be included as part of the line.

We next draw parallels to each of the slant sides, at distances apart which correspond to the number of units for the associated measure; but we continue this only so long as the parallels can intersect the lines we have already drawn. This means there will only be one such parallel, to each side, for the larger measure: there may be more than one, for the smaller.

This divides the plane of our diagram into regions which are bounded by lines parallel to sides of the original triangle: and we need only consider regions which can be reached from the original region by moving always upwards to the left, or always upwards to the right. There will be only one such region, in the one case, but there may be more, in the other: for we cannot fill and empty both measures successively, or the larger measure twice, after the barrel is emptied; but we may be able to do this more than once with the smaller measure.

Each new region then represents a possible earlier state for the measures, and crossing a slant line in an upwards direction implies the filling of an empty measure from the sink. (This is of course the exact reversal of what is a legitimate operation in the forward direction.) On any path which involves more than one region, the crossing of the common boundary will itself correspond to a pouring operation, and each point where a crossing takes place must count as two points—one in each region—associated with different sets of contents: the only difference is that an associated measure is full in one case, and empty in the other.

In each region, once we enter it, we draw paths and obtain further points as in the simple three-measure case: we should proceed outwards and upwards, into successive regions, with the aim of arriving at a vertex, in some region, in the course of the backward path. In different cases, we may find we can reach vertices by proceeding to either side, to one side only, or not at all: for in some regions the path may close cyclically without reaching any vertex. In cases where we can succeed by going to either side, we should consider the shortest solutions for both cases: for the two cases will involve different initial contents for the barrel.

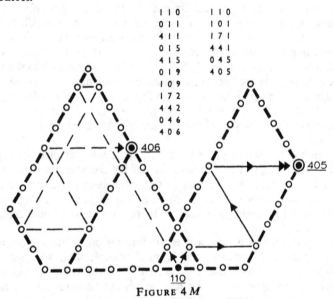

1 1 0	1 1 0
0 1 1	1 0 1
4 1 1	1 7 1
0 1 5	4 4 1
4 1 5	0 4 5
0 1 9	4 0 5
1 0 9	
1 7 2	
4 4 2	
0 4 6	
4 0 6	

FIGURE 4 *M*

If we reach a vertex after a succession of paths in any region, we then can proceed along edges of this region until we reach the uppermost vertex: this vertex corresponds to a situation where both measures are empty and all the fluid is in the barrel. The necessary amount of fluid corresponds to the height of the uppermost vertex, measured from the horizontal baseline, and by reversing the whole of the path by which the last vertex was reached, we obtain a solution which produces the required result if the initial contents of the barrel are in fact what this assumes.

If the initial contents can be assumed to be greater than this, it will not matter what they are: for we can in effect go through the motions of this last solution, having an excess in the barrel until a situation arrives when the barrel should be empty; and at this point we can introduce an extra operation to run off the excess contents. This will require the path to pass at some stage through a point which lies on the horizontal baseline: and if this has not happened otherwise, we can certainly include a point of this type by arranging to call at one of the vertices on the baseline in the course of the edgewise path towards the uppermost vertex.

To illustrate these procedures, we take three cases where the problem is to leave a single unit in each of two measures. If the measures are for 4 units and 7 units, the diagram is as in Figure 4*M*, and we can reach a vertex by proceeding to either side: choosing the best alternative we then have a nine-step solution as in Table 4*f*. If the measures are for

0	0	9+		0	0	12+	3 0 9
4	0	5+		0	8	4+	3 8 1
4	5	0+		4	8	0+	5 6 1
4	5	0		4	8	0	0 6 1
4	0	5		0	8	4	5 1 1
0	4	5		5	3	4	0 1 1
4	4	1		0	3	9	1 1 0
1	7	1					
1	0	1					
1	1	0					

Table 4*f*   Table 4*g*

5 units and 8 units, the diagram is as in Figure 4*N*, and a vertex can here be reached on one side only—the paths close cyclically at the other side; and we then have a thirteen-step solution as in Table 4*g*. If the measures are for 7 units and 12 units, there is cyclic closure everywhere, as Figure 4*P* shows: so there can be no solution here in any case where the initial contents of the barrel are not exactly known.

How to avoid going round in circles

The methods we have just described can be of use in similar problems when the initial contents of the barrel are in fact known exactly. When the methods of the previous section give a solution which is applicable to all initial contents in excess of some known amount, we have only to see if there are shorter solutions for any particular initial contents: if they show that no such solution exists, we have to adopt a different procedure, where similar diagrams can still be of use.

In the first of these cases, we may reach a final vertex more quickly if we can dispense with the requirement to call at a vertex on the baseline, and this can save three operations. With measures for 4 units and 7 units, for instance, we can leave one unit in each measure in only six moves, if initially we have 9 units, but all greater initial contents will require nine moves as in Table 4*f*. With measures for 5 units and

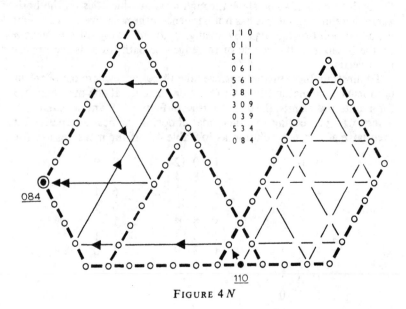

```
1 1 0
0 1 1
5 1 1
0 6 1
5 6 1
3 8 1
3 0 9
0 3 9
5 3 4
0 8 4
```

084

110

FIGURE 4 *N*

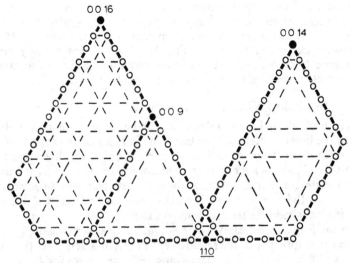

FIGURE 4 *P*

8 units, we can do the same in only ten moves, not only for 12 units initially, but for 17 as well: all other contents in excess of 12 units will require thirteen moves as in Table 4g.

The difference here is that in the first case the minimum solution always pours the full 4-unit measure into the sink: in the second case, the minimum solution empties a full 5-unit measure into the barrel, at one stage, if initially there are 12 units; by diverting this to the sink, we can deal with 5 more units initially, in the same number of steps. The largest initial contents which we can thus obtain will then be the initial contents which will give the required result in the fewest moves, if we are forbidden to pour back into the barrel. Sequences of contents for these solutions are given in Tables 4h, 4k, and 4l.

0	0	9		0	0	12		0	0	17
				0	8	4		0	8	9
4	0	5		5	3	4		5	3	9
				0	3	9		0	3	9
0	4	5		3	0	9		3	0	9
				3	8	1		3	8	1
4	4	1		5	6	1		5	6	1
				0	6	1		0	6	1
1	7	1		5	1	1		5	1	1
				0	1	1		0	1	1
1	0	1								
1	1	0		1	1	0		1	1	0
TABLE 4*h*				TABLE 4*k*				TABLE 4*l*		

If we have a problem where backward paths all close in loops to prevent us from emptying the barrel prior to the final transfer, we then must know the initial contents of the barrel, and these must be a whole number of units. Solutions will here exist for all whole numbers above a certain limit: but we now can set no limit to the number of operations as the initial contents are increased, since the excess in the barrel cannot be run to waste, but must be emptied out in individually measured quantities.

Any solution here must have what we may call a basic phase, and there may or may not be a preceding phase, or a subsequent phase, in addition to this. Initially, both measures must be empty; and just before the last operation, one measure must have its final contents. (The other measure must then be empty, with its contents waiting for it in the barrel.) This means that at some stage of the operation we must start with both measures empty, and produce the desired quantity for the measure which first receives its final contents: this is the basic phase which is inevitable; but we may perform other operations, so long as they do not interfere with this.

We first concentrate on the earliest occasion when the required amount for the chosen measure appeared as a separate quantity; and for the moment we ignore the possibility of subsequently transferring this quantity as a whole from one container to the other, or of using an empty container for removing a further quantity from the barrel. Similarly we concentrate on the latest occasion when there is no fluid in either measure, ignoring for the moment that there may have been earlier operations which served to give the equivalent of a reduction of the initial contents.

If we now think only of the fluid in the measures, we in effect have a problem which we discussed earlier—to produce a required amount using only two measures: so one of the measures must receive fluid repeatedly from the other measure, and be emptied intermittently when it becomes full: and the other measure must be repeatedly filled as it becomes empty in this process. (We can start in either of two ways: and if the two quantities finally required were different, we could look for the first appearance of either of them.)

The refilling of the second measure must draw its fluid from the barrel, but any emptyings of the first measure may be either into the barrel or into the sink. According to how we allocate these emptyings, we can remove from the barrel any of a definite set of amounts between an upper and a lower limit; and in any given case we can determine initial contents of the barrel which are only just sufficient to ensure that no impossible demands are made at any intermediate stage.

If for instance we have to produce a one-unit quantity with measures for 7 units and 12 units, the shortest way involves filling the 12-unit measure three times, and emptying the 7-unit measure five times: in an alternative procedure, we may fill the 7-unit measure seven times and empty the 12-unit measure four times. If there is sufficient fluid in the barrel, the first procedure may remove from the barrel an amount of 1, 8, 15, 22, 29, or 36 units, and the second procedure can similarly remove 1, 13, 25, 37, or 49 units: but restrictions at intermediate stages will make some of these removals impossible for sufficiently small initial contents.

In Tables 4*m* and 4*n* we show contents for the two measures, in both of these procedures, and in a third column we show the cumulative removals from the barrel which must have been made, at various stages, if the minimum demand is to be made on the initial contents of the barrel. This requires all emptyings to be made into the barrel, at the beginning: but not necessarily so, at the end.

At the end of this stage, the barrel must still contain enough to fill the other measure: and if it does not contain this exactly, the excess must be such as can be measured out and rejected, using either one measure or both, but only one at a time, while preserving the already measured quantity in the other.

0	0	−12
0	12	
7	5	−5
0	5	
5	0	−17
5	12	
7	10	−10
0	10	
7	3	−3
0	3	
3	0	−15
3	12	
7	8	−8, −15
0	8	
7	1	−1, −8, −15
0	1	

TABLE 4 *m*

0	0	−7
7	0	
0	7	−14
7	7	
2	12	−2
2	0	
0	2	−9
7	2	
0	9	−16
7	9	
4	12	−4
4	0	
0	4	−11
7	4	
0	11	−18
7	11	
6	12	−6
6	0	
0	6	−13
7	6	
1	12	−1, −13
1	0	

TABLE 4 *n*

To find the minimum initial contents which will allow a solution, we have to examine all initial contents in excess of 17 units, in the first case, and in excess of 18 units, in the second; and we have to consider the different overall reductions which either procedure can provide, according to the alternatives which may be chosen in the final operations.

Barrel contents initially	Barrel contents finally
18	17, 10, 3;
19	18, 11, 4; 18, 6
20	19, 12, 5; 19, 7
21	20, **13**, 6; 20, 8

TABLE 4 *p*

Table 4*p* shows the various final contents of the barrel which are possible for an increasing series of initial contents: the first case where we can arrive at a one-unit quantity is for initial contents of 21 units; the solution in fewest moves comes from rejecting 12 units from a final quantity of 13 units, and we then have a nineteen-move solution as in

Puzzles and Paradoxes

Table 4*q*. Alternatives here arise for a few moves, because either of two emptyings of the 7-unit measure can be to the sink, if the other is to the barrel.

With 22 units initially, we find we cannot reach a solution *in this way*: but we can do it for 23 units, when an earlier emptying of the 7-unit measure can be diverted to the sink, to produce the cumulative removal of 22, which then is allowable, instead of only 15 as given in the table.

```
                0   0  21                        0   0  23
                0  12   9                        0  12  11
                7   5   9                        7   5  11
                0   5  16                        0   5  18
                5   0  16                        5   0  18
                5  12   4                        5  12   6
                7  10   4                        7  10   6
                0  10  11
                7   3  11              0  10  6              0  10  13
                0   3  18              7   3  6              7   3  13
                3   0  18                        0   3  13
                3  12   6                        3   0  13
                7   8   6                        3  12   1
     0  8  6              0  8  13               7   8   1
     7  1  6              7  1  13               0   8   1
                0   1  13                        7   1   1
                1   0  13                        0   1   1
                1  12   1                        1   1   0
                1   0   1
                1   1   0
```

TABLE 4*q*	TABLE 4*r*

We then obtain a one-unit quantity at the end, with nothing further to do, and we can have a sixteen-move solution as in Table 4*r*, with alternatives at one point, for the same reason as in the last case.

If we have 22 units initially, we have to introduce an initial phase—using the same operations as in the other cases, and never emptying measures otherwise than into the barrel—to produce a one-unit quantity in one of the measures. We then reject this to the sink, and in effect this puts us back to the beginning of the 21-unit problem. We finally can have a 35-move solution here, as in Table 4*s*: independent alternatives at each of two stages lead to four variant forms, in all. For other numbers of units initially, we can consider which choices for the three phases will give the fewest operations overall.

As the initial number of units increases, the minimum number of moves for a solution at first fluctuates quite violently, as we have seen:

it later steadies down to a smaller fluctuation superimposed on a regular increase. In Table 4*t* we give numbers of moves which suffice for all initial contents between 87 units and 98 units inclusive, with some additional information to act as a pointer to the nature of the solutions. For larger numbers, we can reckon two more moves for every additional multiple of 12 units. For smaller numbers, we may in some cases be

```
0  0 22        7  8  7                7  3 11
0 12 10        0  8 14                0  3 18
7  5 10        7  1 14                3  0 18
0  5 17    7 0 14      0  1 21        3 12  6
5  0 17        0  0 21                7  8  6
5 12  5        0 12  9        0 8 6          0 8 13
7 10  5        7  5  9        7 1 6          7 1 13
0 10 12        0  5 16                0  1 13
7  3 12        5  0 16                1  0 13
0  3 19        5 12  4                1 12  1
3  0 19        7 10  4                1  0  1
3 12  7        0 10 11                1  1  0
```

TABLE 4*s*

able to use solutions as in Table 4*t* by dispensing with some of the special final removals: in other cases we may have to make an initial reduction of contents in the way we had to do for 22 units. (Note that when the specially measured quantity is emptied out, in any such initial reduction, this still is a reversible move—as we consider these—since the sink is then empty and so is in a terminal state.)

Initial contents	87	88		89	90	91	92	93	94	95	96	97	98
Basic phase removes	36	8	49	36	22	36	36	49	36	15	36	29	36
7-unit measure removes	14	7	14	28	7	42	7	7	21	7	35	7	49
12-unit measure removes	36	72	24	24	60	12	48	36	36	72	24	60	12
Number of moves	27	31	31	29	29	31	27	31	29	31	31	29	33

TABLE 4*t*

Readers may like to obtain isometric paper—it is useful for much else—and to explore further on their own. Alternatively they may rule a set of parallel diagonals to bisect the squares of square-ruled paper: there is then a triangular mesh, and the barrel can be associated with the diagonal direction. Colours can be used in a definite progressive sequence, when drawing paths, in place of giving a common numeral to points which can be reached by the same number of moves.

Customers who mix their drinks: the bartender's guide

In some problems there are two measures, and two different fluids which have to be mixed in proportions which are specified by simple fractions. Any change of relative concentration can here take place only by adding a quantity of one of the pure fluids to a mixture, or, initially, to a quantity of the other; and we shall regard each such operation as a dilution, by assuming that it is the added fluid which dilutes the other fluid. This means that we do not fix our ideas about which of the fluids is diluted by the other: our viewpoint will change if a later operation involves a change of the pure fluid which is added to the existing mixture. We always consider a concentration fraction which gives the proportion of the *non-diluting* fluid, by volume, in the mixture; we can then subtract this from unity if we have to reverse the roles of the two fluids.

There are two distinct ways in which a mixture can take place: we may have to add enough of one of the pure fluids to top up the small measure, or the large measure; or there may be room in the large measure to add one or more fills of the small measure, with some capacity to spare.

In any mixture, our concentration fraction is then always *reduced*, by multiplication by a fraction whose numerator and denominator are given by numbers of units before and after the mixing operation: in a topping-up operation, the denominator will be the number of units in the measure concerned. Fractions whose denominators involve prime factors not present in either measure-number can be introduced only if at least one mixing operation involves a measured addition, rather than a topping-up; and any measured addition of this type will involve a fraction whose denominator (before possible simplification) must be intermediate between the two measure-numbers. As a result of this, a concentration fraction with a denominator prime and larger than the greater measure-number cannot be obtained at all: for instance, no legitimate means can produce a concentration fraction of 1 in 7 if there are measures only for 2 units and 5 units.

With a 2-unit and a 5-unit measure, however, we can produce a mixture whose concentration is any rational fraction $x = p/q$ where p and q are whole numbers such that $p < q \leqslant 6$. For $x = \frac{1}{2}$, we can mix 2 units of each fluid in the 5-unit measure; and since any mixing operation must involve at least 2 units of fluid, we can reject any surplus over 2 units and then halve the concentration for the rest, for any mixture, in similar fashion. For $x = \frac{1}{3}$, we first make use of both measures in order to produce a one-unit quantity of the fluid of which there is to be less, and then to this we add two units of the other fluid; we transform $x = \frac{2}{3}$ into $x = \frac{1}{3}$ by interchanging the fluids. For $x = \frac{1}{4}$ we produce a mixture for $x = \frac{1}{2}$ and then halve its concentration; for $x = \frac{1}{6}$ we do the same for a mixture for $x = \frac{1}{3}$: by exchange of fluids these cover the cases of $x = \frac{3}{4}$ and $x = \frac{5}{6}$. For the various fifths, we can first use both measures to put an appropriate number of units in the 5-unit measure, and then top up with a change of fluid: it can take fewer operations here if some of these fifths are derived by halving a concentration corresponding to some one of the others.

Other cases can be dealt with in similar fashion. Limitations can arise in the attempt to obtain two desired factors successively; for achieving the second factor may require a particular number of units of the earlier mixture which cannot be made available. For instance, with measures for 3 units and 7 units we can obtain $x = p/q$ for $p < q \leqslant 8$, but no fractions with $q = 9$; with measures for 4 units and 7 units we cannot produce concentrations of 2 in 5, 1 in 8, or 1 in 10.

5 *A Gamut of Geometry from A to Y*

School geometry and a vicious circle

Two quite different reasons can justify teaching some geometry to all school pupils: the matter which will be presented, and the manner in which it will be handled. Some familiarity with spatial relationships and some training in deductive reasoning are both desirable in a general education; and each can be given an appropriate emphasis, according to the ages and capacities of the pupils.

Practical work in drawing figures and measuring lengths and angles can serve the first purpose; so also can work with models—and with some forms of puzzles: but mathematics in the true sense enters only when the second objective is in clear view, and with it the need for logical forms of proof.

A typical mathematical argument will take some statements and show how they are logical consequences of others, in a chain going back to some fundamental statements which are not to be questioned: for if we go far enough back, the chain must stop somewhere—it cannot continue indefinitely. Similar logical principles could be applied to construct a dictionary, which would then start with a list of words whose meaning had to be assumed known; it would then proceed to define some words in terms of these, and others in terms of any whose meanings had been earlier established.

No such dictionary appears to exist, and so actual dictionaries provide scope for J. L. Synge's game of *Vish* (from *vicious circle*): contestants choose a word, then another from its definition, and so on; with each new choice they add one unit to their score, until they arrive at a word they have had before. As in golf, the player with the lowest score is the winner: '*the*' defined as '*the definite article*' is a hole in one, and rather much to expect; the best hope is usually a loop between '*begin*' and '*commence*', or between '*state*' and '*condition*'.

The words in the initial list are like the axioms and postulates of a branch of mathematics. Euclid recognized the need for these: in one sense this is the true beginning of mathematics. His pioneer work was imperfect, however, for he makes implicit use of some assumptions which he does not state explicitly; and failing these we can have some familiar geometrical fallacies, which are based on the use of an inaccurate figure.

But the rules of the game are not maintained if an actual figure has to be drawn and examined—its nature ought to be able to be *deduced*: this can be done in terms of more modern (and perhaps more difficult) sets of basic assumptions. So the works of Euclid are now less valued—in the letter—than they were; in the spirit, they win him ever more sincere flattery as their axiomatic treatment is imitated, to provide a firm basis for progress, in other and newer branches of mathematics.

Making do with fewer points

To illustrate our previous remarks, we shall consider a geometry which still exhibits very many of the features of our more familiar geometry, notwithstanding some quite fundamental differences. The most drastic distinction is that we shall no longer have an infinitely extending plane, with points and lines available everywhere in infinite variety: there will be only a very limited number of each. At first we shall have only twenty-five points and thirty lines; later, we shall find it convenient to increase the numbers to give us thirty-one elements of each type.

We shall first have to set out the assumptions which we propose to make: these will specify the inter-relations of these points and lines, and the manner in which we shall define related concepts such as distances, parallelism, and perpendicularity. Some of our demands here may seem strange, and readers should not try to draw figures of the usual type: but strictly speaking there should be no need to draw figures at all—everything must be able to proceed by purely logical arguments, referring everything back to our original assumptions; and this can in fact be done, by those who wish the full rigour of the game.

However, we shall later give a diagram of a more ordinary type; and we shall indicate a way in which this can be interpreted to give a more intuitive appreciation of our basic assumptions. This may make it easier for readers to accept these assumptions—provisionally, at least—before proceeding onwards with us to explore some of their consequences: they may be surprised to find how many of the familiar results of geometry still are true, when reinterpreted in terms of our new concepts. (There are indeed some other results which become false: but readers may be equally surprised to discover how few these are, and how relatively difficult they are to find.)

Our new geometry has one advantage over geometry of the more familiar type: we have a choice of two different ways of proving our theorems. These can indeed be established by logical deduction, as in more conventional geometry; but if we fail here—or prefer otherwise—

an alternative is available: for when the number of cases is finite, a successful verification for all cases will in fact constitute a perfectly valid proof.

The laws of the letters

We shall label our twenty-five points with letters from *A* to *Y*, and group the points in three ways as in Table 5*a*. We shall assume that each row or column here gives a set of points which are to be regarded as lying on one of our lines: so there are thirty lines in all, on each of which there are only five points. Lines are to be considered neither parallel nor perpendicular unless they appear in the same table: in any one table, two rows or else two columns are to give a pair of parallel

A	*B*	*C*	*D*	*E*		*A*	*I*	*L*	*T*	*W*		*A*	*X*	*Q*	*O*	*H*
F	*G*	*H*	*I*	*J*		*S*	*V*	*E*	*H*	*K*		*R*	*K*	*I*	*B*	*Y*
K	*L*	*M*	*N*	*O*		*G*	*O*	*R*	*U*	*D*		*J*	*C*	*U*	*S*	*L*
P	*Q*	*R*	*S*	*T*		*Y*	*C*	*F*	*N*	*Q*		*V*	*T*	*M*	*F*	*D*
U	*V*	*W*	*X*	*Y*		*M*	*P*	*X*	*B*	*J*		*N*	*G*	*E*	*W*	*P*

TABLE 5 *a*

lines, and a row and a column are to give a pair of perpendicular lines. Any two lines then will be found to have one and only one point in common unless they are parallel, when they will have none; and the tables are arranged so that any two points will define a line—to be found in one of the three tables—on which three other points will lie.

In accord with these assumptions, we can then make use of these tables to determine—for instance—that the points *E* and *F* lie on a line together with the points *L*, *R*, *X*; whereas the points *J* and *K* lie on a line together with the points *Q*, *W*, *D*: and we can see that these are parallel lines. Similarly we can find that the line through *A* which is perpendicular to both these lines includes the other points *I*, *L*, *T*, *W*: so the foot of the perpendicular from *A* to *EF* is found to be *L*, and the foot of the perpendicular from *A* to *JK* is found to be *W*.

Distances between points are to depend only on the separation of their symbols in the row or column where these two symbols appear together; and the rows and columns are to be thought of as cyclic, with the first following after the last. There are then only four different distances—one row-unit, or two, or else one column-unit, or two; and we can take these with signs, directionally, if we like; but we must regard row-units and column-units as distances which are different, and indeed incommensurable.

In view of this, for instance, we can determine that $DE = EA$, and hence that *E* is the mid-point of *DA*; similarly we have $FP = PA$, to show that P is the mid-point of FA. The triangles ABI and ABX are equilateral, since $AB = AI = IB = AX = XB$; the triangles ABN and ABS are isosceles, since NA, NB, AS, and BS have a common length, different from that of AB: ABM is a triangle which has all its sides unequal, and we can in fact see that it is a right-angled triangle, with hypotenuse AB.

Similarly, $AFGL$ is a parallelogram, with unequal pairs of opposite sides $AF = GL$ and $AG = FL$, and with diagonals AL and FG which intersect in I: whereas $BFLH$ is a rhombus, formed by two adjacent equilateral triangles BFL, BLH, and diagonals BL and FH of this rhombus intersect at right angles at G. It should be noted that $ABFG$ is a rectangle which has unequal pairs of opposite sides $AB = FG$ and $AF = BG$; for the length of AB (or FG) is a row-unit, whereas that of AF (or BG) is a column-unit: and one of our assumptions has been that these are not identical. Here we see a first important difference from ordinary geometry—there is no figure which can be regarded as a square: for it is not possible to have equal lengths on lines which are perpendicular (and this is true of some other pairs of lines as well).

On the other hand, the six points $N\ U\ M\ R\ F\ S$ are all equidistant from the point A; and when they are taken in this order they form a figure which has all the symmetry properties of a regular hexagon. The six vertices of this hexagon can be considered to lie on a circle—or, indeed, to form a circle: for we can define circles as containing all the points which lie at a given distance from a given point; and each point is then the centre of four concentric circles, on each of which there are six of the other points. For any circle, there are lines which are the radii to its six different points, and we can define tangents as lines which meet a circle in one and only one point: we find then that associated radii and tangents are always perpendicular. But we here discover another difference from our more customary geometry: there are lines through the centre of a circle which do not pass through any point which lies on the circle.

We have given some illustrative examples so that readers may see how a variety of consequences follow directly from our assumptions. We now go on to provide the more intuitive aids which we previously promised; and readers may like to consider our examples again, with this further assistance.

Something to put on the wall

In Figure 5A we indicate a pattern which involves the twenty-five letters from A to Y arranged by fives on a number of lines: rectangles similar to our figure could be put together to cover a plane with this pattern in endless repetition—like a wall-paper design. No letter truly plays a part different from any other; the lines on which there are symbols *A* have been shown heavy only to exhibit the repetitive or periodic nature of the arrangement.

The true pattern-unit is smaller than our rectangle: for the whole pattern is in fact defined inside any rhombus which is formed by the

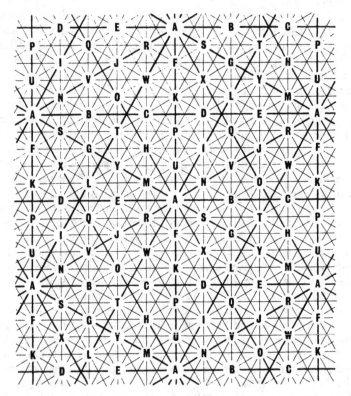

FIGURE 5*A*

union of two adjacent equilateral triangles whose vertices are three neighbouring repeats of some individual letter.

Our figure in fact involves a planar rhombic lattice as considered in crystallography: the pattern here repeats after five lattice steps along any line; and it can be regarded—in three distinct ways—as generated by two sets of equidistant parallel lines, with the addition of the other lines which form the shorter diagonals of the lattice cells, together with three other sets of lines which form longer diagonals of the three sets of identical rhombi which the first three sets of lines produce.

The rectangle of Figure 5*A* has on its boundary a set of six symbols

A which are arranged at vertices of a regular hexagon: intersections of parallels and perpendiculars to pairs of opposite sides indicate three rectangular arrangements identical to those of Table 5*a*; and the whole pattern can be regarded as formed by two identical interpenetrating rectangular lattices whose common pattern-unit is any one of these three arrangements.

In the ordinary way, we would regard our pattern as containing an infinite number of different points which had a common label *A*, and similarly for the other letters: instead of this, we now want to assume that every appearance of each letter relates only to a single point. The diagram is not itself the subject-matter of our geometry—it is to be considered only as a *map* of this: and just as happens with world maps in geography, we prefer to represent points in more than one place in the map, since we then have a more convenient way of showing every point surrounded by its true environment.

If we now assume we have only twenty-five points *A, B, C,...*, *Y*, we can then use our pattern to define thirty lines on which these points lie by sets of five at a time, similarly to their symbols: six of these lines will then pass through each one of the points. Pairs of lines can be defined as either parallel or perpendicular if the like is true of their counterparts in the diagram: two points will uniquely define a line on which they both lie; and two lines must either be parallel or else define a unique point in which they intersect. In this fashion we can obtain again what we have already defined in terms of Table 5*a*.

Basically, a reference to the three schemes of Table 5*a* could suffice; but use of the diagram of Figure 5*A* may be more convenient. The thing to note is that if two lines appear to intersect in an unlabelled point, somewhere else on the diagram two equivalent lines must intersect in a point which *is* labelled: similarly, we may be led to consider two symbols in positions where they are unconnected by any line; if so, the same symbols will be connected by a line somewhere else. We should also note that if two points appear to be an odd number of lattice units apart, there is somewhere else where they are separated by an even number of intervals, which will serve to indicate their mid-point—collinear with and equidistant from them both; and to find points of trisection we can substitute six steps for one, or three for two.

If, for instance, we wish to find the centre of the rhombus *ANBS*, we will not find a label on the necessary point if we look at a rhombus whose sides are only one lattice-unit long: but we can find rhombi, similarly labelled, whose sides—in the diagram—appear four times as large, or six times as large; and in these cases we find a symbol *D* on the point of intersection, in agreement with what we should obtain by direct use of the fundamental assumptions.

Similarly, if we consider the equilateral triangle *AFS*, we find no label for its centroid if we consider the smallest representation which this triangle has in our figure; but if we take a representation six times as large, we find a point which is labelled Q. We then find other appropriately labelled points at the mid-points of the sides, also, which we could equally well have identified by using the basic tables: we could then have determined that Q was indeed a common intersection for AO, FY, and SP, and a point of trisection for them all.

If only three points are involved, we can always find three correspondingly labelled points whose joins appear as actual lines of the diagram. This is not always possible for four points—we cannot choose unique representations of four points A, G, I, Q, for instance, and have all six joins as actual lines; but this need not trouble us: for we can transfer from any point to an equivalently labelled point, at any time, if this is more convenient for what we require.

An incomparable arithmetic

The cyclic recurrence of columns and rows implies that lengths 6, 11, 16, ... units are the same as unit lengths; and that lengths of 4, 9, 14, ... units are to be considered to be unit lengths measured in the contrary direction: the addition of multiples of 5 units must be considered to leave lengths undisturbed. One consequence of this is that numbers need be considered only in terms of the remainders which are left when they are divided by 5: if we have a rational fraction—such as the ratio of two lengths which are multiples of the same unit—the numerator can be increased by any multiple of 5 which will permit division by the denominator without a remainder; and multiples of 5 can then be subtracted from the quotient which so results. All numbers can thus be reduced to one of 0, ± 1, ± 2; or to one of 0, 1, 2, 3, 4.

Lengths on lines—or distances between points—can be distinguished according to the *minimum* separation of associated symbols in our diagram: we can attach signs if we like, and lengths for segments can then be added in the usual way. We can assume we have two units of length, one equal to $\sqrt{3}$ times the other, and lengths can be taken to have magnitude either 1 or else 2, in terms of one or other of these units.

But neither of two unequal lengths can be definitely identified as the larger: this is not really surprising; when a length of $+4$ is equivalent to a length of -1, it is difficult to make comparisons of size with a length of $+2$ which in any case is equivalent to a length of -3. We may note here that we cannot say unequivocally that a length—or number—is positive, or negative: but in appropriate cases we *can* establish that two lengths—or two numbers—have equal magnitudes and opposite signs.

Difficulties in comparing sizes would arise as follows. To obtain a number $\frac{1}{2}$, we divide 1 by 2: but here we can equally well divide 6 by 2, to get 3, which we can then call −2; so for each unit there are two lengths *each* of which would have to be regarded as having double the magnitude of the other—with a change of sign in one case, but not in the other.

To pursue this further would involve some risk of confusing the map with what it represents. The proper view is to note that on any line we may have lengths of either of two magnitudes, directed in either of two directions; and that if any one of these is taken as a unit, the others then can definitely be taken to have lengths of −1, +2, and −2 units.

Whichever choice we make, however, the *ratio* of two lengths then has a value which is independent of the unit chosen; hence we can unambiguously attribute to any such ratio one—and only one—of the four values ±1, ±2: but we may at times have to note that +2 and −2 have to be considered as reciprocals, in the associated arithmetic, since −4 and +1 here have to be considered to be equivalent.

The situation is no different with the incommensurable units for two perpendicular directions. We have said that one unit can be considered to be √3 times the other; and in our diagram we would naturally assume that *AB* was a larger unit, and *AF* a smaller unit. But we could leave *AB* as a unit for the horizontal lines (and their associates), and take *AP* instead of *AF* to be the unit for the vertical lines (and their associates); we could then erase two symbols out of three on every vertical line, and this would leave a diagram with just the same relations as we had before—though the lines associated with the larger and smaller units would then have been interchanged.

So in all there are only four different lengths to consider—or eight, if we introduce considerations of sign, to distinguish different directions: we can tell if two lengths are the same, or different; and we can find numbers to express ratios of lengths, and handle their arithmetic. But we still cannot say that either of two different lengths must be the larger, let alone determine which one this is: and even when we use some numbers, such as 0, ±1, ±2, we shall never find any situation in which there will be any point in saying—or even believing—that +2 is greater than +1.

We had better regard our numbers only as a limited set of labels, which are convenient because we can handle them by the usual rules of arithmetic, if we remember that we can—and must—add some other operations: for we must stop our arithmetic from giving any numbers extraneous to our chosen set; and we do this by arbitrary additions or subtractions of multiples of 5, in the way we have previously discussed.

Triangles old and new

With these preliminaries, we can now consider various figures and various geometrical results in further detail: and we will start with triangles, and continue as far as conic sections.

Any three of our twenty-five points which are non-collinear can be considered as vertices of a triangle, and in all there are 2,000 different triangles possible. These are of one or other of three types, and each type appears in four sizes, each in twenty-five distinct positions: equilateral triangles like *ABX* can have two orientations, and isosceles triangles like *ABN* can have six; scalene triangles like *ABF* can have twelve—but are all right-angled.

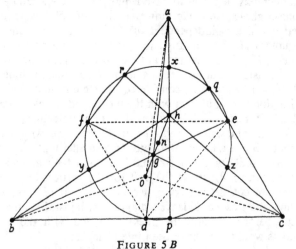

FIGURE 5 *B*

Most of our familiar results for triangles can be found anew in our 25-point geometry, and it is sufficient if we verify this for three particular triangles, one of each different type. There is one notable omission— we can find no point which is the in-centre of other than an equilateral triangle: but each of our triangles has a circumcentre, a centroid, and an orthocentre; and these have the expected properties, in all cases.

Now you see it—now you don't!

In Figure 5*B* we show a conventional triangle, with the Euler line through the circumcentre *o*, the centroid *g*, and the orthocentre *h*; the figure also shows some construction lines involving midpoints and perpendiculars, as well as the nine-point circle, with centre *n*. All this carries over to our 25-point geometry, with symbols corresponding as in Table 5*b*; the specialization of our triangles makes some points coincide, and there is in fact a valid nine-point-circle theorem, in spite of the fact that circles here can have no more than six different points.

But we cannot have Feuerbach's theorem that this circle touches the in-circle and the three ex-circles; for these other circles do not exist for other than the equilateral triangles. In the other types of triangles, some angles occur between sides for which length-units are incommensurable; and the construction to bisect an angle is impossible if we cannot cut off equal lengths on the two arms of the angle. If we could, always, we could bisect angles repeatedly, and we would soon have lines which were not confined to one or other of only six sets of parallels.

a	b	c		d	e	f	p	q	r	x	y	z		o	g	h		n
A	B	X		M	O	D	M	O	D	Y	W	I		S	S	S		S
A	B	N		H	J	D	T	R	D	T	R	X		S	X	I		N
A	B	F		S	P	D	O	A	A	A	D	P		S	M	A		Y

TABLE 5 b

We can next take one specimen of each of our three types of triangle, and consider position-ratios for points taken on each of the three sides, in a cyclic succession. For three position-ratios, we can have a product of -1 (by way of $+4$), if we have one ratio of $+1$, and the other two either both $+2$ or both -2: we can then verify that the associated points are collinear; and so Menelaus' theorem is true. But to have a product of $+1$ (by way of -4) we must have all three position-ratios different, if we are not just to have medians and the centroid, for a trivial case of Ceva's theorem: and we then find that in some cases the Ceva lines are parallel, instead of being concurrent in one of our twenty-five points.

We may note another consequence of our curious (but nevertheless entirely consistent) arithmetic: any four points on a line will form a harmonic range. This is true of B, C, D, E, for instance, if we take the conjugate pairs to be B, E and C, D; for we have equal and opposite position-ratios $BD/DE = +2$ and $BC/CE = -2$. This last result can help us if we wish to find systems of coaxial circles. One set with point circles at B and E also includes the circle $CQTDOL$, in addition to the straight line $AFKPU$ which is the right bisector of BE: this set is orthogonal to another set which consists of the straight line $ABCDE$ and the two circles $BFETKQ$ and $BUEOPL$. One proper circle in the one set is thus orthogonal to two proper circles in the other.

When twice as big is the same size

In Table 5c we classify sets of four points where no three are collinear: there are ten distinct types, and 6,500 in all. The best method of enumeration takes note of symmetry properties and parallelism, and of specifications in terms of angles, since all these are independent of size, position, or orientation.

Angles can be defined as follows: parallels and perpendiculars make angles of $0°$ and $90°$ respectively; non-parallel lines which have *equal* lattice units lie at 60° angles, and non-perpendicular lines which have *unequal* lattice units lie at 30° angles.

We then must note that one type of quadrangle does *not* exist in four distinct sizes, but only in two (*AFGL* is one example): an attempt to double its size only converts it into its reflection, with vertices and lengths permuted. We indicate various distinctions which will assist the selection of appropriate examples for examining various properties of quadrilaterals.

Typical set of vertices	No. of sizes	No. of orienta- tions for each size	No. of pairs of parallel sides	No. of sym- metry axes	Centre of sym- metry?	Four vertices con- cyclic?	No. of different cases
ABFG	4	3	2	2	YES	YES	300
BFHL	4	3	2	2	YES	NO	300
AFGL	2	6	2	–	YES	NO	300
ABKQ	4	6	2	–	YES	NO	600
AGQU	4	6	1	1	NO	YES	600
AKLQ	4	12	1	–	NO	NO	1,200
ABFL	4	12	1	–	NO	NO	1,200
ACGQ	4	2	–	3	NO	NO	200
BFHV	4	6	–	1	NO	YES	600
AGIQ	4	12	–	–	NO	NO	1,200

TABLE 5c

All this—and conics too!

But we are not limited to the simple figures which we can construct with straight lines and circles: we can have conic sections, too; and we shall have more to say of these, later.

Meanwhile we will remark that we can choose a point and a line as the focus and directrix for a parabola; we can then find five points which are equidistant from focus and directrix, and also a line which is an axis of symmetry for this five-point parabola. Through each of the five points there are six lines: four join it to each of the other points, singly, and a fifth coincides with or is parallel to the axis; the remaining line can be regarded as the tangent at the point, and the following theorem is then true for this parabola as for a more conventional one: 'the tangents at the extremities of a focal chord intersect at right angles on the directrix'.

Readers may like to investigate the focus-and-directrix properties of typical conic sections, and we offer them the following assistance: the six points *BNMERS* lie on an ellipse with foci *K* and *P*, associated respectively with directrices *FGHIJ* and *UVWXY*; the five points *JMUNG* lie on a parabola with focus *A* and directrix *FGHIJ*. With this we pass to another problem, which falls into two parts.

A different problem: or is it?

We first suppose that we have to help a race-course owner out of the following difficulty. His track is circular and about 1,000 metres in diameter: it has in fact a centre line exactly 3,100 metres in circumference. He wishes to be able to run trials and races for every exact multiple of 100 metres, with photo-recording of starts and finishes, and he cannot face the cost of thirty-one sets of photographic equipment.

He has just realized that he may well manage with fewer, since he need not have a common starting or finishing point, and each camera can be used either for a start or for a finish. How few equipments need he buy, and how should he locate them, if every length of race is to be possible from some one of them to another?

That was the first part of the problem. The second part is to discover what this has to do with our 25-point geometry—for there is in fact a connexion, as we shall later see.

6 Race-track Problems and Legal Fictions

Making the circuit of the race-tracks

If as few as possible camera equipments are to be placed round a 3,100-metre track, in such a way that races of any exact multiple of 100 metres can be started opposite some appropriate camera, to finish opposite some one of the others, this requires thirty different courses each of which is less than a full circuit: each pair of camera stations will divide the circuit into a shorter arc and a longer arc, and will thus provide two different courses; so we will require a minimum of fifteen different pairs in all.

Six stations could suffice to give us fifteen pairs, but we must then find a way to arrange the stations so that no two pairs are the same distance apart; every pair must here be used on a unique task of its own, as nothing can be spared to cover duplications. If we take 100 metres as our unit of length, our problem is then to determine six points on a 31-unit perimeter, to make arcs of all numbers of units from 1 to 30 appear between different pairs of points.

We can note that one pair of adjacent points must be one unit apart, and another pair must be 2 units apart; if these two arcs are adjacent, they will jointly provide a 3-unit arc, which must not then appear elsewhere; but if these two are not adjacent, there must be a 3-unit arc somewhere else.

We can proceed in this fashion, determining lengths and contiguity for possible arcs: after five adjacent arcs have been chosen, the sixth is determined; and we can see if any allowable permutation of the arcs can give us a solution. With a substantial amount of labour, we can then determine that the lengths of arcs between adjacent stations must in fact occur in one of the cyclic orders (12, 4, 7, 2, 1, 5), (10, 1, 3, 2, 7, 8), (14, 1, 7, 3, 2, 4), (13, 1, 2, 5, 4, 6), or (14, 1, 3, 6, 2, 5).

In doing the work—or in checking these solutions—it is sufficient to verify that contiguous arcs can sum to give all numbers from 1 to 15; if so, the associated larger arcs must then supply the rest. The way we have written the cyclic orders, any combined arc involving a connexion of the last and first numbers would exceed 15; so the verification can be done wholly in terms of numbers which are actually adjacent as we have listed them.

Race-track Problems and Legal Fictions

Once we know one of these solutions, we can in fact readily derive the others: if we have a solution, we can not only proceed once round the track, measuring arcs and locating stations in the obvious way; we can take any number *r* from 1 to 30, and proceed *r* times round the track, laying out *r*-fold multiples of the segments in our solution, and this too will locate stations appropriately for a solution.

Round a total length equivalent to *r* circuits, we shall then have pairs of stations spaced with all the intervals *r*, 2*r*, 3*r*,..., 30*r* units; and when we find the remainders on division by 31, to obtain the corresponding spacings round a single circuit, these remainders must all be different, because none of our multipliers can have any factor in common with the divisor 31: as a result of this, the thirty different remainders can only be 1, 2, 3,..., 30, in some order or another, as required.

Six multipliers including *r* = 1 will here produce a solution equivalent to the original, with an unaltered cyclic succession of the individual arc lengths; the other twenty-four multipliers are grouped in four sets of six, such that each set gives a cyclic succession of arcs for one of the other four essentially distinct solutions.

A procedure of limited variety

Readers may wonder what happens if we have other numbers of points dividing the circuit: with *n* points, we would have $\frac{1}{2}n(n-1)$ pairs, and we might hope to cover all possibilities for a circuit of n^2-n+1 units. This can certainly be done in all cases where $n-1$ is either a prime, or some power of a prime: in other cases the question remains open, but only for quite large numbers; it is known that there are no solutions of any other type if $n \leqslant 1,600$.

The prime-power case is rather beyond our limits here. We shall assume that $n = p+1$, where *p* is a prime; there is then a solution for a circuit of *N* units, with $N = n^2-n+1 = p^2+p+1 = (p^3-1)/(p-1)$. Solutions are lacking only for cases $n = 7, 11, 13, 15, 16, 19, ...$: but fortunately we can more easily give explicit directions for solving our problem, with $n = 6$, $p = 5$, $N = 31$, than we can for any higher numbers prior to $n = 18$; the reason is that here we have *N* a prime, as well as *p*.

The theory involves sequences of numbers where each new number is formed in the same way, by additive or subtractive combination of fixed multiples of its three immediate predecessors. Here, however, we are not interested in the actual numbers, but only in the remainders which they leave when divided by *p*; so we can conveniently drop multiples of *p* at any stage in the work.

We then have a situation similar to what arises for digits of repeating decimals: later results must repeat cyclically, since we cannot continue to have variety indefinitely. All our numbers, like the remainders for

89

the decimal, must be less than a given divisor: with the decimal, there is recurrence as soon as any remainder is repeated; here the recurrence begins as soon as any *set of three successive numbers* is repeated.

Each of our numbers may be any of the p different numbers from 0 to $p-1$, so there are only p^3 different triads of numbers possible: from these we exclude the triad 0, 0, 0 which gives all zeros thereafter; and we are left with p^3-1 triads which will give non-trivial continuations.

Some recurrence relations will generate longer periodic sequences than others: when p is a prime, we can in fact find recurrence relations which have $N = p^2+p+1$ terms in their period, such that in these cases there will be $n = p+1$ zero terms, spaced just in the way we want our n points on a perimeter of N units.

When N is a prime as well as p, the finding of a suitable recurrence relation is a much simpler matter. We can examine all the expressions x^3-Ax-1 for different values of A from 1 to $p-1$: if some x chosen between 1 and $p-1$ makes the expression a multiple of p, we reject the corresponding value of A; each other value of A gives a recurrence relation

$$u_{r+3} = Au_{r+1}+u_r$$

which is of the type we want. To find each new number, we ignore its immediate predecessor (or multiply this by zero), and add A times the next earlier to the one next earlier still: and we reject multiples of p from the result—or before this, if we wish.

We can assume that $u_0 = 0$, $u_1 = 0$, $u_2 = 1$; for p^3-1 triads other than $(0, 0, 0)$ are generated by sets of p^2+p+1 in $p-1$ different series; a sequence of two zeros followed by a non-zero will occur only once in each, and the zeros will have an identical cyclic distribution in them all.

For our case of $p = 5$, we cannot use $A = 1$ or $A = 2$; but we can use either $A = 3$ (or -2), or $A = 4$ (or -1). These respectively give periods of

0 0 1 0 3 1 4 1 3 2 0 4 2 2 0 3 2 4 4 4 1 1 2 4 2 4 0 4 4 2 1

and

0 0 1 0 4 1 1 3 0 3 3 2 0 1 2 4 4 3 0 1 3 4 3 4 1 4 3 2 1 1 1

where the zeros are at positions (0, 1, 3, 10, 14, 26) in the first, and at positions (0, 1, 3, 8, 12, 18) in the second. We see that cyclic orders for the intervals are (1, 2, 7, 4, 12, 5) and (1, 2, 5, 4, 6, 13), equivalent to those in two of our five solutions; the other three cases can be obtained from recurrence relations where the immediate predecessor is *not* ignored.

Pointers towards a true direction

We promised that we would relate all this to the remarkable 25-point geometry which we described earlier: so in Figure 6*A* we repeat the diagram of the geometrical relations for the 25 points, *A, B, C, . . ., Y*; to accompany this, Figure 6*B* has a ring of twenty-five letters and six numerals, in the centre of which we assume there is a rotary dial which carries six pointers.

These six pointers are located around the dial like the points in one of the solutions of our race-track problem, and in the position shown

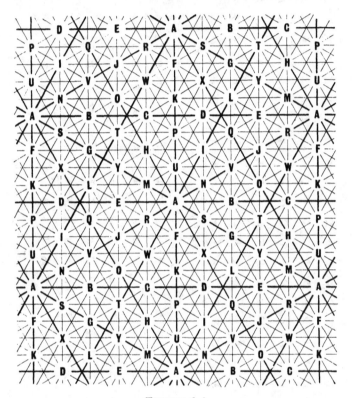

FIGURE 6*A*

in the drawing the pointers all point to numerals on the outer ring. If we now consider all the thirty other positions of the central dial, five of the six pointers will point to letters which are aligned on some line of Figure 6*A*; and a sixth pointer will then point to a numeral which will indicate the slope of the line, with reference to directions radially to corresponding numerals on a clock face.

The sets of symbols indicated by the pointers—for successive positions of the rotary dial—are given in the columns of Table 6*a*: the cyclic succession of symbols is here the same for every row, but there

Table 6a

1	1 2 A 3 J C F S Y W 4 V D I 5 N B G U Q O M X K P T 6 R E H L 1
2	2 A 3 J C F S Y W 4 V D I 5 N B G U Q O M X K P T 6 R E H L 1 2
3	3 J C F S Y W 4 V D I 5 N B G U Q O M X K P T 6 R E H L 1 2 A 3
4	4 V D I 5 N B G U Q O M X K P T 6 R E H L 1 2 A 3 J C F S Y W 4
5	5 N B G U Q O M X K P T 6 R E H L 1 2 A 3 J C F S Y W 4 V D I 5
6	6 R E H L 1 2 A 3 J C F S Y W 4 V D I 5 N B G U Q O M X K P T 6

TABLE 6a

Table 6b

1						3						5				
A	I	L	T	W		A	B	C	D	E		A	X	Q	O	H
S	V	E	H	K		F	G	H	I	J		R	K	I	B	Y
G	O	R	U	D		K	L	M	N	O		J	C	U	S	L
Y	C	F	N	Q		P	Q	R	S	T		V	T	M	F	D
M	P	X	B	J		U	V	W	X	Y		N	G	E	W	P
4	4	4	4	4		6	6	6	6	6		2	2	2	2	2

TABLE 6b

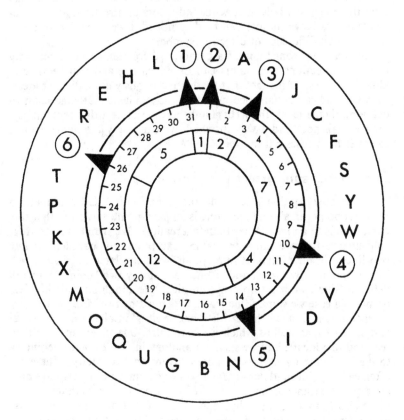

FIGURE 6*B*

are progressive displacements in the different rows, arranged to give a set where six different numerals all appear together.

Apart from this last set, there are thirty other sets, each containing five letters and one numeral: and these can be arranged to form the rows and columns of three schemes as in Table 6*b*. Row numerals and column numerals both change by steps of 2 between any two schemes, and differ by steps of 3 in any one scheme, when we consider that 1 follows cyclically after 6.

These schemes are then the basic schemes of our 25-point geometry, with new symbols added, to associate the lines in each of the six parallel sets: these new symbols then act as indicators of direction; and appropriate angles between lines can be determined if we allow 30° of angle for each unit difference of direction symbols.

This indicates something of a paradox: there seems to be some way in which directions and points can be mixed up, and still be treated alike, regardless of the fact that these are obviously quite distinct ideas. This can indicate what once motivated an eminent mathematician to define mathematics as 'the art of giving the same name to different things': for we shall now find a way in which we can apply the name 'point' to cover both cases alike.

Legal fictions in correct perspective

Let us now say that a letter denotes a *real* point, and a numeral a *fictitious* point (an alternative name is an *ideal* point, to signify that this corresponds to an *idea* rather than to a reality). We then have the great convenience that we can stop making exceptions for parallelism: *any* two lines will now intersect in a 'point'—we can later consider which kind of point, if we wish; and to ensure that any two 'points' will still define a 'line', we must now add an ideal line containing all the ideal points—in case we want a line which is defined by *two ideal points*.

Once this is done we have thirty-one 'points' in all (twenty-five real and six ideal), as well as which we have thirty-one 'lines' in all (thirty real and one ideal); and we have an analogy in our 25-point geometry to the ideal points and lines of more conventional geometry. These are often called points and lines *at infinity*—when unnecessary disputes may arise from extraneous implications of the words: here perhaps we see more clearly that no metaphysics is involved, but only a device whose fundamental justification is the linguistic abbreviation which it can produce.

'*Fictitious*' is perhaps a better introductory term than the others ('fictitious', 'ideal', 'at infinity' all mean exactly the same, here). It correctly suggests that this procedure is entirely on a par with *legal fictions*—the convenient devices by which shore establishments are treated as ships for purposes of the Naval Discipline Act, and by which typewriters are (or were) considered as musical instruments for purposes of railway freight. The basic reason is the same—to simplify statements by omission of tedious distinctions in cases where they are immaterial.

With thirty-one points and thirty-one lines, we can now look for correspondences with the more usual type of *projective* geometry—the geometry which developed out of the discovery of the true rules for perspective drawing, in the later Middle Ages.

In this type of geometry we consider transformations which resemble perspective representations, inasmuch as 'points' remain 'points', and 'lines' remain 'lines', with collinearity of points and concurrence of lines being preserved in *all* cases: a *vanishing point* in a picture is then the real point in the picture which corresponds to the ideal point of two actually parallel lines; and the *horizon* is the real line in the picture which corresponds to the ideal line which contains all the ideal points which lie in any horizontal plane.

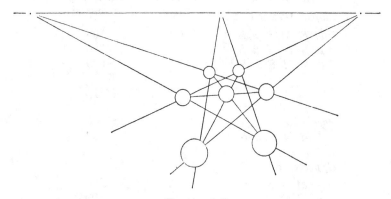

FIGURE 6 *C*

Thus from one point of view Figure 6*C* gives a perspective view of something like an airfield with three runways concurrent where seven beacons and nine of their joins define the two triangles and three diameters of a star-of-David. There are then three vanishing points and a horizon line, which correspond to ideal points and to the ideal line in the plane of the airfield. But in the plane of the picture they are real points and a real line, and if we include them with the others we then have ten points and ten lines, arranged with three points on every line and with three lines through every point. This configuration was first considered by Desargues in the seventeenth century. It is of far-reaching importance in all geometry.

Making use of inside information

We shall have more to say about the Desargues configuration later: but meanwhile we wish to indicate briefly how the consideration of conic sections in our 25-point geometry is best done by extending this to a 31-point (and 31-line) geometry, with inclusion of ideal points and lines as given by the numerals which we have earlier considered.

95

Once the extra points and lines are included with the others, we can then state without exception that if we select any five points all of whose joins are distinct, there will always be exactly one other point which does *not* lie on *any* of these joins. We can define these six points as lying on a conic section, or as forming a conic; and at each point we can define a tangent as the only line which has no other point in common with the conic: for through each point there is one other line,

Typical conics	Symmetry	Number of
Ellipses (*incl. circles*)	axes	examples
N U M R F S	6	100
B N M E R S	2	300
B V U E J F	–	600
		1,000
Parabolae		
J M U N G 6	1	600
Hyperbolae		
N M R S 1 5	2	300
B U E F 1 5	2	300
B Q E O 1 4	–	300
G H Y X 1 6	–	600
		1,500

TABLE 6 *c*

in addition to the five which give connexions to the other points of the conic.

Apart from the six points and six tangent lines of the conic, there are fifteen secants, each through two of the points of the conic, and these secants intersect in fifteen 'exterior' points from which *two* tangents can be drawn, in each case: the remaining lines provide ten non-secants which intersect in ten 'interior' points from which *no* tangents can be drawn; and in the latter case there are three of the points on each line, and three lines through each point—arranged in exactly the same way as in our picture of the airfield.

In all, there are 3,100 conics, of eight different types as in Table 6*c*. Ellipses (including circles) have six real points; parabolae have five real points, and also one ideal point which gives the direction of the axis; hyperbolae have four real points, and two ideal points which give the directions of the asymptotes. Only parabolae have the 'interior' points all real; for the parabola *JMUNG6*—for instance—they are the real points of two congruent parabolae *ORASL* and *EHPIB*: readers can verify that these are connected as in a Desargues configuration.

Putting it all on a rational basis

We hope that what we have given will tempt readers to explore this geometry further. It may seem paradoxical that so many theorems of ordinary geometry can still make sense in a quite different context; but we can briefly indicate some relevant considerations.

Many (but not all) of the axioms of ordinary geometry will apply—in identical terms—to our new concepts *as we defined these*: so theorems which do not use the other axioms will be true in both geometries; and the falsity of others can be a means of showing that they involve the need of using some of the other axioms—a point of some interest to geometers.

In another interpretation, we can relate our 25-point geometry more closely to ordinary geometry. We can assume that we have been considering a co-ordinate geometry where we take every point to have co-ordinates $(p\sqrt{3}, q)$ and decide to ignore points other than those for which p and q are both rational fractions (ratios of whole numbers): to be strictly correct, we should add that we require the rational fractions to have no factor of 5 in the denominator, so that our arithmetic can reduce each of them to a value which is one of 0, ± 1, ± 2. We then effectively classify the other points into twenty-five different classes, in terms of the pairs of reduced values, and we then decide to make no distinction between different members in each of our classes.

In this interpretation, what we then refer to as a point means 'some member of a particular class of points—the particular member doesn't matter', and similarly for lines. Valid theorems will then imply that our constructions lead only to points of the type we allow; and others which are false will imply that we would require to consider points of the type we decided to ignore—namely, those for which p and q are *not* rational numbers of the required type. This is why we find Ceva's theorem false, and why we cannot find foci for those of our conics which have no axes of symmetry.

Our whole procedure forms an additional example of 'the art of giving the same name to different things' (and however paradoxical some results may seem, they all represent valid mathematics). In this process, things are given the same name because they resemble one another sufficiently in some aspect which is of immediate concern: this name then emphasizes this resemblance, and makes for economy both in writing and in thinking. But the things must still remain different in some otherwise essential respect—or else they would already *have* the same names, because they *were* the same things: in other contexts these differences will force themselves upon our attention; and we then must respect them, if we are not to be led into error.

It may seem paradoxical to talk of lines through the centre which have no points in common with a circle, or of angles which cannot be bisected; but it is not logically absurd, when we remember that these are not ordinary circles or angles: we have merely chosen to use these terms in what we might describe as a Pickwickian sense. What *would* be logically absurd—and consequently *not* mathematics—would be if we did this where it could lead to *Pickwickian* contradictions: as for instance if we could use one line of argument to show that we could have a Pickwickian square, and another to show that we could not. But this is what *cannot* happen: for we would then have corresponding contradictions in our co-ordinate geometry—which is geometry of the ordinary type.

What establishes all this as proper mathematics is the proof that contradictions cannot occur: after this, any debate on the merits or demerits of the assumptions is no longer a matter of mathematics. In some cases we may still have to ask whether some mathematics is suitable for some intended application to the physical world: in less utilitarian cases—as here—the decision may be more a question of aesthetics, involving the variety and richness of chains of argument which they allow.

Not non-decimal, but undecimal

Before we turn to other subjects, we should perhaps make clear that our 25-point (or 31-point) geometry is not the only specimen of its type: it is merely the one which seems best to combine variety of theorems with economy of apparatus.

Our recurrence-relation procedure can be used to produce other 'finite geometries', with other numbers of points on a line, involving other total numbers of points; and by introducing one further term in our recurrence relations, we can indeed produce three-dimensional finite geometries: but few of these give much scope for recreational activity. Possibilities are unduly limited if lines have only three points: on the other hand, the tables of alignments become somewhat tedious to handle, if lines have seven points or more. An exception might perhaps be made for the finite geometry which uses the prime number 11 in the way our previous geometry uses the prime number 5: we here have 121 real points (and we can add twelve ideal points, if we like).

The most convenient way of identifying individual points is then to use eleven symbols (the digits 0, 1, 2, ..., 9 supplemented by an X, say) and to assign a unique *pair* of symbols to each point. This gives us a series of 121 labels

00, 01, 02, ..., 09, 0X, 10, 11, ..., ..., 99, 9X, X0, X1, ..., X9, XX:

when considered in this order, these in fact would represent consecutive whole numbers written in the scale of eleven—the undecimal scale, from the Latin *undecim*, eleven—if we assume that the X is the additional digit which this scale would need, with a numerical value of *ten*. (Ideal points could then be represented by initial letters of the alphabet, in a regular sequence such that each step could be made to represent a change of direction by 15°.)

Basic geometrical relations for the 121 points can then be defined by reference to three 11 × 11 schemes as in Tables 6*d*, 6*e*, and 6*f*. Alignments are now given not only by rows and columns, but also by either set of diagonals, with continuity along broken diagonals, such as would occur if the schemes were used as units for repeating patterns. Again there are two incommensurable units (which here can be thought of as involving a ratio of $\sqrt{2}$, in either direction—or simultaneously in both directions): one unit now applies alike to rows and to columns, and the other unit applies to all the sets of diagonals.

00	01	02	03	04	05	06	07	08	09	0X
10	11	12	13	14	15	16	17	18	19	1X
20	21	22	23	24	25	26	27	28	29	2X
30	31	32	33	34	35	36	37	38	39	3X
40	41	42	43	44	45	46	47	48	49	4X
50	51	52	53	54	55	56	57	58	59	5X
60	61	62	63	64	65	66	67	68	69	6X
70	71	72	73	74	75	76	77	78	79	7X
80	81	82	83	84	85	86	87	88	89	8X
90	91	92	93	94	95	96	97	98	99	9X
X0	X1	X2	X3	X4	X5	X6	X7	X8	X9	XX

TABLE 6*d*

00	35	6X	94	19	43	78	X2	27	51	86
58	82	07	31	66	90	15	4X	74	X9	23
X5	2X	54	89	03	38	62	97	11	46	70
42	77	X1	26	50	85	0X	34	69	93	18
9X	14	49	73	X8	22	57	81	06	30	65
37	61	96	10	45	7X	X4	29	53	88	02
84	09	33	68	92	17	41	76	X0	25	5X
21	56	80	05	3X	64	99	13	48	72	X7
79	X3	28	52	87	01	36	60	95	1X	44
16	40	75	XX	24	59	83	08	32	67	91
63	98	12	47	71	X6	20	55	8X	04	39

TABLE 6 *e*

00	85	5X	24	X9	73	48	12	97	61	36
53	28	X2	77	41	16	90	65	3X	04	89
X6	70	45	1X	94	69	33	08	82	57	21
49	13	98	62	37	01	86	50	25	XX	74
91	66	30	05	8X	54	29	X3	78	42	17
34	09	83	58	22	X7	71	46	10	95	6X
87	51	26	X0	75	4X	14	99	63	38	02
2X	X4	79	43	18	92	67	31	06	80	55
72	47	11	96	60	35	0X	84	59	23	X8
15	9X	64	39	03	88	52	27	X1	76	40
68	32	07	81	56	20	X5	7X	44	19	93

TABLE 6 *f*

Each scheme gives four sets of parallel lines, with eleven lines in each set and eleven points on each line; and we have twelve such sets in all, and twelve lines through every point. Lines are perpendicular if they correspond to a row and a column, or else to two oppositely sloping diagonals, provided that both occur in the same scheme.

These larger tables are somewhat more troublesome to use than the 5×5 tables for the 25-point case: a convenient procedure is to copy them on squared paper, so that alignments can be determined by using a straight-edge—or a set-square—as an index. Even without this, points are not too difficult to find in the schemes, if rows or columns are scanned successively to find a symbol which has a correct digit in either the first position or the second: there is one such symbol in each row or column (or diagonal); but only in one case will the other digit be correct as well.

In one of the schemes, the order is obviously systematic, with unit steps horizontally for one symbol, and vertically for the other. There are similar regularities involving multiple-unit steps for both symbols, in the other cases; and these can be used to assist a rapid finding of desired symbols in the schemes. Here, as in the arithmetic, the cyclic properties of the symbols make arrival at *eleven* equivalent to a resetting to *zero*: as we search the tables, we may—for instance—see a regular progression by double-unit steps, through values 0, 2, 4, 6, 8, X, 1, 3, 5, 7, 9, in a cyclic sequence; any two consecutive values then indicate where each of the other values can be found.

But searching for symbols in the tables is the only case where—in effect—we have to do arithmetic with numbers which are *written* in the scale of eleven: when we mention numbers hereafter, these will be ordinary numbers written in the scale of ten; and the number whose multiples we can neglect will then be written as 11—to mean *eleven*. (In the scale of eleven, 11 would, of course, mean *twelve*.)

We shall not discuss this geometry as fully as the other; in particular, we shall not discuss ideal points, or conics: but we shall give a few brief indications which may tempt more hardy readers to explore further.

Here we may have equal lengths on perpendicular lines, so we now can have four points which form a square: and we can have more variety in our triangles, for there now are twelve different types—each available in ten sizes, with 121 different positions possible in every case. Equilateral triangles of given size and location then have four possible orientations; four types of isosceles triangle (one is right-angled) each have twelve; and there are seven types of scalene triangle (two are right-angled) which each have twenty-four. Each point is surrounded by ten concentric circles, each of which has twelve points which form a regular dodecagon.

If we take distances without distinction of sign, we can have multiples of either unit by 1, 2, 3, 4, or 5, after which we have the equivalent of negative multiples in a reversed order: and Pythagoras' theorem will hold if we note that we have

$$1^2 = \ \ 1 \equiv 34 = 3^2+5^2 \qquad\qquad (\sqrt2)^2 = \ \ 2 \equiv 13 = 2^2+3^2$$
$$2^2 = \ \ 4 \equiv 26 = 1^2+5^2 \qquad\qquad (2\sqrt2)^2 = \ \ 8 \equiv 41 = 4^2+5^2$$
$$3^2 = \ \ 9 \equiv 20 = 2^2+4^2 \qquad\qquad (3\sqrt2)^2 = 18 \equiv 29 = 2^2+5^2$$
$$4^2 = 16 \equiv \ \ 5 = 1^2+2^2 \qquad\qquad (4\sqrt2)^2 = 32 \equiv 10 = 1^2+3^2$$
$$5^2 = \quad 25 \quad\ = 3^2+4^2 \qquad\qquad (5\sqrt2)^2 = 50 \equiv 17 = 1^2+4^2$$

as well as some more conventional results involving $\sqrt2$, since we can add or subtract multiples of 11 if we wish.

We now have enough points on our circles to be able to have a nine-point circle with all points distinct: we show this for one of the scalene triangles, in Figure 6D. Once again, we cannot bisect all angles, and consequently some triangles have no in-centres: but we now can have in-centres for some triangles other than equilateral triangles.

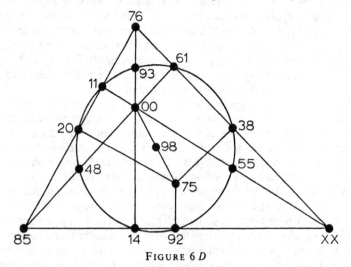

FIGURE 6 *D*

The *pedal* triangle of a given triangle—formed by the feet of the altitudes—must have the orthocentre for its in-centre, and the vertices for its ex-centres: but in the 25-point geometry, all pedal triangles either were equilateral, or else had two coincident points, and a side of zero length.

We now have more variety for pedal triangles; and taking the one from Figure 6D, we can show its in-circle and its ex-circles as in Figure 6E, with the nine-point circle touching all four of them: so Feuerbach's

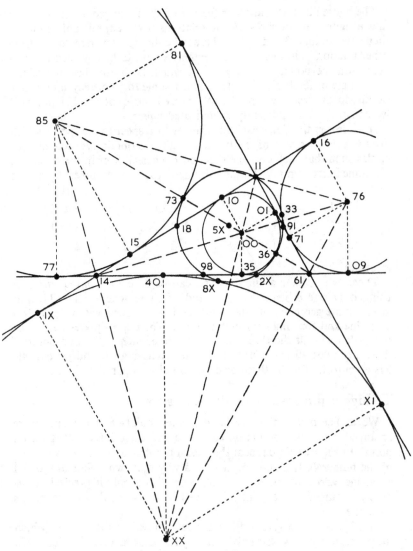

FIGURE 6 E

theorem applies when the necessary circles exist. On the Feuerbach circle, the basic nine points and the four points of tangency would give thirteen points in all: but our circles only have twelve different points; and in fact the nine points are *not* all distinct, here, because the basic (pedal) triangle is right-angled.

Puzzles and Paradoxes

The figure illustrates another feature of the finite geometries—we see that a figure cannot show *all* the relations involved, but only some of them: two points 33 and 77 have here to be shown elsewhere, to illustrate other relations, although they nevertheless have to be regarded as collinear with the points 00, 11, and XX which lie on the bisector of the right angle of the basic triangle. Failing some form of recycling of our points, in this way, we could easily exceed our quota of 121 points if we constructed a sufficiently complicated figure.

If we invert the Feuerbach diagram with respect to any point which does not lie on a side of the basic triangle, we obtain two sets of four circles such that each one in either set touches all four in the other set, but none in its own set. This applies here, too: we can invert by noting that

$$1 \times 1 \quad = \quad 1 \qquad\qquad \sqrt{2} \times (-5\sqrt{2}) = -10 \equiv 1$$
$$2 \times (-5) = -10 \equiv 1 \qquad 2\sqrt{2} \times 3\sqrt{2} \quad = \quad 12 \equiv 1$$
$$3 \times 4 \quad = \quad 12 \equiv 1 \qquad 4\sqrt{2} \times (-4\sqrt{2}) = -32 \equiv 1$$

in our arithmetic.

Those who prefer a simpler task can explore the consequences of using only one scheme 3×3, instead of three schemes 11×11: this gives a finite geometry of nine points and twelve lines, with three points on a line and four lines through a point. There are squares here, too: but little else. Of the three points on a line, each is the mid-point of the other two: all triangles are isosceles right-angled; and no triangle has a centroid, for the three medians are always parallel.

To higher dimensions, with Desargues

We earlier had a diagram in which ten points and ten lines were arranged with three points on each line and three lines through each point. In Figure 6F we repeat this: each point is now labelled with two of the numerals 1, 2, 3, 4, 5, in such a way that two points are joined by a line, and three points are collinear, if and only if precisely *three* different numerals are jointly involved in the symbols for the points concerned.

In Figure 6G we give a different but equivalent diagram in which the points in collinear sets have precisely the same labels as in Figure 6F: this is easily constructed with no aid other than an ungraduated straightedge. We draw any three lines concurrent in a point 12; on these we take any pairs of points 13 and 23, 14 and 24, 15 and 25, respectively; and we associate these to give a pair of triangles whose vertices are 13, 14, 15 in one case, and 23, 24, 25 in the other.

For these two triangles we can define corresponding vertices as those which lie on the same line through the point 12: this lets us determine

104

corresponding sides for the two triangles, whose sides we draw and produce as necessary; corresponding pairs of sides then intersect in three points which we must label 34, 35, 45 in accordance with our system. It will *always* be found that these points are collinear, and we can draw a line which completes our diagram as we want it.

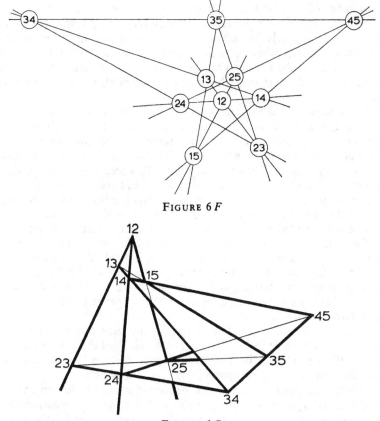

FIGURE 6*F*

FIGURE 6*G*

One way of seeing this is to think of Figure 6*G* as a picture of a three-dimensional arrangement. Our first point is then the vertex of a trihedral solid angle of which our first three lines are the edges: corresponding pairs of sides of our triangles then lie in one of the planes which form the trihedral angle; the planes of the two triangles intersect in a line, and our final three points are those where this line intersects the three planes of the trihedral angle. (Line thicknesses have been varied in our diagram, to make this clearer.)

Once our diagram is complete, however, there is nothing to show which was the point with which we began: to duplicate the diagram, we could start with *any* point, and on the three lines through this point we would find pairs of other points which we could associate to form triangles, in such a way that we could then proceed exactly as before, finally obtaining three points—not joined to our first point—which would be collinear on the last line we would have to draw.

Alternatively we may label our figure in 120 different ways for which the ten sets of labels for collinear points are exactly the same: we can choose any of ten labels for a first point, any of six labels for a second point joined to the first, and any of two labels for a third point joined separately to the first two; this then determines all the other labels in the way that we require.

Each point is labelled with a pair of different symbols chosen from 1, 2, 3, 4, 5, and each line is associated with a set of three symbols which are taken in pairs to label the three points on the line: we can then pair off each point with the line which involves the three symbols which are *not* involved in labelling the point. This means associating each point with the line which our construction would draw *last*, if we started from the point concerned; and if two points are thus associated with two lines, the line joining the two points will be found to be the one which is associated with the point of intersection of the two lines.

On this basis we can describe another way to draw our figure, starting with a line on which we take three points, instead of a point through which we take three lines: we interchange the words 'point' and 'line', also the words 'concurrent' and 'collinear', in our previous description; and we finish up with three lines which we can prove to be concurrent in a common point.

All these results show that our diagram—the Desargues configuration—has a very high degree of symmetry indeed. We here have explained some of its properties by considering space of three dimensions; we can do even better by proceeding one stage further still.

When we regard geometry as a deductive science based on axioms and postulates, there is nothing to stop us from making the assumption —or postulate—that space has *four* dimensions: we can assume, for instance, that we can have *four* lines each perpendicular to all the others, and see where this leads us. Admittedly, we cannot make exact models to check our logical deductions; but we can (if we like) draw three-dimensional perspectives or sections of four-dimensional objects, just as we can make similar two-dimensional representations for three-dimensional objects.

To appreciate some four-dimensional relations, we can argue as follows, proceeding upwards by steps of one dimension at a time.

Two points define a line, which forms a one-dimensional figure: the simplest two-dimensional figure is the triangle, which is based on three non-collinear points; taken two at a time, these define three lines. The simplest three-dimensional figure is a tetrahedron, based on four non-coplanar points: the four points are the vertices; six pairs of points define lines for edges, and four triads of points define triangles for faces which meet in pairs at the edges.

Similarly, the simplest four-dimensional figure is based on five points. In each of five different three-dimensional sub-spaces there are only four of the points, and each set defines a tetrahedron which lies in its own three-dimensional space: ten pairs of points each define edges which are common to three tetrahedra, and to three triangular faces which pairs of these three tetrahedra have in common; and ten triads of points each define triangular faces which are common to pairs of tetrahedra. In the four-dimensional space there then are ten lines and ten planes; each plane contains three of the lines (which form edges of the triangular face which is in this plane), and each of the lines lies in three of the planes.

Just as we can take a section of a three-dimensional figure by a plane, which has one dimension fewer, we can similarly take a section of our four-dimensional figure by a three-dimensional space. In general cases this replaces lines by points, and planes by lines: and a line which lies on a plane will be replaced by a point which lies on a line. We can choose a three-dimensional space which contains *none* of our five points (just as we might section a tetrahedron by a plane which avoided all the vertices, to obtain the four lines and six points of a complete quadrilateral); and we then obtain a three-dimensional figure similar to the one we assumed was pictured in Figure 6*G*.

Alternatively, we can argue as follows. We can project a tetrahedron on to a plane in such a way that its vertices are replaced by the vertices of a triangle, together with one of the interior points; and we can use this representation to appreciate inter-relations of vertices, edges, and faces, for the original tetrahedron, even though faces have been distorted, to bring them all into a single plane. Similarly, we can project our five points from four dimensions into three, to make them the vertices and an internal point of a tetrahedron; this allows us to see inter-relations of five points, ten lines, ten triangles, and five tetrahedra, and we can finally section this figure by a plane which avoids all five points, to obtain a Desargues configuration in the plane. This amounts to a three-dimensional shadowgraph of the procedure we have just described for four dimensions.

This now provides an explanation of why the labelling of our points with *double* numerals turned out to be so systematic and convenient. Each single numeral 1, 2, 3, 4, 5 could represent one of our five points, in four dimensions, and the double numerals could then represent the lines which are defined by *pairs* of these points; the three symbols which suffice to label any line in our diagram are then labels for three points which define one of the ten triangular faces in our four-dimensional figure: and the points and lines of our Desargues configuration are traces of these lines and planes as they pass through a particular three-dimensional space. For in four dimensions, different three-dimensional spaces exist in infinite abundance—as planes do, in a three-dimensional space: and lines, planes, and other three-dimensional spaces will intersect a given three-dimensional space in points, lines, and planes, respectively, as they pass through it, proceeding from one (four-dimensional) side of it, to the other.

The 120 equivalent re-labellings of our two-dimensional figure exactly correspond to the 120 ways we can permute the labelling of our five basic points in a space of four dimensions: if we take our five points to form a regular figure (which would be bounded by five regular tetrahedra), we have sixty ways of rotating this as a whole, to replace it a different way round, in an unchanged position; and we have sixty ways of doing the like with its mirror image.

In the three-dimensional argument which proved that a straight-edge construction would succeed, we required only assumptions (of obvious type) indicating how points, lines, and planes were defined and inter-related. Two-dimensional beings would similarly assume only that two points defined a unique line, and two lines a unique point. These two postulates would not be falsified if their lines behaved like rays of light passing from air to water; but if one of the ten points were in a different medium from the other nine, there would be a refraction effect which could make the final three lines cease to be concurrent if a diagram was drawn so as to make this point the last point to be found.

To guarantee that they could have a Desargues configuration, two-dimensional beings would either be forced to supplement their plane geometry by additional postulates, or else extend it to cover a third dimension outside of their physical experience. In three dimensions a corresponding refraction effect could not be present without falsifying some of the assumptions about inter-relations of points, lines, *and planes*; these concepts here are more firmly interlocked, and a corresponding difficulty does not arise. So we might say that understanding the Desargues configuration is easier for beings like ourselves who have physical experience of space of three dimensions; and that it would be even easier still, for beings who had direct experience of four-dimensional space.

In Figure 6*H* we show another way of having ten points arranged by sets of three on ten lines of which three go through each point. This appears to have more symmetry than the other diagrams, but for our present purposes it actually has less: there are only ten equivalent labellings which give unchanged collinear sets; we can advance all numerals cyclically by the same amount, and we may also exchange corresponding dashed and undashed symbols throughout.

A perspective drawing of this figure would have the same properties; but no diagram of *this* type can be drawn with only a straight-edge—the last alignment will *not* come automatically, here. Finding how to construct this figure with ruler and compasses makes a good exercise which involves properties of the golden-section number $\tau = \frac{1}{2}(1+\sqrt{5})$.

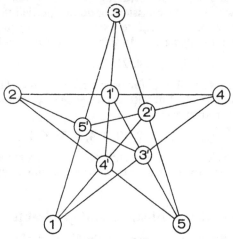

FIGURE 6 *H*

A very evident distinction from a Desargues configuration is that a point can here be taken on each of the three lines through any given point, in such a way as to provide three points which are collinear on another line.

Best ways of getting the feel of it

Selecting sets of symbols as if for a finite geometry is a procedure which is sometimes convenient in statistical design: this provides a means of arranging a balanced representation of all members, in a limited number of combinations. (Some familiar forms of gambling can offer scope for similar activities.)

Sets of numbers determined as for our race-track problems can help to solve other problems also. We might ask how to arrange five thickness gauges on a key-ring, to measure thicknesses of from 1 to 20 units by unit steps. This is a prime-power case, not covered by the theory we were able to give, earlier; but examination of all possibilities is not unduly difficult. The solution is unique, and gauges must here have thicknesses (10, 2, 5, 1, 3), in this cyclic order; we can remember this as the equivalent of writing 1, 2, 3, 5, 10 in succession, at vertices of a pentagram.

If we wish to have thickness gauges arranged on a common spindle, in the more usual fashion—like blades of a pocket knife—we no longer have a cyclic system, and no generally applicable theory seems to be known. Small numbers can be dealt with empirically: some of the best results so far found appear to arise by choosing a particular solution for some cyclic case, before breaking the ring—possibly directly, but more usually with suitable omissions or duplications at the broken ends.

Thus, for instance, if we require a set of thickness gauges to measure by units from 1 to 60, we can do this with twelve gauges arranged in a set

$$(26, 3, 11, 2, 4, 21, 7, 5, 10, 8, 1, 35)$$

which is a race-track solution for twelve cameras ($p = 11$), split so that the first omission is 61. But with twelve gauges we can actually get up to 61, in another arrangement

$$(6, 16, 14, 9, 2, 10, 3, 4, 1, 26, 6, 16)$$

which in fact has less thickness overall: this comes from a (prime-power) race-track solution for ten cameras, with two sections duplicated at the split.

Steps to take with yard-sticks and quadrants

With the thickness gauges, the overall thickness of the set is allowed to be greater than the largest measurement in the desired series: we can now consider similar problems where this possibility is ruled out. If we required a yard standard to be graduated to measure all whole numbers of inches from 1 to 36, we might wish to have as few graduations as possible, if each graduation involved a lengthy and expensive procedure: or we might seek to arrange a minimum number of graduations—or targets—over an arc of a quadrant, to allow the determination of angles of every exact number of degrees from 1 to 90, by selection of an appropriate pair.

Here, too, there seems to be no complete theory; but the best results appear to come from using several repetitions of identical segments in the middle, with appropriately arranged terminations at the two ends.

For the yard-stick, it is known that fewer than nine segments will not suffice, and that the problem can be solved by using graduations at the inch-divisions

$$0, 1, 3, 6, 13, 20, 27, 31, 35, 36$$

to provide nine segments arranged in a succession

$$(1, 2, 3, 7, 7, 7, 4, 4, 1).$$

Whether nine segments could do the like in another arrangement—or similarly provide for 37 inches, or more—seems to be an unsolved problem. For the quadrant, a solution has been found which uses graduations at degree-positions

0, 1, 2, 8, 14, 20, 31, 42, 53, 64, 75, 80, 85, 88, 89, 90

to provide fifteen segments arranged in a succession

(1, 1, 6, 6, 6, 11, 11, 11, 11, 11, 5, 5, 3, 1, 1).

Whether fifteen segments could provide for ninety cases otherwise—or for more than ninety—again seems to be an open question.

Our concentration on a yard and on a quadrant was in fact less arbitrary than might at first appear: for it seems quite possible that each of the numbers 36 and 90 is an optimum case.

7 Cubism and Colour Arrangements

'*Plus ça change*—': the Tantalizer through the ages

Many different puzzles call for the arrangement or assembly of some actual geometrical objects in a way which will comply with some stated condition: an attractive feature of the type we shall now discuss is that they are particularly easy for anyone to make—all that is needed is a few pieces which have more or less the form of cubes, and a method of marking faces with symbols or colours, to identify the members of various associated sets.

A familiar puzzle of this type provides four cubes which have to be assembled in a block $4 \times 1 \times 1$ with four different designs all showing somewhere on all four sides of the assembly: misdirection is provided by designs being repeated on some of the cubes.

At different times, faces have been marked in many different ways. Commercial designs or trademarks have sometimes been used for purposes of sales promotion: a version has recently been circulating in which the four designs are a red triangle, a blue triangle, a bottle, and a glass—and most English readers will need no further clue to its source. Some few years ago another version was on sale, with coloured dots; a still older example (Provisional Patent 18945) had coloured faces. The two more recent ones bear the name of 'Tantalizer'; an earlier one was 'The Great Tantalizer'. There was an American version—the Katzenjammer Puzzle—with card-suit symbols. All of these were in wood: another (British) version had cardboard cubes decorated with facsimiles of labels for soup, gravy, table cream, and custard powder. The earliest of these must be over fifty years old.

Yet these are not five puzzles, but one puzzle. As mathematicians would say, they are abstractly identical: we can list sets of correspondences as in Table 7a. The present author has examples of all five; and cannot resist remarking that not the least tantalizing feature, to him, is how this puzzle can be brought out again and again, with trivial variations, while many other good puzzles appear once and vanish, or circulate only privately, if at all!

With some versions (including current ones) a pictorial solution is supplied, or can be obtained: but the Great Tantalizer does no more than reassure its victims that it can be done; and Mr. Katzenjammer is supplied with a monologue, addressed to his wife, in which he says 'It comes easy, Katerina, if you look at the picture on the box, because that has one spot of each kind on two sides already yet.' (Need we tell readers that this picture is designed with some skill, to send her—and them—up a blind alley?)

	A	B	C	D
Groceries (dry)	Soup	Gravy	Table cream	Custard powder
Faces (The Great Tantalizer)	Natural	Brown	Red	Blue
Suit-symbols (Katzenjammer)	Club	Spade	Heart	Diamond
Dots (as recently on sale)	Green	Yellow	Red	Blue
Groceries (licensed)	Glass	Bottle	Red triangle	Blue triangle

TABLE 7 *a*

Try this—it may well work!

A pictorial solution with no obvious system is rather tedious to follow, and it can be somewhat awkward to memorize, unless some systematic rules are derived from it. We hope the solution procedure which we give here will enable readers to produce cubes from their pockets and put them together as required—with no need to consult pieces of paper—before onlookers lose interest in their efforts.

The Katzenjammer puzzle makes the individual cubes easily identifiable by a use of fainter background colours peculiar to the individual cubes (possibly as some compensation for its wilfully misleading picture): with other versions, there is no such simple help. Our instructions as in Table 7*b* will permit the cubes to be first identified quickly, and then positioned appropriately. These instructions produce a solution which is essentially unique apart from interchanges of the cubes and rotations of the assembly, provided that the four cubes are marked as in the traditional form of the puzzle.

One point to notice here is that if any cube is replaced by its mirror image, the solution is essentially unaffected: only four faces are actually used; and the other two (which provide the false trails) can be interchanged indifferently. In the traditional form, two of the four cubes are unchanged by reflection, and two others can each exist in distinct left-hand or right-hand forms; our directions have been arranged to apply independently of mirror-image variations.

113

The five versions are all equivalent, but mirror-image distinctions make some more equivalent than others: in this respect the Katzenjammer and packet-food versions are identical, and the Great Tantalizer is an exact mirror-reversal of these; the two modern ones are also identical, but different from both the other types.

Find a cube which has three faces all alike: call this the No. 1 cube, and call these faces the *A* faces. Then one of the other cubes will have two *A* faces, together with another pair of identical faces which we may call *B* faces: call this the No. 2 cube. Of the two remaining cubes, one will have one *A* face and two *B* faces, and the other will have only one face of each of these types: call these the No. 3 and No. 4 cubes in this order.

Assemble the cubes in the numerical order so determined, in a block 4 × 1 × 1, and turn the cube No. 1 so that a join of two opposite *A* faces lies along the long axis of the assembly. This cube will then expose an *A* face on one side of the assembly, and a *B* face on a neighbouring side.

Now turn the remaining cubes so that there are four *A* faces along one side face of the assembly, and four *B* faces along another. For cubes No. 2 and No. 3, a choice between right and wrong alternatives is required: for No. 2, choose the alternative which conceals an *A* face and a *B* face by aligning their join with the long axis of the assembly; for No. 3, choose the alternative which exposes a pair of identical faces (of yet a third type) on the remaining side faces. For No. 4 there is no choice; there is only one way it can go, as required, once No. 1 has been placed.

This fixes the concealed faces for all cubes, and the exposed *end* faces for No. 1 and No. 4. These will not now be changed: but we still have to rotate some cubes about the long axis of the assembly.

First give the two middle cubes, jointly, a 180° half-turn about the long axis, leaving the other cubes undisturbed. Once this has been done, divide the assembly at the middle, and rotate the two cubes of one half through a 90° quarter-turn with respect to the two of the other half: the particular direction to choose will be evident; the other will be seen to be incorrect.

These instructions will lead to a solution which is essentially unique— provided that the four cubes are marked as in the traditional form of the puzzle.

TABLE 7*b*

In Figure 7*A* we show the design pattern for the faces, and the method of assembly of the cubes: to avoid favouring one set more than another, we have staked our own claim to further inessential variety by using the remaining mirror-image alternative for our figure; in this we use symbols *A*, *B*, *C*, *D* (which have apparently not yet appeared on actual cubes).

Of course, it is quite possible that a similar puzzle could have four cubes with designs arranged in a way totally different from what we have assumed here; yet a further possibility is that there might be another number of cubes altogether. But in our experience, whenever we meet a puzzle of this type—possibly hand-made—with four cubes, the first thing we do is to see whether it is just a new version of our old friend: and we have met no strangers this way as yet.

Suppose that there is a set of four cubes where four different designs all appear at least once on every cube, and that with this set our directions make sense, and lead to a correct solution. (By this we mean that there is no doubt which faces are the *A* faces, and which cube is No. 1, as only one cube has three faces the same; and that there is similarly

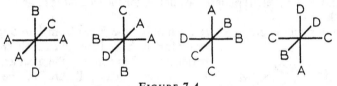

FIGURE 7*A*

no doubt about which are the *B* faces or about the numbering of the other cubes: likewise that alternative choices do arise and require decisions consistent with our rules):

If this is so, the set of cubes can then have only one or other of two distinct designs (mirror-image variations apart). One of these is the traditional design, for which the solution obtained is essentially unique: but there is another possibility—a very similar design which admits of two other solutions besides the one to which our directions lead.

Some readers may like to determine just what this other design is, and how it may best be distinguished from the traditional design; and they may find it instructive to consider differences between the three possible solutions. (We shall have more to say about this in what follows.)

Marshalling five Allied Flags, or more

There is a five-cube puzzle of the 'Tantalizer' type which dates from the first World War—the 'Flags of the Allies' puzzle. The five patterns here were the national flags of Belgium, France, Japan, Russia, and the United Kingdom; we denote these respectively by the symbols *B*, *F*, *J*, *R*, and *U*. The symbol *U* may be assumed to refer to the United Kingdom, or to the Union Flag—which is less correctly known as the Union Jack: since we wish to use *B* for Belgium, we cannot here use *B* for Britain; and we know better than to solve *this* problem by making an improper substitution of *E* for England.

With this terminology, the five cubes can be sufficiently specified by giving symbols for the three pairs of opposite faces on the different cubes: these are here (*BR, BU, FJ*), (*FB, FJ, RU*), (*FB, FU, JR*), (*RF, RJ, BU*), (*UB, UR, FJ*), for the five different cubes involved.

Puzzles and Paradoxes

(We may note that this method of specification will not distinguish between a cube and its mirror image, either of which would give identical symbols; but it makes no difference if the two inessential faces are interchanged, to replace any cube by its mirror-image counterpart.)

We shall use this puzzle as a basis for explaining a general method which can be used to find solutions—if they exist—for corresponding problems with other numbers of cubes. With n cubes, there must of course be n different patterns available, for the side faces of an $n \times 1 \times 1$ block.

In our chosen example, we can number the cubes from 1 to 5 in the

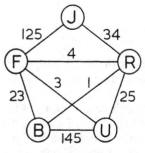

FIGURE 7 *B*

order in which we have given their specifications, and then combine the specifications into one diagram as in Figure 7*B*. We thus obtain a network of points interconnected by lines, similar to what we have used in other problems: a point labelled with a corresponding symbol is associated with each of the individual patterns; lines joining pairs of points are then marked with numerical symbols to show which cubes have the two associated patterns on a pair of opposite parallel faces.

We have here assumed that the two points—and the corresponding patterns—are distinct, as they always are for our present puzzle; but in other cases, where two parallel faces have the same pattern, we can draw a loop away from and back to the point which represents the pattern in question, and we can mark this loop with the numerical symbol of the relevant cube.

A diagram of this type then shows all the mutual inter-relations of the patterns and the cubes, in just the way we require for solving the puzzle.

We now assume that we have a solution of our problem, and we concentrate separately on what this implies for the two pairs of parallel side faces of the assembly block. In either of the two pairs, the two side faces must both show all the different patterns: so starting with any pattern on one of the two faces, we can note the number of the cube concerned, and the pattern on the opposite face of this cube; and if this second pattern is not the same as the first pattern, we can then find it elsewhere on the first side face of the assembly, on a different cube. We can next note the number of this new cube, and the pattern which it in turn contributes to the opposite face; and we can continue in this fashion.

A time must come when we arrive at the same pattern as the one with which we started, this time situated on the opposite face. We have then closed a cycle in which pattern symbols and cube symbols alternate: each cube symbol lies between the symbols of the patterns which it contributes to the two opposite faces of the assembly, and each pattern symbol lies between the symbols of the two cubes which contribute this pattern to the two different faces involved.

The cycle may close only when all cubes have been involved, or alternatively it may close earlier: it could close immediately, with only one pattern symbol and one cube symbol, if the solution made use of the same pattern on opposite sides of one of the cubes. But if it does close with less than the full number of cubes, we can begin again with another pattern and another cube; and we can do this again, if need be, until it can be done no longer.

At the end of this procedure, we will have made use of every pattern symbol and every cube symbol, once and once only in each case, to form one or more closed chains of the type which we have just described: and there must be a chain or set of chains of this type twice over, once for each of the two pairs of opposite faces of the assembly block. We must now examine our diagram to determine how these two arrangements can be obtained.

Referring to Figure 7*B,* we note first that here there are no loops, so there can be no one-step chains, with only one symbol of each type: apart from having a complete five-step chain, we could only have two chains, one a three-step chain and the other a two-step chain.

We can in fact find *one* arrangement which connects one specimen of each pattern symbol and cube symbol jointly into a combination of a three-step chain and a two-step chain: but we require *two* compatible arrangements each of which assembles a complete set of symbols into one or more closed chains; and this is impossible here unless we use a five-step chain for both arrangements.

One way to discover this is to draw up a table which has a column for each junction line which is included in the figure: at the head of each column we can list the associated choices which are available for a cube, and we can then consider each possible circuit in turn, to see if we can find a method of selecting a complete set of different cube-symbols. It is obviously preferable to start with any choices which are forced—some segment may allow only one cube, or some cube may be available only from one segment—and as consequences of these, there may be further forced choices elsewhere, and so on, progressively: failing this we consider alternative possibilities in succession; and some circuits may allow no complete set of symbols at all. For our present puzzle, we then obtain a scheme as in Table 7*c*, from which it is easy to see that though there are six possible individual circuits, these give rise to only two compatible pairs.

SEGMENT:	BR	FU	FR	FB	UR	JR	FJ	BU	
ALTERNATIVES:	1	3	4	2 3	2 5	3 4	1 2 5	1 4 5	
Circuit *BFJRU*	·	·	·	2 ·	· 5	3 ·	1 · ·	· 4 ·	(a)
,,	·	·	·	· 3	2 ·	· 4	1 · ·	· · 5	(b)
,,	·	·	·	· 3	2 ·	· 4	· · 5	1 · ·	(c)
,,	·	·	·	· 3	· 5	· 4	· 2 ·	1 · ·	(d)
Circuit *BRJFU*	1	3	·	· ·	· ·	· 4	· 2 ·	· · 5	(e)
Circuits *BU, FJR*	·	·	4	· ·	· ·	3 · ·	· 2 ·	1 · 5	(f)
Circuits *FJ, RUB*	No complete set of symbols possible								
Circuits *JR, UBF*	No complete set of symbols possible								

Only two pairs of compatible circuits: (*a*) and (*c*); or (*a*) and (*e*).

TABLE 7 *c*

How to use two chains if you can find them

The two compatible pairs lead to the two solutions which we illustrate in Figures 7*C* and 7*D*: in these figures we have used single dashes to

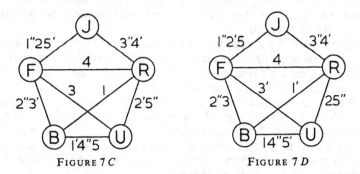

FIGURE 7 *C*   FIGURE 7 *D*

identify the symbols which are associated in one chain, and double dashes to identify those for the other chain (which is the same in both solutions). Each numerical symbol must appear three times over in any such diagram, corresponding to the three pairs of opposite parallel faces on its associated cube; so once the chains are identified by the single and double dashes, a complete set of unaltered cube symbols will remain, to identify the pairs of parallel faces which do *not* appear on side faces of the assembly block.

These symbols *without* dashes indicate the first step in finding the solution: we take the cubes in numerical order and put them together in any way which aligns the correct pair of faces with the long axis of the assembly.

The second step is then to achieve a pair of opposite faces as specified by *one* of the two compatible arrangements. We consider cubes in the cyclic order of their symbols in the associated chain, and turn them appropriately about the long axis of the block, to make each successive cube exhibit the same pattern as its predecessor, but in the opposite face of the assembly; the second face of the last cube in any chain must finally correspond to the first face of the first cube: we do this for each chain in the arrangement, if multiple chains are involved.

The third step is to do the same for the remaining pair of assembly faces, as specified by the other of the two compatible arrangements: cubes are here taken in their cyclic order as in the second arrangement, and are now rotated through 180°, if necessary, about the join of the

> First assemble the cubes so that from left to right the successive cubes can be identified from the presence of
>
> (1) two Belgian flags (*B*);
> (2) two French flags (*F*), one opposite a Japanese flag (*J*);
> (3) two French flags (*F*), one opposite a Union flag (*U*);
> (4) two Russian flags (*R*);
> (5) two Union flags (*U*).
>
> Next turn the cubes until the top faces, from left to right, are *FBJUR*: the bottom faces will then be *JFRBU*. Finally, rotate cubes about vertical axes, if necessary, until the front faces are either *URBJF* (with associated back faces *BUFRJ*), or *RFUJB* (with associated back faces *BJFRU*).
>
> This gives the two essentially distinct solutions of the puzzle: others are derived from these by permutations of cubes and rotations of the assembly as a whole.

TABLE 7 *d*

two faces which have already been located in the first pair of side faces. The half-turns do not disturb the selection of patterns for the different positions in the first pair of faces; cubes which are neighbours in the cycle once again contribute the same pattern to opposite faces, this time in the remaining pair of faces of the assembly block; and once again the cyclic closure of any chain or chains is guaranteed as required.

On completion of these three steps the cubes will be assembled in a way to solve the puzzle. By this means we obtain directions as in Table 7*d*, for the two solutions illustrated in Figure 7*E*. (In both solutions the inessential faces are shown as they are on the actual cubes of the puzzle.)

Mutations and natural selection

We once discussed the 'Flags of the Allies' elsewhere, and remarked that the only specimen we knew was in the Museum of Childhood in Edinburgh. A generous correspondent (Mr. Walter Schofield) was led to look out a specimen which he had had for some time: it proved to differ from the Edinburgh exhibit by the omission of the cube which we have labelled '5', with a duplication of the cube which we have labelled '3'.

Curiously enough, this does little to spoil the puzzle: though we imagine it is the result of a mishap, rather than an application of

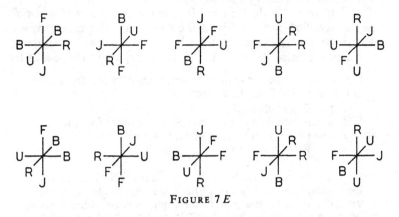

FIGURE 7 *E*

production engineering! We leave it to readers to show that in this new version there are four individual circuits, which again give only two compatible pairs: we might consider that a solution is equally difficult to find, in practice. The chances of partial success—on a single pair of opposite faces—are somewhat reduced: it may be doubtful whether this is a disadvantage, or an improvement!

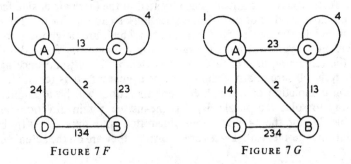

FIGURE 7 *F*   FIGURE 7 *G*

The four-cube 'Tantalizer' puzzle leads to a diagram as in Figure 7*F*: the solution directions we first gave would be equally applicable to a puzzle with a diagram as in Figure 7*G*. (To obtain cubes for this second puzzle, we need only change the inessential faces of cube 1 from *A*–*A* to *A*–*B*, and of cube 2 from *A*–*B* to *A*–*A*, before interchanging the numbers for these cubes.)

The method we have explained will then show that the original puzzle has a unique solution, whereas the other has three distinct solutions. In both of the cases there is a solution involving two four-step chains; in the second case there may also be a four-step chain combined with a three-step chain plus one loop, or with a two-step chain plus two loops.

It seems a pity that no more than two puzzles of this type are at all well known; and we may ask whether other forms could be as good, or better. The number of possibilities for different colorations of a set of even a few cubes is so immense that we may well seek to impose some restrictions before we begin our search.

One idea which readily arises here is as follows. In working with a set of cubes, it may prove difficult to select a desired cube, or to distinguish the individual cubes from one another: but it is usually easier to note which faces have the *same* colour, and how the identical colours are disposed, than to remember and recognize patterns which involve recognition of individual colours.

We can therefore ask how many types of cube are distinguishable, if faces involve n different colours, but attention is paid only to the dispositions of identical colours, without regard to the particular colours involved. Both for $n = 1$ and for $n = 6$, there obviously is only one type, in this sense: for $n = 2, 3, 4$, and 5, the corresponding numbers are 5, 8, 6, and 2. For $n = 5$ the like-coloured faces must be either adjacent or opposite: in Figure 7H we illustrate the greater variety which is possible for $n = 2, 3, 4$.

If individual cubes are to be distinguishable as we have suggested, they must correspond to different diagrams in our figure—no two must become equivalent merely by permuting the colours which the letter symbols represent: and we may well prefer to have every colour represented somewhere on every cube. There are not enough different types of cubes, if $n = 5$; and for $n = 2$ the problem is trivial when it is not impossible: but we can hope for better from $n = 3$ and $n = 4$.

When we have a choice, we may have grounds to prefer one type of cube to another. Since our object is to make the solution difficult, we may well wish to reject cubes which can take different orientations and still present the same patterns on the faces which are of interest. This applies to all the cubes for $n = 2$, since any one of these can show an identical pattern in some other orientation: in the other cases some cubes are inevitably ambiguous and some cubes cannot be, whereas for other cubes this will depend on which ring of faces is needed in the solution.

Again, we may well prefer—if possible—to have a set where each colour appears as often as any other, overall: for otherwise there is a clear hint to choose the more frequent colours for the inessential faces.

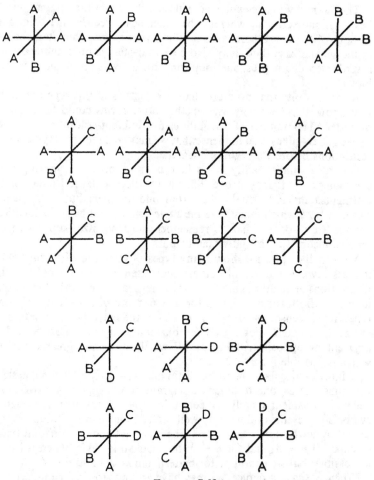

FIGURE 7 *H*

In the 'Flags of the Allies', it may be noticed that the French flag is favoured at the expense of the Japanese; and the Tantalizer similarly has one pattern seven times, and another only five times. (With as many patterns as cubes, the average number of appearances of the same pattern must be six, overall: and all the other patterns appear exactly six times.)

Forming threes and forming fours

We find that we cannot succeed in all our aims, if $n = 3$. A possible form is as in Figure 7*K*, but this has colours divided 8, 6, 4, and one cube can be rotated through 180° without disturbing the solution. With six appearances of each colour, we either have sets like the one in Figure 7L, with three solutions—for here we can have solutions if we align the cubes in each of the other possible directions, without rotating any cubes: or we have sets like the one in Figure 7M, which may tempt some readers to anti-social behaviour—for cubes made to this specification will allow no solution at all.

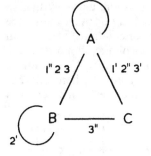

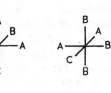

FIGURE 7 K

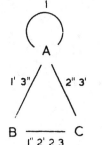

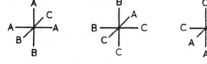

FIGURE 7 L

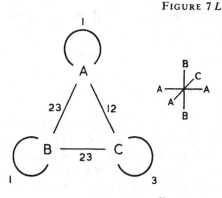

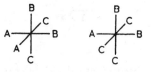

FIGURE 7 M

With $n = 4$, we have precisely the same trouble. From various possibilities we select as in Figure 7*N*; the evilly disposed may rejoice to find three circuits, none compatible with either of the others. In Figure 7*P* we select a set with a three-way solution, which would be a preferable set to manufacture. To have a three-way solution, we cannot ignore mirror-image distinctions—all cubes must be as illustrated, or we must have reflections for all four simultaneously: otherwise there are three distinct ordinary solutions, only, and no three-way solution is possible.

However, with colours divided 7, 6, 6, 5—no more unevenly than in the traditional Tantalizer—we can still succeed in our other aims. We can reject the cube which has two equivalent orientations, and we can avoid using the one which has *two* pairs of like-coloured opposite faces. With the other four we can have a diagram as in Figure 7*Q*, leading to cubes which assemble for a solution as in Figure 7*R*: here all four cubes are distinguishable in the way that we required. One cube has

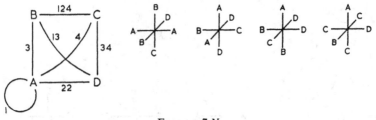

FIGURE 7 *N*

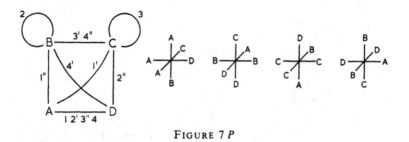

FIGURE 7 *P*

three identical colours round a vertex—something not present in the older form; another cube has three colours the same with two of these on opposite faces, and a third cube has an opposite pair of one colour and an adjacent pair of another, as in the other version; here only the fourth has two adjacent pairs with different colours for each pair, whereas the traditional form has two cubes of this type.

We think our new form is an improvement—especially since it can tantalize the more, because here there are four circuits with only one pair compatible. In the usual form, the two compatible circuits are in fact the only circuits possible, and if you already have four different colours arranged on two opposite faces, you are necessarily fairly near to a solution: with the new version you may be, or you may not be.

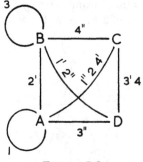

FIGURE 7 *Q*

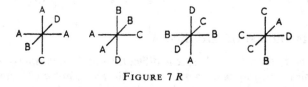

FIGURE 7 *R*

The figures make another difference clear: two of the four colours are each used for a single pair of like-coloured opposite faces, in both versions; but every pair of different colours is now used for at least one pair of opposite faces, whereas one pair is missing, in the traditional version.

All or nothing in five-way agreements

For $n = 5$, we can allow all cubes to be of identical type, since we here can have a very simple distinction in terms of colours: each cube can display the full set, with a different colour repeated on each cube. In this special case, we can use identical symbols for cubes and for colours, without confusion: cubes can be named after the colours which they have in duplicate; or colours can be numbered similarly to the cubes which show them twice. Here, we prefer to have the like-coloured faces adjacent—rather than opposite—on every cube; and we prefer to have opposite faces showing every possible pair of colours.

125

Puzzles and Paradoxes

We can offer three designs, as in Figures 7S, 7T, and 7U. These give two sets each with a unique three-way solution, but different in other respects, as well as a third set for which no solution is possible: we leave it to readers to discover which is which. They may also note that one of the three sets of cubes can be converted into either of the other two by replacing only a single cube—different in either case.

These sets could be regarded as variants of the 'Flags of the Allies'. There might be some point in using national symbols on the impossible set: the Olympic rings could be used if there was hope of exhibiting multilateral agreement.

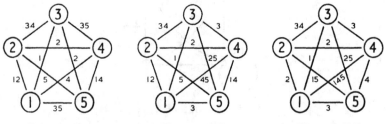

FIGURE 7 S   FIGURE 7 T   FIGURE 7 U

Uses for non-standard dice

For more than five cubes, it is difficult to find—or apply—selection principles which appeal on grounds of elegance: but one form for six cubes seems worthy of special mention. This has been described by E. M. Wyatt, who gave it in an equivalent form which conceals some symmetry which we can illustrate here: the attractive feature is that

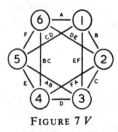

FIGURE 7 V

every cube exhibits all the six different patterns. In a later book he gave a variant which appears less interesting: but we like his idea of making the cubes like dice, with the usual patterns of spots (he points out that the dice are non-standard, as there is not the usual sum of 7 for opposite faces). The diagram for the six cubes is as in Figure 7V, and the requirement is to produce a solution of the three-way type.

Here we can first note that most forms of multiple-loop circuits are impossible, and the only possibilities are circuits of six, or else pairs of triads. Further consideration leads to association of symbols either as in Figure 7W or as in Figure 7X: these give two possible solutions as in Figures 7Y and 7Z. Further examination of these figures will show that we can retain one solution, and remove the possibility of

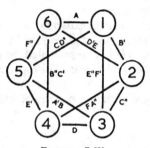

FIGURE 7 *W*

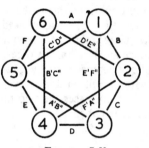

FIGURE 7 *X*

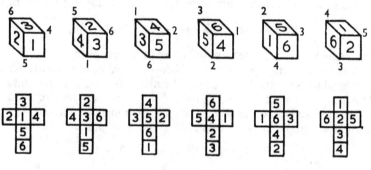

FIGURE 7 *Y*

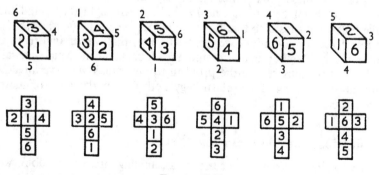

FIGURE 7 *Z*

the other, if we replace every alternate cube by its mirror-image; and we would consider this to be an improvement.

In these figures, we have used numerals for the patterns, with letters for the cube-symbols, contrary to our earlier practice: it may be easier to replace the numerals by dice symbols. We have represented the cubes by oblique perspective views, together with related nets for the faces, as in Wyatt's book, and we have added symbols to indicate the hidden faces. In some cases the two figures have different but equivalent nets for the same cube.

Addition sums as further complications

Yet another possibility for puzzles of this type is to put numerals on the cube faces, and then require a specified sum over the assembly faces. If this sum can be made only from *different* numerals—as for the cases

$$1+2+4+8 = 15, \quad \text{or} \quad 2+3+5+8 = 18,$$

for instance—there is then no difference in the problem.

A correspondent—Mr. C. H. Parker—has told us he has a four-cube puzzle which was purchased at the Wembley International Exhibition. This involves numerals 3, 4, 5, and 8, with a required sum of 20, and it turns out to be the Tantalizer, in yet a sixth metamorphosis: we can relate the symbols to our previous diagram, if we put

$$A = 8, \quad B = 3, \quad C = 5, \quad D = 4;$$

but we have now to consider whether or not we can have 20 as

$$4+4+4+8, \quad \text{or as} \quad 5+5+5+5.$$

Actually, these possibilities are merely further distractions: for the important point here is that no symbol appears eight times, and the symbols are disposed so that there are no opposite pairs (4, 4) or (4, 5). From these considerations we can easily show that we can ignore ways of making 20 other than by summing four numbers which are all different: we thus reduce the problem to one which we have already solved—a profitable form of strategy both for puzzles and for more serious mathematics.

Don't just tumble them together!

To find the chances of success by assembling cubes at random, we should first note that a cube can have twenty-four different orientations: it can occupy the same position sitting on any of six faces in any of four different ways; alternatively, any of twelve edges can be put in a standard position, either of two ways round. On this basis we first discuss a case where there is a unique solution which cannot remain a solution if the orientation of any cube is changed.

In a case like this, if we specify the long axis for the assembly, we have a 1/3 chance of placing the *first* cube correctly—for we have only to make the right pair of faces have their planes perpendicular to the long axis: after this we have only a 1/24 chance for each later cube, since each of these then has only one orientation which is allowable. By multiplying the probabilities for these independent choices, we have probabilities of 1 in 41,472 for four cubes, of 1 in 995,328 for five, and of 1 in 23,887,872 for six.

Four-cube and five-cube versions which we illustrate have solutions which in no case will allow a change of orientation for any isolated cube; but with other forms we might have to allow for this: we would then have to take note of the increased multiplicity of the favourable cases. Similarly, the two distinct solutions for the 'Flags of the Allies' allow about two chances in a million, for success by random assembly, in place of only one.

Intelligent use of trial and error is better than random assembly, of course; and the Tantalizer can yield to this—combined perhaps with a little luck: the author's daughter succeeded with it, at the age of 10. But four cubes are about the limit: empirical methods had produced no solution of the 'Flags of the Allies', for the Museum of Childhood. Here—as with some puzzles of greater moment—some theoretical study may finally prove a lighter burden than conscientious but ill-directed perseverance.

8 Gamesman, Spare that Tree

Games: and when they are impartial

We shall now consider a class of games which require only the simplest of apparatus—a number of small objects which are easily handled and counted. Matches, counters, beans, buttons, screws—these or anything similar will do (even small stones, if nothing else is at hand). Our aim is to find guiding principles which will indicate how to play any such game to best advantage.

All the games will involve two players only: at all times, information of all relevant considerations will be available equally to both players; and the course of a game will be wholly determined by decisions which they make, with nothing dependent on chance events which might favour one player rather than the other. This places our chosen games in a different category from many familiar games, such as card games where each player knows his own cards, but is unaware whether his opponent has—or has not—some of the others; or from dice games where each player may have unexpected benefit or disadvantage from particular falls of the dice.

We may characterize all our chosen games as *two-person games of perfect information with no chance moves*. Among games of this type we find some other familiar games: both chess and noughts-and-crosses (otherwise, tick-tack-toe) are further examples, notwithstanding their noticeable dissimilarity in other respects—such as complexity of structure and variety of interest. We shall derive some results which are applicable to all such games, and consequently to noughts-and-crosses and chess also: but in complex games like chess—fortunately, as we may well think—there are virtually insuperable barriers of complication which will prevent practical realization of the theoretical possibilities.

Apart from this we shall find other results which will apply to our chosen games only, and *not* to chess or noughts-and-crosses: these results will be dependent on yet a further property which our games have, in addition to what we have so far considered. For a characteristic feature of our chosen type of game is that the objects which are used are not used as *pieces* which belong to one or other of the players only—they are rather to be considered as *markers* which the two players use in common, to record the state of the game, and to determine the allowable moves.

The important point here is that the possibilities for moves must be determined from the state of the markers *alone*—in precisely the same way—quite independently of which of the players is to make the next move: this must be true also of the rules which decide when the game is over, and what is the final result.

Games of this type have been called *impartial* games: for they make no distinction between the players other than the obviously necessary one, that one player will have the right to make the first move. No game can be an impartial game, in the sense in which we use the term, if either player has pieces of his own, distinguished from those of his opponent; and impartial games can be readily identified by the presence of the following characteristic.

In some games it can happen that the joint effect of two successive moves is that the markers are left in a state in which they could have been left in one move, with a different choice of the earlier of the two moves. As between these two cases, in an impartial game, there must be a complete reversal of the possibilities and prospects for the two players: and if the player who made the later of the two moves goes on thereafter to an inevitable victory, the other player will then have the added annoyance of a realization that he could have defeated his opponent in an absolutely identical way, had he made his move in a fashion which would have combined the effect of the two moves as they occurred in the game which he in fact lost.

Wythoff's game, and how to lose it

As a first example, we can take a game described about fifty years ago by W. A. Wythoff. In Wythoff's game the objects are divided into two heaps: the two players play alternately, and at each move the player must either diminish one heap alone, or else diminish both heaps by equal amounts. He must take at least one object; he can remove a heap completely if he likes, possibly removing a like number from the other heap: and he has an independent choice—to diminish either heap, or both, and to what extent—at each different move. The player who removes the last object—singly, or with others—becomes the winner.

Wythoff's game has the features which we said were characteristic of an impartial game. At any stage, all that matters is the current pair of numbers in the two heaps. What the one player can do, the other could do in his place, if the heaps were the same when he had to play. The detailed course of the previous moves no longer matters; all is just as if a new game started with the current heaps as initial heaps and the same player to play. If one player can win by making a move which his opponent could have combined with his own move, his opponent could have won instead, had he so combined it (and then continued correctly thereafter).

As a result of this, we can divide the heap-combinations into two classes which we distinguish as *safe* or *unsafe*—from the viewpoint of the player who has left them after his move. These are such that a player who is faced with a combination which is safe (for his opponent) must inevitably leave one which is unsafe (for himself), no matter what move he makes; whereas a player who plays when the position is unsafe for his opponent has only to look and he will certainly be able to find one move—possibly more—which will produce a position which is safe for himself. Among experts the winner is thus the one who can first seize and hold the chain of safe combinations.

To determine the safe combinations, we start from the end of the game, and work backwards, noting that the total number in the two heaps will continually increase as we take note of each preceding move. When the winner is the one who takes the last object, the heap-combination (0, 0) is obviously *safe*: for the player who leaves it has then won. We now look for other safe leaves.

Any combination which can be converted into (0, 0) in one move must be *unsafe*: for it must be assumed that the other player will do this, and so win. This rules out leaving only one heap empty, or both heaps equal (but not empty). Among heap-combinations not yet ruled out, any which have the minimum total number of objects possible must be safe: for they cannot be reduced to (0, 0) in one move, or they *would* have been ruled out; but the next move must reduce them, and anything else to which they can be reduced is necessarily unsafe.

There are no safe combinations with a total of one or two objects; for (0, 1) (0, 2), and (1, 1) are all convertible to (0, 0) in a single move. So also is (0, 3): but (1, 2) is not. This provides the next combination which is safe, and anything reducible to this in a single move becomes unsafe. This means any combination with 1 in one heap and more than 2 in the other; or with 2 in one heap and more than 1 in the other; or with a difference of 1 between larger heap numbers.

The next safe combination is then the pair with the smallest total which do not include a heap of 0, 1, or 2, or have a difference of 0 or 1. So the smaller heap must have the smallest number not yet excluded—namely, 3—and the heaps must differ by the smallest difference not yet excluded—namely, by 2. The next safe combination is thus (3, 5). The heap numbers now excluded are 0, 1, 2, 3, 5 and the excluded differences are 0, 1, 2; the first gaps are respectively at 4 and at 3, and so we have (4, 7) as the next safe combination.

In this way we can continue a sequence (0, 0), (1, 2), (3, 5), (4, 7), (6, 10), (8, 13), (9, 15), (11, 18), (12, 20), ... as far as we like. This gives all the safe combinations. The heap differences always increase by unit steps, and the smaller heap increases either by two or by one, according as the next higher number has or has not already been used for the larger of two heaps in an earlier combination: the larger heap correspondingly increases by three or by two.

After this, we can consider a different but related game, where the rule is that the one who takes the last object is to be the loser. In effect it is then as if our earlier game were being played with both players purposely trying to lose: and it is surprising how little difference this makes.

When it is the loser who takes the last object, (0, 0) now becomes unsafe, since he who leaves it has lost; and (0, 1) becomes safe, since he who leaves it forces his opponent to take the last object. Working back from (0, 1) we find that (0, 2), (1, 1), (0, 3), (1, 2), (0, 4), and (1, 3) are all unsafe: but (2, 2) is safe. We now have two safe combinations, (0, 1) and (2, 2).

Between them these rule out higher-total combinations with a smaller heap of 0, 1, or 2, or a heap difference of 0 or 1. But this is precisely what the first two safe combinations (0, 0) and (1, 2) jointly ruled out in the other game: we have simply taken the first two differences in the reverse order. It follows that all other safe combinations are identical in the two games.

The expert player will therefore proceed as follows. He will memorize the safe combinations (0, 0) and (1, 2) for the first game, and the safe combinations (0, 1) and (2, 2) for the second; from these he will readily derive the higher safe combinations (3, 5), (4, 7), (6, 10), ... applicable to both games alike.

If he is faced with a combination which is not in the sequence of safe combinations, he will know that he can convert it into one which is; and being aware of this he will readily determine how to do it. Sometimes he will have no choice—for instance, he can leave only (4, 7) if he is faced with (6, 9): but in other cases he may be able to vary his play. Faced with (5, 6), he can have a longer game by leaving (3, 5), or a shorter game by leaving (1, 2); he can be sure of winning with either choice.

If the initial course of the game has given him no chance to obtain a safe combination, he will probably take one object—or very few—and hope his opponent is not another expert. He may then pick up the series at a later move: but an expert opponent will not give him the chance.

The expert cannot play this game with a novice for long, if they take turns to start. If the expert takes no unnecessary risks, the novice may well begin to see—and play for—the safe combinations; if the expert takes risks, to conceal his strategy, the novice will sometimes win—by chance, or luck, or developing skill—with a similar result. The task of finding an expert's strategy makes a good practical intelligence test for a novice—but only if he can be guaranteed to be previously uninstructed!

Readers may think the series of safe combinations has a curious blend of regularity and irregularity: and they would be right in this belief. In the game where the winner takes the last object, the safe combinations are slightly the more regular. Each of them can in fact be specified individually, without recursive reference to earlier combinations, by a quite uniform procedure.

We first select two numbers which differ by 1, namely 1·618 033 989... and 2·618 033 989...; we then find that if we take their multiples by whole numbers 0, 1, 2, ..., *and reject all fractional parts*, we thus obtain number-pairs (0, 0), (1, 2), (3, 5), ..., exactly as we want.

An equivalent graphical procedure is illustrated in Figure 8*A*, where we have three uniform scales starting from a common zero. The scale ratios are proportional to

$$1 \ : \ 1 \cdot 618... \ : \ 2 \cdot 618...,$$

involving the same numbers as above. (Readers may note we have not said whether the proportionality is direct or inverse.) To find safe combinations, we first choose one of the graduations of the coarsest scale, and then move towards the common zero, to take the labels of the graduations we first encounter on each of the other two scales.

Just what our numbers 1·618... and 2·618... are, and why they work as we have said they do, is a problem which is of some interest in its own right.

Never mind the fractions!

Divorced from any reference to Wythoff's game, our last problem can be stated as follows:

Prove that we can find two numbers 1·618... and 2·618... such that if we take corresponding multiples in pairs, in increasing order, and reject the fractional parts, we get a series of pairs of whole numbers (1, 2), (3, 5), (4, 7), ... with these two properties: the differences in successive pairs increase by units; and the smaller number of any pair is the smallest whole number which has not occurred (in either position) earlier in the series. This latter property implies that if we continue far enough, *every* whole number will appear either as the smaller or as the larger of a pair, but *no* number will appear in both capacities.

We first require a theorem about rational numbers and irrational square roots. (The number p/q is *rational* if p and q are whole numbers. We can assume p and q have no common factor, as we could find and remove this, without changing the number.) This theorem states that no rational number can be the square root of a whole number N, if N

is not itself a perfect square: its proof is as follows. If we had $p^2/q^2 = N$, then $p^2 = Nq^2$ would be an equation between whole-number products, so that the prime factors of p^2 and Nq^2 would have to be the same. Since we can assume that no factor is common to p and q, the same is true of p^2 and q^2. If N is not a perfect square, it has some prime factor which appears an *odd* number of times. The same factor would have to appear at least as often in p^2, but an even number of times in all; yet it cannot appear in q^2.

This is impossible. We have reached a contradiction, by correct reasoning: so our first assumption must have been unjustifiable. Hence we *cannot* have $p^2/q^2 = N$, with p/q rational, if N is a whole number but not a perfect square.

It follows from this that we can never get a whole number (or indeed a rational number) by multiplying an irrational square root by a whole number or a rational number: for if we could, this would imply an equation which could be solved to give a rational equivalent for the irrational square root.

(Since a square of unit side has a diagonal of length $\sqrt{2}$ units, it follows that both side and diagonal cannot simultaneously be exact whole-number multiples of any unit, however small. The Pythagoreans in Greece in the fifth century B.C. knew this result, but regarded it as a scandal, or a paradox; they sought to conceal it from others, like a skeleton in a cupboard. Its proof appears in Euclid, about a century later.)

Our mystic numbers are in fact

$$\tfrac{1}{2}(1+\sqrt{5}) = 1{\cdot}618... \quad \text{and} \quad \tfrac{1}{2}(3+\sqrt{5}) = 2{\cdot}618... \,.$$

The first of these is commonly denoted by the Greek letter τ (*tau*). Among other things it is the ratio of a diagonal to a side in a regular pentagon—that is, the ratio of the sides of a *pentagram* to the sides of the pentagon which circumscribes it. From this we can deduce that $\cos 36° = \tfrac{1}{2}\tau$.

It is easily verified that

$$\tau^2 = (1{\cdot}618...)^2 = \tfrac{1}{4}(1+\sqrt{5})^2 = \tfrac{1}{2}(3+\sqrt{5}) = 2{\cdot}618... = 1+\tau,$$

so that τ is the positive root of the quadratic equation $x^2-x-1 = 0$. The usual results for sums and products of roots then indicate that the negative root is $-\tau^{-1} = 1-\tau = -0{\cdot}618...$ Geometrical application of these results, in relation to rectangles and squares, leads to the *Golden Section* of the Greeks, and the *Modulor* of the modern architect Le Corbusier.

From the basic result

$$\tau^2 = \tau + 1$$

we derive
$$\tau^3 = \tau^2 + \tau = 2\tau + 1,$$

$$\tau^4 = \tau^3 + \tau^2 = 3\tau + 2,$$

$$\tau^5 = \tau^4 + \tau^3 = 5\tau + 3,$$

and so on: also

$$\tau^{-1} = \tau - 1 = 0.618...,$$

$$\tau^{-2} = 1 - \tau^{-1} = 0.381... = 2 - \tau,$$

$$\tau^{-3} = \tau^{-1} - \tau^{-2} = 2\tau - 3,$$

and so on. In this way we can reduce any (positive or negative) integral power of τ to a combination of an integer and an integral multiple of τ.

If we start with 0 and 1, and derive new numbers by adding the last two to get the next, we get a series 0, 1, 1, 2, 3, 5, 8, 13, 21, ... which is very closely related to τ. Consecutive terms are the whole numbers which appear in the reduced expressions for the powers of τ; and the ratio of any term to the one before it becomes the more nearly equal to τ the further the series is continued. (Actually, the numbers in the series can be derived by removing a factor $\sqrt{5}$ from differences of rth powers of τ and of $-\tau^{-1}$, for $r = 0, 1, 2, 3, ...$: the powers of τ increase, and the others diminish, as we proceed to higher values of r.)

The series and the numbers included in it take their names from Fibonacci, otherwise Leonardo of Pisa, 'the only outstanding European mathematician of the Middle Ages'. He learned much from Arab sources in North Africa, and promoted the spread of the Hindu-Arabic numeral system which we now use, by his book *Liber Abaci* (A.D. 1202). Like τ, Fibonacci series and numbers appear in many different contexts. We shall now see how they arise in our present problem.

Since $\tau^2 = \tau + 1$, numbers $\tau = 1.618...$ and $\tau^2 = 2.618...$ will differ exactly by 1, so that multiples of τ and of τ^2 by any whole number n will differ exactly by n. The two multiples must therefore have the same fractional parts, and when these are removed, the whole numbers left must also differ by the whole number n. This proves that in our series of pairs of whole numbers, the differences increase by the unit steps which are needed to satisfy the first of our two requirements.

For the rest, we next seek to find how many numbers less than a given whole number N are included in the two series together—the series of smaller numbers derived from multiples of τ, and the series of larger numbers derived from multiples of τ^2.

We here ignore the zero which more strictly forms the first term of each series: a unit is then contributed to the joint total for every multiple of τ which we can take without exceeding N, and similarly for multiples of τ^2. The number we want is thus the sum of the *whole-number parts* of the two quotients N/τ and N/τ^2.

Since we have $1 = \tau^{-1} + \tau^{-2}$, we also have $N = N/\tau + N/\tau^2$: and consequently the two *exact* quotients must sum exactly to N. Because of the $\sqrt{5}$ involved, no multiple either of τ or of τ^2 can exactly equal any whole number, so each individual quotient N/τ or N/τ^2 must have a fractional part which is not zero (but which of course must be less than 1).

Before we remove the two fractional parts, the sum of the *exact* quotients is the whole number N: after we remove them, the resulting sum must again be a whole number. We have definitely reduced the sum, and we cannot have removed as much as 2. The two fractional parts must therefore sum exactly to 1, and the number of non-zero terms less than N in the two series together must thus be $N-1$.

Since this last result holds for every whole number N, the dropping of the upper limit by one unit must always exclude one term and one term only. This is possible only if all whole numbers appear once and once only in the two series jointly: and our proof is now complete.

If we were not given our two mystic numbers, we could find them if we first assumed that there were two suitable numbers x and y, of which x was the smaller.

Unless we had $y-x = 1$, the differences $ny-nx$ would differ from n by increasing amounts as n became larger, and this would make it impossible to have a difference of n after dropping the fractional parts.

Similarly, unless we had $1/y + 1/x = 1$, the number of terms less than N in both series jointly would differ from N by increasing amounts, and either duplications or omissions would be inevitable.

This shows that the only possible numbers are positive numbers which satisfy $y-x = 1$, $1/y + 1/x = 1$. These equations lead to $x = \tau$, $y = \tau^2$, and $x = -\tau^{-1}$, $y = \tau^{-2}$, of which only the first solution gives both numbers positive as we require here. Having proved that no other numbers can do what we want, we then must prove that these numbers will, in the way we did earlier.

In Figure 8A, the scale intervals have lengths in the ratios of $1 : \tau : \tau^2$, that is,

$$1 \ : \ 1{\cdot}618... \ : \ 2{\cdot}618...,$$

or equivalently $\tau^{-2} : \tau^{-1} : 1$, that is,

$$0{\cdot}381... \ : \ 0{\cdot}618... \ : \ 1,$$

and the three scale-ratios are in geometric progression.

137

We may notice that our series of pairs includes (among others) the pairs which are formed by grouping all the Fibonacci numbers in consecutive pairs in one of the two possible ways. In these cases the excluded fractional parts are particularly small. Pairs formed from consecutive Fibonacci numbers in the other pairing are all excluded, but only just: here the fractional parts very nearly amount to a unit.

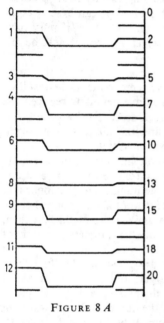

(It follows that the series includes all pairs in which both numbers are one unit less than in the excluded Fibonacci pairs.)

Figure 8*A* shows this for the included pairs (1, 2), (3, 5), (8, 13), as well as for the excluded pairs (5, 8) and (13, 21)— with corresponding included pairs (4, 7) and (12, 20).

FIGURE 8 *A*

Contests of tree surgery

The procedure which we have adopted with Wythoff's game indicates what we can try to do in other two-person games also. With perfect information and no chance moves—whether the game is impartial or not—we can work backwards to determine safe and unsafe positions. When the game is not very complicated, this may be all we need do, if the safe positions are few enough—and simple enough—to be readily memorized.

Sometimes—as with noughts-and-crosses—it may be possible to take advantage of obvious symmetries (and of hidden symmetries, if these can be found), to reduce the number of essentially distinct cases which have to be examined. Even with noughts-and-crosses this becomes a somewhat laborious task, and for a game like chess the full task is well outside the speed and storage capacity of any computers which can currently be imagined.

If this procedure is to give fruitful results for playing other than very trivial games, it becomes necessary to have some other way of finding the safe positions than working backwards to every one individually. This means that we must find some more easily determined property which they all have—in some such fashion as we did for Wythoff's game, where we showed they could all be defined in terms of corresponding multiples of τ and τ^2.

At a later stage, we shall find that many *impartial* games—played with collections of objects—are of such a type that we can imagine that they consist of either a fixed or a variable number of component games which are carried on simultaneously, with each move being a move in only one component game at a time. When the loser is the one who finally cannot move in any of the component games, we shall find it possible to combine results for the component games to give results applicable to actual games: and in cases of common occurrence—where all components are identical—this can lead to quite simple methods of infallible play for what appear to be quite elaborate games.

Before we reach this stage, however, we shall consider inter-relations of moves and positions for several simpler games. What we say here will apply to all games of perfect information with no chance moves. In many cases our examples will in fact be impartial games, chosen for their comparative simplicity: but we shall not make any use of this consideration for the present.

As a suitably simple example, we shall take *Grundy's game*. Here two players start with a single heap of objects, and no objects are removed: the first player divides the original heap into two heaps, which must be unequal; and each alternately thereafter does the same to some single heap which is present when it is his turn to play.

The game proceeds until finally every heap has either one object, or two, when continuation becomes impossible. In the standard form of this game, the player who first cannot play is held to be the loser: but as with any other game, we can also ask what happens if both players purposely *try* to lose; this gives a related but different game, as with *misère* declarations in solo whist. We did this for Wythoff's game, and we shall consider the *misère* variant of Grundy's game also; here the rules for dividing heaps are the same, but a player *loses* if he fails to leave a move for his opponent.

Here, as with any other two-person game with perfect information and no chance moves, we can—in principle, at least—make use of the following procedure: beginning with the starting position we can draw a diagram similar to a genealogical tree. Below each position in the game we can list all the possible next positions, according to the different moves which are then possible: there are branching points similar to the generations in a line of descent; alternate generations here correspond to moves of different players. A single branch is possible, instead of a fork, for a forced move (this would correspond to an only child): and each line ultimately terminates—as for a descendant without issue— where the game is over, with a known result.

Figure 8*B* shows this done for Grundy's game with seven objects initially. Multiplicity of alternatives can make it impracticable to do this for many other games we have in mind (try it even for noughts-and-crosses!): but there is no difficulty in principle—a tree of this kind is implicitly specified by the rules, for every game of the type which we consider here.

Once this is done, the far end of every branch represents a situation where the game is over, with a known result: and each player will know when this would be favourable to him, or otherwise.

So each player can start at the far end of all the branches, and work backwards: the first to find a fork where he has a choice between moves leading to results of different value will in fact resolve to prune the offending branches from the tree, if ever he has occasion to make the

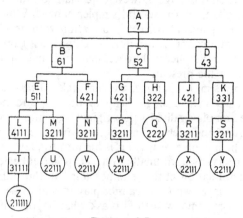

FIGURE 8 *B*

move which is associated with this fork; the other player at the next fork may have occasion to do the same, remembering that he has no prospect of subsequent play going along a branch which his opponent will decide to remove. After this they take turns until all branches have been reviewed.

The only time there will be no pruning is when all alternatives are equally favourable—or equally unfavourable—to the player whose move gives him his turn with the shears. At the end, all the branches left will lead to results of identical value (otherwise someone will not have pruned as he could and should); and if both players are expert, the game may then take various courses, but can have only one final result.

Applying these principles to Figure 8*B*, we may conclude that in the standard game the first player would cut the branch *EM* and the second player the branches *BE* and *CH*, after which the second player would win at *V*, *W*, *X*, or *Y*: in the *misère* game, the first player would cut *EL* and the second player *CG*; the first player would then cut *AC*, and would win at *U*, *V*, *X*, or *Y*.

This procedure would be applicable with an actual genealogical tree if alternate generations formed teams which had opposing views of the preferable sex for the final recipient of an inheritance (assuming they all could know the whole *subsequent* structure of the tree!): members of the one team would co-operate to cut off lines leading to boys, if girls were available, and those of the other team would act precisely oppositely.

How best to split heaps unequally

The tree model is unnecessarily complex if equivalent positions can be reached after different sequences of moves: with the tree, the equivalent positions must be repeated identically on different branches (as in Figure 8*B*); space can be saved if we use a network, with a single representation of equivalent positions, as in Figure 8*C*.

The situation here is as if the diagrams were plans of a railway marshalling yard, where junctions at each successive level down a slope are switched by points which are alternately under the control of one or other of two shunters who have opposed views on preferable sets of sidings to which to direct the trucks: one of these shunters then can have his way, and the other must finally acquiesce; it may be the one who has first choice, or his opponent, according to the plan of the yard.

In Figure 8*C*, the left-hand diagrams display all the possible moves in Grundy's game, for the cases of six, seven, and eight objects, initially. Diagrams in the centre column are for the standard game, and those in the right-hand column are for the *misère* game; dotted lines indicate junctions which one player or the other will decide to cut, and heavy lines indicate the only courses of play possible between two expert players.

The first player is *A*, the second is *B*; and starting from the end, we can label each position with the symbol of the player who *will* win, or *can* win, if this position arises: this indicates not only how the game should be played between experts, but also how an expert may sometimes manage to gain more than he deserves, if a non-expert opponent fails to make an optimum move.

For Grundy's game with six objects, the first player should win the standard game, and the second player the *misère* game; with seven objects it is the other way round, and with eight objects the first player should win either game. For larger numbers of objects, the associated diagrams soon become too complicated: we shall return to this problem later, and show how to determine winning lines of play for larger numbers of objects, without having to draw any networks.

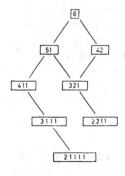
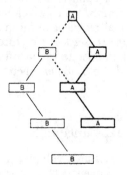
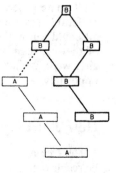

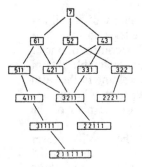
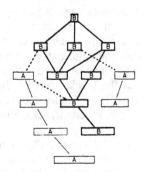
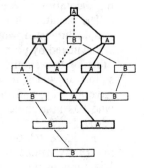

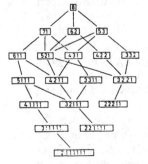
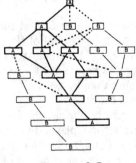
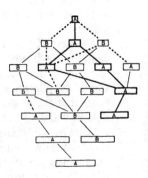

FIGURE 8 *C*

Games for optimists and pessimists

To illustrate the situation where the game may end otherwise than in a simple win or loss, we can consider a different set of rules for a new game with eight objects, in a case where the game is no longer impartial: the first player wins if there is *one* two-object heap at the end, the second if there are *two*, and the game is a draw if finally there are *three*. Here each player will prefer a win to a loss or a draw, and a draw to a loss: these preferences will be found to give precisely the same diagram as for the *misère* game; but the guaranteed result will here be a draw. Similar procedures will apply in cases where there are distinctions of value between different modes of winning, or losing.

It follows from what we have shown that it can only be the lack of expert players which ensures that games of this type do not always finish the same way. Which way this is, we cannot tell without the analysis: but in effect the rules must either present the game to one player—maybe the first, or maybe the second—or else deny a win to either unless by his opponent's mistake. We should be glad that for all but very simple games the analysis seems safely beyond the speed and storage of any conceivable computer; it would be a tragedy if chess were analysed out of existence, or reduced to the exploitation of the uninformed!

For readers who may wish to experiment with network diagrams, we can give two other games where the rules provide possibilities of a draw as well as of a win and a loss. In both cases there is a single heap of objects, and at each move a player may remove objects up to a maximum number of three. When all objects are finally divided between the players, they reject sets of three from their collections, and consider how many objects remain. In both cases, two objects remaining will identify a winner.

In *the optimist's game*, the number of objects is a multiple of 3: both players may have no odd objects left, which gives a draw; and a single object remaining will here identify a loser. In *the pessimist's game*, the number of objects is of the form $3n+2$: here a player with no objects remaining is a loser, and there is a draw when both players finally have one object each.

We give the games these names because in the optimist's game a suitable strategy is to secure a collection of the form $3n+2$, and to retain it in this form by taking three objects at later moves; if you can do this to the end, you will win—and when you cannot, you will be able to have a draw. In the pessimist's game, a suitable strategy is to secure a collection of the form $3n+1$, taking three objects at later moves: you are sure of at least a draw, if you do this; and any time you cannot do it, you can have a win.

As suitable numbers of objects, we suggest nine or eight, for a short game, and eighteen or twenty for a longer game, in the respective cases. The longer games give scope for some initial concealment of tactics: for any move is as good as another if all choices would leave six objects or more. In both games the result should be a draw if both players are expert.

(We should remark that these are *not* impartial games, as we use the term. Removed pieces here have to be retained by the players, whereas in an impartial game they could be put in a common discard heap: each player here *acquires* pieces of his own as the game proceeds; and the result depends on how the objects thus become the property either of one player or of the other.)

Marks of favour and disfavour

For games where one player must win, and the other lose, without further distinction, we saw how we could label the junctions with a symbol for the player who *would* win—or *could* win—if the corresponding positions materialized in an actual game; but since we know which player has the move at any junction, we can also label positions in a different but equivalent fashion, as follows.

Positions will be labelled either *F* or *U*: a position is to be labelled *F* only if it is a winning position for the player who has just moved, or if all routes from it go next to *U* positions; a position is to have a label *U* if one or more routes go next to *F* positions. All positions thus acquire one label or the other, and labels can be determined by working backwards after labelling every final dead end with an *F*; no position can be labelled until every position which can follow it in the game has already been labelled.

This symbolism will then denote that an *F* position is *favourable*—and a *U* position *unfavourable*—for the player who has completed a move; they are of course precisely the reverse from the viewpoint of the player who is then about to move. This means that we rank positions as favourable, not if a player *can* make a good move, but only when he *has* made a good move—which seems the better choice; and since the players play alternately, we may effectively regard any starting position as one which is left by the second player. A simple device lets us assume that every game ends with a move which produces a win for the player who makes it: if the game as ordinarily understood can end with a losing move, we then supply an additional notional move, of a compulsory type, equivalent to the making of a claim of victory by the winner.

If either player can leave an *F* position after his move, he need never do otherwise thereafter: every move by his opponent must then leave a *U* position, and from every *U* position a move can be found which will again leave an *F* position. This can continue, until an *F* position representing a win is finally obtained. If the starting position is an *F*, the first player must leave a *U*, and the second player can then continue with further *F* positions, and so win; but if the starting position is a *U*, the first player can win, for he can then secure a chain of *F* positions.

What to do if you may want to lose

Every game of the previous type has an associated but different game —the *misère* game—where in effect both players are purposely trying to lose. We can consider both games together, by using a different labelling. Positions are now marked with one or other of *four* symbols *E, S, M, N*, according to these rules: (1) a point is an *E* point only if all routes go next to *N* points; (2) a point is an *S* point only if it is a final dead end, or if some route goes next to an *M* point but none to either an *S* point or an *E* point; (3) a point is an *M* point only if some route goes next to an *S* point, but none to either an *M* point or an *E* point; (4) a point is an *N* point only if some route goes next to, an *E* point, or if there are routes going next to an *S* point *and* to an *M* point. All points thus receive one or other of the four labels, and labels can be determined by working backwards as before; the first step is to label every dead end with an *S*.

More concisely, we can summarize: non-final *S* positions must go to *M* positions and must not go to *E* or *S* positions; *M* positions must go to *S* positions and must not go to *E* or *M* positions; *N* positions must go to *E* positions—with or without *S* or *M* positions as well—or, failing this, both to *S* and *M* positions. For positions of these three types, it is immaterial whether or not they go also to *N* positions: but *E* positions must go *only* to *N* positions.

With this labelling, all routes from an *E* or an *S* must go next to either an *M* or an *N*, and from either an *M* or an *N* a route *can* be found which will go next to either an *E* or an *S*: so he who can leave an *E* or an *S* need never do otherwise thereafter, and must finally be able to reach an *S* at a dead end, and so win the standard game; but he who leaves an *M* or an *N* will find an expert opponent doing the like to him.

With the *misère* game, the object is to reach the *M* which precedes a final *S*. We now note that all routes from an *E* or an *M* must go next to either an *S* or an *N*, from either of which a route *can* be found which will go next to either an *E* or an *M*. It follows that he who can leave an *E* or an *M* can then reach an *M* which makes his opponent next take a final *S*; and he who leaves an *S* or an *N* gives his opponent the chance to do this in his place.

The meaning of the symbolism is now apparent: with expert play, an

E, *S*, *M*, or *N* position is a favourable leave in either game, in the standard game only, in the *misère* game only, or in neither game, in the respective cases: and once again the starting position should be regarded as being left by the second player.

For readers who know something of Boolean algebra, the labelling rules can be put more simply. If the logical variables 0 and 1 are used in place of *F* and *U* respectively, each label is then the *Sheffer-stroke* combination of all immediately following labels: this implies an 'and' function which is followed by a 'not' function. The 'and' produces 1 only where every successor is 1, and otherwise it gives 0: the 'not'

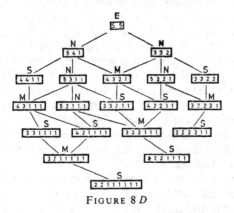

FIGURE 8 *D*

replaces any 1 by 0, and any 0 by 1. In the other labelling, we can put *E* = (0, 0), *S* = (1, 0), *M* = (0, 1), *N* = (1, 1): we then have pairs of Boolean variables (*X*, *Y*), where the *X* and *Y* components combine as in the last case, quite independently of one another.

In Figure 8*D* we show a labelling of the fourfold type for a game which starts with *two* heaps each of five objects, but otherwise proceeds as in Grundy's game. When heaps must be divided unequally thereafter, the first player can either be forced to make the last division, or can be denied any chance of doing so.

Nim—for beginners

We shall now consider what is perhaps the best known of all the games which are played with heaps of objects such as matches or counters. This is the game of *Nim*—which may derive its name from a pseudo-Chinese variation of the German imperative '*nimm!*' (from *nehmen*, to take) or possibly from a revival of an old English word which had a similar meaning, with associations of trickery. (Sometimes the game has been called *Fan-Tan*, but a gambling game which is quite different has a better claim to this name.) Our purpose here is twofold: Nim is an interesting game in its own right; and it has a mathematical theory which can be useful in the discussion of many other games.

The theory of playing Nim first appeared about sixty years ago: in more recent times it has formed a basis for constructing some special-purpose machines which can play as good a game as any expert; there was a machine of this kind at the Festival of Britain in 1951. A 'do-it-yourself' model has appeared in the handbook for a form of educational toy which provides a set of multi-pole multi-throw switches, with lights and a battery; and many computers can now play Nim, with various facilities for audience participation.

Over the years, the game has passed into popular tradition, to be intermittently rediscovered and reported (this happened recently from Tasmania, in our experience). In various places all over the world one can indeed find it played for amusement—or for the price of drinks: in both cases the contest may well be quite genuine, and not necessarily the exploitation of a victim by an expert!

The rules are very simple: the objects concerned are initially grouped into a number of heaps, usually three; the two players play alternately, and each move must remove at least one object, and may remove any larger number, up to and including the whole content of one of the heaps; each player must confine himself to one heap at a time, but at each move he can choose whichever heap he likes.

A distinction should here be made between a standard game in which he who takes the last object wins, and a *misère* game in which he who takes the last object loses; the standard game is more commonly discussed, and the *misère* game is more commonly played. We shall here find a situation similar to the one we found for Wythoff's game: the two forms of game are identical in the opening stages of play, and differ only when a recognizable terminal stage begins.

We first consider the standard game, realizing that all positions can be unambiguously classified as either favourable or unfavourable to the player who leaves them, as we discussed earlier. From a favourable position, *all* moves must lead inevitably to unfavourable positions; but from an unfavourable position, one or more moves must be possible which will leave favourable positions. A win defines *one* favourable position, and all others can then be classified, working backwards: the practical need is for a method which gives an equivalent labelling of positions, without our having to do all this work.

The usual way to find such a method is to work backwards empirically, looking for regularities: these may suggest a rule which further work can justify, in which case the theory of the game has been found; but wrong theories can arise if apparent but actually limited regularities are accepted as universal, without proof.

A little experimentation with Nim can suggest the following rules: reduce the heaps to two equal heaps, if you can; or else arrange that two heaps have *different* numbers whose sum gives the number in the third heap. The game is often played with fifteen matches, in three heaps initially (3, 5, 7); if you play first yourself, and make this either (2, 5, 7) or (3, 4, 7), you will find that you have a chance next time of leaving either two equal heaps, or else some one of the arrangements (2, 4, 6), (1, 4, 5), or (1, 2, 3), either directly or with the numbers permuted; and you should thereafter see how to continue in such a way as to win.

Some players of Nim know no other rules: but these rules cannot be the whole story. If you leave (2, 5, 7), your opponent may leave (2, 5, 3), but still you can beat him; the same is true if he changes your (3, 4, 7) to (3, 4, 1). If he changes your (2, 5, 7) to (1, 5, 7), you must choose (1, 5, 4) and *not* (1, 5, 6): and even if you leave (3, 5, 6) with your first move, you can still beat him. We should now ask what is common to (2, 4, 6), (1, 4, 5), (1, 2, 3), and (3, 5, 6), but not present in (2, 3, 5), (1, 3, 4), (1, 5, 6) or any other losing leave.

Nim—for experts

Many readers nowadays will know the answer to our last question. Each heap number can be written in a unique way as a sum of different powers of 2 from the sequence $2^0 = 1$, $2^1 = 2$, $2^2 = 4$, $2^3 = 8$, ...; and a position is favourable if and only if there is then an *even* number of appearances of every separate power of 2, over the whole set of heaps. (Zero is, of course, a possible even number!) This means that if we express the heap numbers in the binary scale, and write them aligned vertically as if for addition, there must then be an even number of unit digits in every column, over the whole set.

More generally, we can do this for arbitrary heap numbers; we can then consider the individual powers of 2, and their associated columns. We shall say that a power of 2 is *balanced* if and only if it appears an even number of times, in which event there will be an even number of unit digits in the associated column; and we shall say that a set of heaps is a *balanced arrangement* if and only if there is a balance for *every* power of 2, individually, over the whole set.

If we are given all the heaps but one, there is only one number in the remaining heap which can give a balance overall: we can determine this number by taking each power of 2 separately, and seeing if it is balanced over the other heaps, or not; if it is, it must be omitted from the last heap, and if not it must be included. The sum of the otherwise unbalanced powers of 2 thus gives the number which is required (this number will in fact be zero, if the others are all already balanced): and since the number concerned is unique, it follows that the change of any single heap in a balanced arrangement must inevitably give rise to an unbalanced arrangement.

In an unbalanced arrangement, at least one power of 2 must be unbalanced, and there may be others as well: we concentrate on a heap in which the *largest* unbalanced power of 2 is included. There may be only one such heap, or three, if there are three heaps—possibly a larger odd number, if there are five heaps or more: any such heap will do if there are more than one; and a change to a balanced arrangement will then result from a move which gives the joint effect of simultaneous operations with different powers of 2, in the following manner.

The largest unbalanced power of 2 will have to be removed from the chosen heap; and for other powers of 2 we must compare the actual content of the heap with what is required to produce a balance. This may indicate that one or more powers of 2 can be left as they are— either included, or absent; but in some cases powers which are present may have to be removed, and in some other cases powers which are absent may have to be supplied.

The fundamental consideration which makes the theory depend upon the balance in the binary representation is the fact that even if every other power of 2 has to be *supplied*, the overall result is still a possible and legitimate move—a *removal* of one piece: apart from this, all other possibilities of unbalance can be dealt with by making larger removals, up to the removal of the whole heap, which is the other extreme case.

The complete theory of both forms of the game now requires only a simple application of these last two results—that every balanced arrangement can be changed only to an unbalanced arrangement, and that a suitable choice of move can turn any unbalanced arrangement into a balanced arrangement.

In the standard game, the winner must leave all zeros, which is a balanced position. It follows that all balanced positions are favourable leaves here and all unbalanced positions are unfavourable leaves. We can readily appreciate the optimum strategy, and which player should win: whichever player *can* first make a favourable leave, *will* do so; he can then keep doing so thereafter—regardless of what his opponent does—until finally he must win. Our discussion will have shown not merely what he has to do, but how he can in fact do it: the mental arithmetic can be quite rapidly done in actual practice.

In the game where the last player loses, the balanced positions *not consisting solely of unit heaps* are still favourable positions, just as in the standard game; no difference arises until all heaps but one are reduced to unit heaps (or else empty). The pairing of powers of 2 makes it impossible for a balanced position to contain only one heap with more than a single object—there must either be two or more, or else none: so if a player can seize and hold a chain of balanced positions, he can be sure that it will be his turn to play when first there is only one heap remaining which is not a unit heap.

At this stage in the standard game, he must secure another balanced position, and he will either remove the large heap completely, or else reduce it to a single object—whichever will produce an *even* number of unit heaps. In the *misère* game the unbalanced positions now become favourable positions, and he must take one object less, in the first event, or else one more, in the second—to produce an *odd* number of unit heaps which will force his opponent to make the final removal. (In either form of game, the result is a foregone conclusion if all remaining heaps are unit heaps.)

In an earlier section, we gave certain rules for applying labels E, S, M, N to the different positions in a game. For Nim, we can give simple rules for distributing these labels. The E positions are the balanced positions where not all the heaps are unit heaps (we noted that these must have *two* non-unit heaps, or more); the S positions consist solely of an even number of unit heaps, or none, and the M positions have nothing but an odd number of unit heaps; the N positions are the unbalanced positions where at least one heap contains more than one object. (We assume here that empty heaps are to be ignored.)

It is not difficult to show that these have just the forms of inter-connexion which the rules of our labelling system require, to ensure that positions are favourable in either form of the game, in the standard or *misère* forms only, or in neither form, when labels are E, S, M, N, respectively.

9 'NIM' you say—and 'NIM' it is

When no two are equal among four

In the previous section, we have described Nim as it is usually played, when it requires only a collection of small objects, and nothing else. However, the introduction of a simple form of board gives a precisely equivalent game which may be more convenient when larger numbers of heaps or objects are involved. We here require only a series of adjacent cells which are numbered (actually, or notionally), to replace the heap numbers, and a collection of markers equal in number to the proposed number of heaps: the presence of a marker in a particular cell can then indicate the current contents for one of the heaps.

If we then require that each move must displace only one marker at a time, in a direction towards the terminal cell which is associated with the number 0, we shall have a game which is precisely equivalent to Nim, provided that we do not object to the simultaneous occupation of a cell by more than one marker; for this will be necessary to represent cases where two or more heaps contain equal numbers of objects: and we must also be able to move markers over other markers, without restriction.

We may now consider games similar to this last game, but with restrictions imposed which we must forgo to represent Nim. In the first event we shall forbid only the multiple occupation of cells: we shall here leave pieces free to pass over one another if desired. We shall call this *Welter's game*, since the relevant theory has been worked out in detail by C. P. Welter. The general case is beyond our limits here: we confine ourselves to two particular cases which have been considered by R. Sprague.

The first of these cases is where there are only four markers, or fewer; and in this case we place no restriction on the number of cells. If there are exactly four markers, any such game then proceeds exactly as if it were a game representing Nim: for in Nim a balanced position must have either two pairs of equal heaps, or none—it cannot have one pair only; and since a move alters only one heap, there can never be any need to produce balanced arrangements with two pairs of equal heaps, unless the previous unbalanced position *already* had one pair of equal heaps. So if an unbalanced arrangement has all its heaps unequal, it must be possible, at the next move, to change it into one balanced arrangement at least—and perhaps into others—where all the heaps are still unequal.

In Welter's game, when the player who makes the last move wins, the set of cells finally occupied must be (0, 1, 2, 3), which is a balanced position in Nim: this will be automatically attained by the player who seizes and holds a chain of positions whose cell numbers give balanced positions for four-heap Nim; and if we watched an expert playing Welter's game with four markers, we might equally well think he was playing the equivalent of Nim which we first discussed, against an opponent who for some reason avoided making two heaps equal, but who could recognize defeat a little before the actual termination.

After this it is easy to see how Welter's game should be played if there are fewer markers. With three markers we can number the actual cells from 1 upwards, instead of from 0 upwards: we can then play three-heap Nim with the numbers concerned—for this is equivalent to a four-marker game with one piece already occupying a cell labelled with 0. With only two markers, we can similarly assume notional occupation of cells labelled 0 and 1; the favourable positions then consist of any two adjacent cells where the lower-numbered cell has an even number; and this remains true when the cells are renumbered to make 0 the terminal cell of the actual board.

Here again the change to a *misère* game makes a difference only in the closing stages. In the four-marker *misère* game, we need only make heaps of four and three objects correspond to the cells which would be numbered 3 and 4 in a serial order, with heap numbers equal to cell numbers everywhere else; and if we choose cells as if we were playing *standard* Nim with the heaps thus concerned, we shall then find that we are employing an optimum form of strategy for the *misère* form of Welter's game for four markers.

Until the final move, or the final two moves, this means that we seek to play an optimum form of the corresponding standard game, with the addition of a rule that each of the exceptional cells must be assumed to take the place of the other. This exchange makes no significant difference if a piece only occupies either cell while in transit to another cell: for with or without the new rule, it can pass in two moves from the same earlier position to the same later position—or in three moves, if it has to move from one exceptional cell to the other as part of its path. The difference can only affect a piece which finally occupies one or other of the exceptional cells, at the end of the game, without being able to pass through to a non-exceptional cell; and there can be only one such piece—not two—since all three cells 0, 1, 2 must then be filled.

What our device has secured is that at this stage the winning heap of three in the standard Nim will be associated with a position which leaves one move which is forced upon the loser, in the *misère* game here discussed; whereas the losing heap of four in standard Nim will correspond to the final position where the *misère* loser leaves no move for his opponent. With the *misère* game for only three markers, or two, an identical inversion applies to the notionally extended board, and consequently to positions one cell earlier, or two cells earlier, on the actual board.

The difference a fifth one can make

When Welter's game is played with five markers, a simplified rule can be applied if the board has no more than sixteen cells. This was pointed out by Sprague: we modify his procedure slightly, and provide a proof.

Instead of numbering cells with increasing numbers starting from 0 for the terminal cell, we here number them with decreasing numbers starting from 16 for the terminal cell: with our limitation to not more than sixteen cells, we shall not then require to have a cell labelled 0. Some of the lower-numbered cells may be lacking; or equivalently we may suppose the game is started with every piece on a cell with a number which is higher than 1. When the last player is the winner, the rule is to ignore any piece which is transferred to cell 16, and apart from this to play an *additive* form of standard Nim with the cell numbers: the player who here seizes and holds a chain of balanced arrangements will then ultimately arrive at the final position (16, 15, 14, 13, 12), which will rank as a balanced arrangement.

In effect we must here start with five non-zero heaps, which can only be increased; all must be—and remain—unequal, with not more than sixteen objects in each. A heap of sixteen is allowable only once, and counts virtually as a removal of one of the heaps, with a reduction to a four-heap game thereafter.

To see how to obtain a balanced arrangement from an unbalanced arrangement, we again must examine powers of 2, just as in standard (subtractive) Nim; after this, we make an additive change in any heap which does *not* contain the largest unbalanced power of 2 (we here exclude the 16 which we treat as 0). To secure the balance, we here must *add* the highest unbalanced power of 2 to this heap, combining this with a balance of all the lower powers of 2 done in the same way as before: so even if all other powers of 2 have to be subtracted, we still have an additive move as the final combination; and even if all other powers of 2 have to be added, we cannot require a final heap number in excess of 15.

This procedure fails only if the highest unbalanced power of 2 is present in every one of the five heaps; and in this event the unbalanced power can only be 8—five *different* numbers are impossible with a limitation to any lower power. In this event we can show that four of the heaps must necessarily form a balanced arrangement; and the appropriate move is then to increase the fifth heap to sixteen, and so remove it from consideration. (After this the trouble cannot recur: for with only four effective heaps, an *unbalanced* power of 2 cannot be present in all four.)

We can prove this by geometric arguments, in which simplifications derive from symmetries of a cube. If we label the vertices of a cube as in Figure 9*A*, we find that three types of arrangements of vertices represent

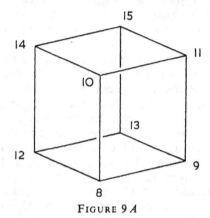

FIGURE 9 *A*

balanced arrangements of four heaps: six sets—like (8, 9, 10, 11)—correspond to vertices of a cube face; six other sets—like (8, 9, 14, 15)—correspond to vertices at the ends of a pair of body-diagonals; and two sets—(8, 11, 13, 14) and (9, 10, 12, 15)—correspond to vertices of inscribed tetrahedra. All have the common feature that any cube face contains an even number of their points (or none).

It is then a simple matter to check that no' way of omitting three vertices will fail to leave one of these fourfold configurations among the five vertices which remain. There are only three distinct cases. The joins of the omitted vertices may be two edges and a face-diagonal, which will leave four vertices of a cube face remaining; they may be an edge, a face-diagonal, and a body-diagonal, which will leave ends of two other body-diagonals remaining; and they may be three face-diagonals, which will leave a tetrahedral set remaining: in every case the fourfold balanced set which remains is unique.

This means that in the five-marker game, when all heaps have eight objects or more—and thus will include 8 as an unbalanced power of 2—a unique set of four of the heaps must form a balanced set, and the appropriate move is to increase the remaining heap to sixteen, and so reduce the game to a four-heap game with the remaining heaps.

It only remains to show that we can always change an unbalanced arrangement to a balanced arrangement, in one move, without requiring two heaps to be equal; and we can assume the unbalanced arrangement itself has no heaps equal. This result can be established as follows.

If we had five heaps, A, B, C, D, E and a balanced arrangement could arise by making $B = A$, the set (C, D, E) would have to be a balanced set after the move, and therefore before the move also. But in this event all three of C, D, E could not contain the highest power of 2 which was unbalanced over A, B, C, D, E—it would have to be two of them only, or none—and so a balanced arrangement must have been possible by making a move in one of the three heaps C, D, E instead. Suppose the heap concerned was C.

If this move had to change C to make it equal to A, then (B, D, E) would have to be a balanced set; but since we assumed (C, D, E) was a balanced set, we should then have to have $B = C$, and hence there would have been equal heaps in the original unbalanced arrangement: similarly if C had to become equal to B.

If this move had to change C to make it equal to D, then (A, B, E) would have to be a balanced set; but since we assumed (C, D, E) was a balanced set, this would imply that (A, B, C, D) was a balanced set, and we could then change E to 16, and so in effect remove it, to leave a balanced set: similarly if C had to become equal to E. (If we already had a heap of sixteen, we would in effect have the situation for only four heaps, where we already have shown there is no difficulty.)

This completes our proof of the rules which Sprague gave for the five-marker game on the sixteen-cell board. For a *misère* game, we need only exchange the heap numbers for cells 11 and 12. Our account may allow readers to share our admiration for the fact that Welter could find a method of dealing with all forms of this game, with no restriction either on the number of cells or on the number of markers. The games for cases just beyond our limits would admittedly require something more than mental computations—but not much more than could be done on the back of an envelope!

When you can put, as well as take

Suppose that we now extend the rules of Nim to allow arbitrary additive moves, as well as the more usual subtractive ones; in particular, this will permit the supply of a new heap at any stage, for we may regard this as making an addition to a zero heap. The mode of inter-relation of balanced and unbalanced positions is then essentially unaffected: but it then becomes possible to secure a balanced arrangement by making a change in *any* heap, or by adding a new heap; and in each case the amount and type of alteration is unique.

To secure a practical game, however, it will be necessary to impose some limit on the additive possibilities, to ensure that heaps must ultimately diminish, to provide a termination to the game: and if this is done without placing any restriction on the subtractive moves, the strategy of the winning player will be unaffected. Even if his opponent makes additive moves, he can always answer them with subtractive moves as in the more usual game; in particular, he may remove any addition immediately after it is made, and sometimes he may have no alternative: apart from this he may himself make any additive moves which will allow him to leave a balanced arrangement.

When only the odd ones matter

One way of achieving this result is to secure that each object must be involved in a subtractive move more often than in an additive move, and we can do this if its initial and final moves are made subtractive, in a chain of moves of alternate types. This will be the case if we play a game of Nim with a set of heaps to which we give odd numbers, and arrange that between these heaps we make provision for auxiliary heaps with even numbers, all originally empty, with another similar heap labelled 0: we then assume that only odd-numbered heaps are actually involved in the game of Nim, and require that any objects removed from the odd-numbered heaps must be placed in the auxiliary even-numbered heap which is labelled with one unit less, and that transfers to the odd-numbered heaps must be made only from the auxiliary even-numbered heap which is labelled with one unit more.

This ensures that all objects must finally arrive in the auxiliary heap which is labelled 0; and there are limitations on additive moves, but none on subtractive moves. We can regard this as a means of allowing some additive moves in a game of Nim played with the odd-numbered heaps, which will finally have their contents reduced to zero.

We have shown that this will make no difference to the expert Nim player: he can play his usual game—with no change, if he wishes, or with additive variations of his own, when he sees that these are safe. This situation is unaffected if we start with something in the auxiliary heaps also; and as a result we can now see how to play some other games which appear quite different from Nim at first sight.

In the first of these we have a board with a single row of cells, as before, and multiple occupation of cells is allowed: but the only moves permitted are those which take an arbitrary selection of the pieces in one cell and deposit them in a cell one stage further towards the terminal end. (An equivalent description—which Sprague used for this game—involves the moving of sets of coins downwards by one tread, on a staircase.) This exactly represents what happens over the sequence of heaps of *both* types together—real heaps and auxiliary heaps—in our game of Nim: so we can play this game infallibly by imagining we are playing Nim with the contents of a set of alternate cells; and the set concerned is the one which does *not* contain the terminal cell.

This is also equivalent to playing a game with several heaps, where no heap can be diminished by more than one, but where any arbitrary set of *equal* heaps can be simultaneously diminished. Here we play Nim not with *contents* of heaps, but with the *numbers* of heaps whose contents have each of the different *odd* numbers; and we arrange to change some odd heaps to even heaps, or else to change some even heaps to odd heaps, in a way which will guarantee final success.

A more interesting observation—also due to Sprague—is that we here have the same situation as in playing the equivalent of Welter's game with a restriction added that no piece is to leap over another. Here the numbers of vacant cells between pieces act exactly like heaps in our game with the auxiliary heaps, if we assume the final dump is at the non-terminal end: for every move will increase an interval on this side of the moved piece by just so much as it diminishes an interval on the terminal side. So the rule here is: play Nim with the set of *alternate* gap-numbers which include the one for the gap between the two pieces which start *farthest* from the end where all the pieces will finally be collected together.

Nim-sums and faulty adders

When we discussed the balance of the powers of 2 for heaps in Nim, we mentioned the possibility of expressing heap numbers in the binary scale, and writing them with their digits aligned in columns, as if for addition: a balanced arrangement then required that there was an even number of unit digits in every column.

We also showed that if we were given all the heaps except one, there was a unique number in the final heap which would produce a balanced arrangement overall. This number was obtained by examining the balance of the individual powers of 2 in the other heaps; and each power of 2 had to be included in the balancing heap if it was unbalanced over the others, but omitted, if it was already balanced: we can see that if the other heaps already formed a balanced arrangement, this procedure would indicate a zero content for an additional heap.

If we write the first heap-numbers in the binary scale as if for addition, the binary representation of the content of the balancing heap has then to have a unit digit in any place where the number of unit digits in the corresponding column is odd, and a zero digit if the number of unit digits in the column is even; and we may notice that this is precisely the result that we should obtain if we performed this addition by a binary adding mechanism which was faulty to the extent of suppressing all transfers of carry digits.

If only two heap numbers were concerned, we should require our result to have a unit digit in each place where these two numbers had different digits, and a zero digit in each place where they had identical digits. This means that the digit in each position has to be obtained from two other digits in the same position by use of the 'Exclusive-*Or*' function of Boolean algebra; and the resulting binary number is derived from the others by what many readers will recognize as the 'Not-Equivalent' operation—an auxiliary feature to be found in many computers which also have adding facilities of the ordinary type.

In contexts like the present, the 'Not-Equivalent' operation is said to perform *Nim-addition* on the two numbers, giving their *Nim-sum*: for the operation has many characteristics of ordinary addition. The order of the numbers is immaterial; and the result is the same, no matter whether numbers in a series are combined simultaneously or successively. A Nim-addition of zero produces no change in a Nim-sum; and a Nim-addition of the same number to different numbers will always give different Nim-sums: but two identical numbers will always have a Nim-sum of *zero*—and for this reason we have no need to consider Nim-differences, or Nim-subtraction!

We shall use the symbol $\oplus$ to connect the numbers for our Nim-sums. We then have some results which resemble ordinary addition, like

$$0 \oplus 3 = \quad 000 \oplus 011 \quad = 011 = 3,$$
$$2 \oplus 4 = \quad 010 \oplus 100 \quad = 110 = 6,$$
$$1 \oplus 2 \oplus 4 = 001 \oplus 010 \oplus 100 = 111 = 7,$$

and others which differ from ordinary addition, like

$$3 \oplus 3 = \quad 011 \oplus 011 \quad = 000 = 0,$$
$$5 \oplus 6 = \quad 101 \oplus 110 \quad = 011 = 3,$$
$$2 \oplus 4 \oplus 5 = 010 \oplus 100 \oplus 101 = 011 = 3,$$
$$3 \oplus 5 \oplus 6 = 011 \oplus 101 \oplus 110 = 000 = 0.$$

Here we have given three-digit binary representations of our numbers, so that readers may easily appreciate the procedure, and check the results: we shall omit the binary numbers in future. After a little practice, Nim-sums for small numbers can be found mentally, like ordinary sums; and we shall want to make some use of them, in what follows.

In terms of Nim-sums, we can summarize the theory of Nim as follows: balanced arrangements have heap numbers whose Nim-sum is zero; and balanced arrangements will be obtained by moves which change some heap to give it a content which is the Nim-sum of the contents of all the other heaps.

When a heap is not a heap

We have already seen that some games can be discussed in terms of an equivalent game of Nim; and we shall now show how this can be done for many other games also. The essential requirement here is to decide what corresponds to a heap; and we must do this in such a way that there is an exact correspondence of allowable moves between the Nim-picture and the other game. In many cases this will require that there are some possibilities of additive moves, in the Nim; but we have already seen that this will make no real difference to the manner of play for the winning player—the only essential, for him, is a complete set of subtractive moves. For reasons which we shall discuss later, the Nim-picture will be in terms of *standard* Nim, in all cases.

First of all we consider what we can represent in terms of a single Nim heap which may contain several objects. Admittedly there is no problem in deciding how to *play* Nim with a single heap: but unless we can establish this correspondence, we shall have no hope of representing other games in terms of corresponding games of Nim.

One essential point here is that a position from which no moves are possible must correspond to a zero Nim-heap with no possibility of additive moves; and since we are seeking a representation in terms of standard Nim, such a position must imply that the player who cannot play then becomes the loser. There are other points of resemblance which also are essential.

From any position which is represented by a Nim heap with non-zero contents, it must be possible to move to positions which jointly have representations by Nim heaps of every lower content, including zero: this is necessary if all the usual subtractive moves of Nim are to have their counterparts; and it will not matter if there are some possibilities of additional moves also. Moreover, in the single Nim heap, removal of more than a unit may be made in one move, by one player, or else in two moves, one by each player; and in the two cases, the positions and prospects of the two players are exactly reversed: for Nim is an impartial game, in the sense in which we used the term earlier. It follows that a precisely similar feature must be present in the game which is being represented, and so this must be an impartial game also; and since Nim has perfect information and no chance moves, the other game must resemble it in this respect as well.

Puzzles and Paradoxes

If we have a game of this type, we can represent it in terms of a single-heap game of Nim if we introduce *labels* for positions, in the following way: a final dead end is to be labelled with 0; positions which must immediately precede dead-end positions are to be labelled with 1; and working backwards from these we proceed to label every position with the smallest label which is *not* to be found among the labels of all the positions which can be reached from it in one move. (This will then imply that zero labels will have to be given to positions which are found to have no successor positions with zero labels.) In Figure 9B we show

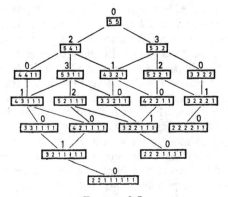

FIGURE 9 B

this done for a game we discussed earlier—the game which starts with two heaps each of five objects, and requires an unequal division of some single heap at every move.

Once a labelling of this type is introduced, all moves proceed exactly as if Nim were being played in a single heap, with the labels giving contents of the heaps. Not all the zero labels will represent terminations of the game; for some will merely represent positions where the other player is allowed to make one or more additive moves: but each such position represents the only balanced arrangement here possible, and the player who first secures one will be able to secure a sequence of others until he finally wins by obtaining one which has no successor. (We are tacitly assuming that there is no possibility that the game could continue indefinitely.)

In the single-heap representation, the positions with zero labels are the favourable positions, and the others the unfavourable positions, with the properties which we discussed earlier. The reason for making distinctions among the unfavourable positions—by the use of different non-zero labels—will become apparent as we proceed to consider a Nim representation in terms of several heaps.

How Nim-sums give the right labels

If we are to be able to have a Nim-representation in terms of several heaps, we must be able to split the game concerned into a number of entirely distinct component games—one to correspond to each heap—such that each move in the game consists of selecting one component game arbitrarily, and making a move in this game only.

There are in fact many games for which this can be done. In some cases the number of component games is fixed, and all are identical; in other cases all are identical, but their number may increase: in other cases various component games may be of different types. In all cases we have only to provide all the component games with our chosen type of labelling: and after this the optimum strategy of the game must be exactly equivalent to playing an optimum strategy of standard Nim, with the labels considered as heap numbers.

From this point of view, Nim is itself the simplest game of this type. Each component game can be taken to be the arbitrary reduction (or, possibly, increase) of a single heap: so the theory is simpler than for other games—and Nim gives a suitable representation of other games—precisely because the labels in Nim are identical to the heap numbers.

For games which we can consider as a set of component games—with each move being a move in one selected component game only—the important property of the labels is that if we divide one component game into two or more, or if we combine two or more component games into one, the label for any position when components are combined is simply the Nim-sum of the labels for the constituent positions of the components considered separately.

We need prove this only for the representation in terms of Nim. We first note that Nim-sums of zero will identify a final position, as well as balanced positions; and that these have no balanced positions among their immediate successors: we must next show that every unbalanced position has immediate successors with all labels smaller than its own. We can do this if we note that the label gives a heap number for an auxiliary heap which would produce a balanced position.

If we diminish the auxiliary heap, the largest power of 2 which is changed must be one which is *removed*: this must have been present in one at least of the real heaps also, when there was a balance; and a move in this heap can balance the whole set once more, in which case the real heaps will have a Nim-sum which is equal to the reduced content of the auxiliary heap. This shows that positions with all smaller labels can indeed be obtained, and that a Nim-sum will produce a single overall label in just the way that we want.

For games where heaps can be split, or where certain reductions have been prohibited, we can start with a zero heap, which can be labelled with 0 (no moves can be made with no objects): in turn thereafter we can take larger heaps of 1, 2, 3, ...; and for these we must consider all possibilities, but we need do this only for a single move. When heaps are split, we can form Nim-sums of labels which we already know for single heaps, to find labels for the different successor positions which are possible; and when labels for all successors are thus known, the first gap in the series 0, 1, 2, ... gives the label appropriate to each new size of single heap.

Developing a line of winning numbers

We first take two examples where the number of heaps remains constant, with identical rules applicable to every heap. Here we need no Nim-sums to *find* the labels, and we need work only with a linear sequence of numbers.

If we play as in Nim, but with removals limited to a maximum of three objects, a heap of four cannot then be reduced to zero: so if we note what successor positions are possible, and what their labels are, we can then select the smallest missing label and complete a series of labels for increasing heap numbers. Here this takes a form

HEAP NO. 0 1 2 3 4 5 6 7 8 ⁻ ⁻ ⁻

LABEL   0 1 2 3 0 1 2 3 0 ⁻ ⁻ ⁻

with labels which repeat indefinitely, and each heap has a label which is the remainder if its heap number is divided by 4. For a single heap, this game is well-known, but less so, for multiple heaps. (Modifications for limits other than three will be obvious.)

Alternatively, we might play as in Nim, but require that if a heap were not removed completely, the number removed and the number left had to have no common factor. We then would find

HEAP NO. 0 1 2 3 4 5 6 7 8 9 ⁻ ⁻ ⁻

LABEL   0 1 2 3 2 4 2 5 2 3 ⁻ ⁻ ⁻

where labels increase only for *prime* numbers, and each composite number takes the same label as its smallest prime factor.

Once we have thus found a label for every heap number, we have all we need for the optimum strategy, which is to play the equivalent of Nim with the labels; and we can make use of Nim-sums *here*, if we wish.

Take them, or split them—just as you like!

Nim-sums become of greater importance when we consider games in which heaps can be split. As a first example of this type we will take a variant of Nim considered by Emanuel Lasker: here a player can split a heap into two, as an alternative to diminishing it. (Lasker was unable to solve this completely: the theory is due to his associate R. Sprague.)

The important point here is that $(3, 2, 1)$ can no longer be a favourable position, for it can now be converted into $(2, 2, 1, 1)$—which *is* still a favourable position; and this possibility has its effect on positions with larger heap numbers also. To find labels for increasing heap numbers, we can here proceed as follows—enclosing heap numbers in parentheses, to make them readily distinguishable from labels, which will be given as simple numerals.

A heap (0) has no successors, and must have label 0. A heap (1) has no successor but (0), with label 0: so a heap (1) must have a label 1. A heap (2) has the two previous heaps as successors, and also $(1, 1)$ whose label must be $1 \oplus 1 = 0$: the split makes no difference here, and (2) has a label 2. But a heap (3) can be changed to $(2, 1)$, with label $2 \oplus 1 = 3$, as well as to all smaller heaps: and its label must therefore be 4. A heap (4) can be changed to heaps $(3), (2), (1), (0)$, with labels 4, 2, 1, 0, respectively, and also to $(3, 1)$ and $(2, 2)$ with labels $4 \oplus 1 = 5$ and $2 \oplus 2 = 0$: so a heap (4) receives the label 3.

If we proceed in this fashion to larger heap numbers, we are led to conjecture that labels are identical with heap numbers except when heap numbers are of the form $(4n+3)$ or $(4n+4)$: and that any heap $(4n+3)$ has a label $4n+4$, and a heap $(4n+4)$ a label $4n+3$. To establish this, we have two things to prove: that from every label we can reach every smaller label in one move; and that we cannot similarly reach an identical label.

The first task is simple. From all heaps except those of the form $(4n+3)$, the required labels can all be secured by diminishing the heap, with no need to split it: and for heaps $(4n+3)$—which have labels $4n+4$—the only label missing from the smaller heaps is a label $4n+3$, which can be secured by making a split $(4n+2, 1)$. The labels for the two heaps are here identical to the heap numbers, and the Nim-sum gives the same result as ordinary addition: we note that in binary representations of labels and heap numbers, the two least significant digits are unaffected by changes of n.

For the second task, we need only consider what possibilities arise from *splitting* of heaps: for quite obviously we cannot have an identical label after any *reduction* of a heap. Here we neglect zero heaps entirely, for a split must change the position by providing two non-zero heaps. We shall consider heap numbers and labels in binary notation, in both cases; and we shall consider only the two lowest binary places, which are independent of the choice of n.

In Table 9 a we show the various possibilities for binary digits in the two lowest places. For each type of heap, we show in a left-hand column the different types of pairs of heap numbers which are possible after a split: the *ordinary* sum for each pair must here correspond with the original heap number. Opposite to these, in a right-hand column, are the final digits of the corresponding labels, according to the system we are considering.

For each possible type of split, we show the final digits of a label applicable to the combined position formed by the two heaps; this label

$(4n+1)$ HEAP	$4n+1$ LABEL		$(4n+3)$ HEAP	$4n+4$ LABEL	
01	01		11	00	
00	11	10	00	11	11
01	01		11	00	
10	10	10	01	01	11
11	00		10	10	

$(4n+2)$ HEAP	$4n+2$ LABEL		$(4n+4)$ HEAP	$4n+3$ LABEL	
10	10		00	11	
00	11	01	00	11	00
10	10		00	11	
01	01	00	01	01	01
01	01		11	00	
11	00	00	10	10	00
11	00		10	10	

TABLE 9 *a*

is found by taking the *Nim-sum* for the component labels: we see that in no case can a split give the same two final digits as for the label of the original heap; and this establishes that the conjectured system of labelling is indeed the correct one.

Lasker's Nim is a game where we can extend our discussion to cover a *misère* form of game also: for just as in ordinary Nim, we here have a unique stage at which all positions can be reduced to a diminishing set of unit heaps, each of which allows only one move thereafter; and at this point the same change of strategy can be applied as in the *misère* version of ordinary Nim.

In more general cases we may not be able to handle the *misère* game in this way; for we need more information than is given merely by the labels which we use in the standard game. These labels give nothing to show whether positions with *higher* labels are attainable, or not, and give no indication whether or not a position is in effect a combination of two components which individually would have *larger* labels: and both these questions can be vital, in the *misère* game.

How to divide and conquer

For games where a heap can be split into two, we can find labels for individual heaps by working in a two-dimensional scheme. Along both a vertical and a horizontal border we indicate successive heap numbers; we then work progressively to heaps of increasing size, determining labels. At the intersection of each row and column, we put the Nim-sum of labels already determined for constituent heaps, thus obtaining an appropriate label for their combination; and for each new heap number there will be an appropriate region in which to look for labels of all possible successor positions, before determining a label for a new size of single heap.

We here provide a row and a column for a zero heap, and this then secures that labels for single heaps are found in the border columns of the scheme: in effect we represent them as labels for a combination of an actual heap with a zero heap. If we like, we can limit our working to one side of the diagonal of zeros which is formed by the labels for positions which have two equal heaps.

In Figure 9C we show this done for two games: *Grundy's game*, where component games are identical, with only one rule—a heap must be divided unequally; and *Kayles*, invented by Dudeney, where objects are put in a row, like pins in a skittles alley, and any single object or adjacent pair of objects can be removed (as presumably a sufficiently skilful player could remove them, with a ball whose size was suitably related to the clearance between adjacent pins).

In Grundy's game each move must sub-divide a heap into two; in Kayles this may be true actually, and can always be assumed to be true provided that if need be we assume that there is an additional zero heap. We indicate the way in which internal labels can be obtained from the boundary labels; we also show typical regions in which the relevant successor labels are to be found, before the determination of a new label for a next larger heap number. In Grundy's game these relate to pairs of *unequal* heaps which sum to the new heap number itself; in Kayles, to pairs which sum to a number either one unit or two units less, with no other restriction.

In the play of a game, the Nim theory will indicate a heap in whose associated game a move has to be made to secure some prescribed label. In a diagram like those we illustrate, this label will be found in the successor-label region corresponding to the label for the heap number concerned; and finding the corresponding boundary labels will then indicate the particular move which should be used to split the heap.

For Grundy's game, as an alternative way of finding appropriate labels for successive single-heap numbers, we can use two overlapping strips as in Figure 9*D*. The squares for heap-sizes 0, 1, 2 are first labelled 0, and as the strips are made to overlap farther and farther, sets of

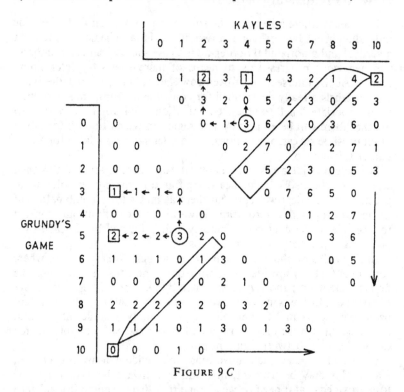

FIGURE 9 *C*

Nim-sums are determined so that the smallest number which is missing can be entered as a new heap-number label. The diagrams show why we enter the labels 3 and 0 for heaps of thirteen and twenty respectively. Nim-sums need be found for half the overlap only, and none is formed for an equal pair in the middle, since heaps must be divided unequally.

For the case of thirteen objects there is a unique 0 to show that the first player can win only if he first divides them 8–5; otherwise he can be beaten: in other cases more than one form of division may be allowable.

Once his opponent has moved, a player must see if he can divide any heap such that the Nim-sum of the labels for its two parts will equal the Nim-sum of the labels for the undivided heaps: and if his last position had a label 0, there is bound to be *some* way that he can thus get another of the same type. For example, if the opponent makes 8–5 into (6–2)–5, either 6–2–(3–2) or (5–1)–2–5 will do; but if the opponent chooses 8–(3–2), the only correct reply is (6–2)–3–2.

Two mobile strips could be used similarly for Kayles, if one of the mobile strips had *two* rows of cells, for entering labels twice over, with a one-unit displacement.

Series of labels can have curious properties, as we should see if we were to continue our figures to higher heap numbers. In the case of

0	1	2	3	4	5	6	7	8	9	10	11	12	13
0	0	0	1	0	2	1	0	2	1	0	2	1	(3)
(3)	1	2	0	1	2	0	1	2	0	1	0	0	0
13	12	11	10	9	8	7	6	5	4	3	2	1	0

$$\text{(1)} \quad \text{(1)} \quad \text{(0)} \quad \text{(1)} \quad \text{(1)} \quad \text{(2)} \quad \text{(1)}$$

0	1	2	3	4	5	6	7	8	9	10	11	12	13	14	15	16	17	18	19	20
0	0	0	1	0	2	1	0	2	1	0	2	1	3	2	1	3	2	4	3	(0)
(0)	3	4	2	3	1	2	3	1	2	0	1	2	0	1	2	0	1	0	0	0
20	19	18	17	16	15	14	13	12	11	10	9	8	7	6	5	4	3	2	1	0

$$\text{(3)} \quad \text{(3)} \quad \text{(3)} \quad \text{(3)} \quad \text{(3)} \quad \text{(3)} \quad \text{(3)} \quad \text{(4)} \quad \text{(3)}$$

FIGURE 9 *D*

Kayles, the labels recur in a sequence of 12 once a heap number of 71 is reached. Grundy's game shows some curious irregularities—for instance, the heap numbers which have 0 labels begin 1, 2, 4, 7, 10, 20, 23, 26, 50, 53, but after this there are none between 53 and 270, and yet between 270 and 392 there are no less than sixteen! (It seems to be unknown, whether the labels ultimately recur, or not.)

Readers may like to try these techniques on two variants of Lasker's Nim. If only the odd heaps can be split, labels are unchanged, and there is no significant difference from Lasker's game, other than in the prohibition of some moves which a winning player will not require. It can in fact be seen from our earlier discussion that the same would apply if we prohibited any split other than the $(4n+2, 1)$ split of a heap $(4n+3)$.

If no odd heaps can be split, but even heaps can be split arbitrarily, the labels are identical with the heap numbers except when the heap numbers are sums of two different powers of 2, or one unit more, as with $(6, 7)$, $(10, 11)$, $(12, 13)$, ..., in which event an inversion occurs in the series of labels.

We now leave readers to explore the theory of other games which they may know, or may care to invent!

10 *Ten Divisions Lead to Easter*

Back rooms and their problems

The variation of Easter from year to year is regarded as something of a puzzle—or paradox— by many: we propose to discuss some of the considerations which lead to the apparently arbitrary variations; and we shall give a purely numerical rule—subject to no exceptions of any kind—which calculates the date of Easter from a knowledge only of the year number, with no reference to any other rules or tables. This rule is an arithmetical equivalent of the various types of tables which have been employed by religious authorities and others: it includes a mathematical formulation of the procedure by which these tables have been constructed. (Simpler rules are sometimes found, and may be useful if limitations to their validity are known and acceptable. Such rules may apply to some particular century only, or to a longer—but still limited—period: they may include exceptional procedures for certain rare cases; or errors may arise in these cases, because these are omitted.)

The Easter rules may be regarded as an entirely creditable piece of applied science: here—as sometimes elsewhere—we have to remember that the technologists responsible for the solution were not themselves responsible for the specification of the problem; for they had to meet requirements laid down by others to whom the scientific aspects were by no means the only questions at issue.

The basic problem derives from the wishes of the Christian churches to commemorate the Resurrection annually on a suitable date: but difficulties arise because of certain astronomical considerations which are implicitly involved, though not immediately apparent; and further complications have arisen from various causes which are attributable to various human imperfections.

Wheels within wheels within wheels

Astronomical considerations become important in various ways, as soon as increasing civilization requires days to be arranged in an ordered succession, related to periodicities of natural phenomena. Agriculture requires attention to annual events like sowing and harvesting, or major

168

variations of water supply: hunting and travelling are activities in which the presence or absence of light from the moon may be important—and this is true also of warfare, even in modern times.

In arranging days in a calendar, the natural units to employ are therefore months as defined by successive new (or full) moons, and years as defined by the seasons—or, more precisely, by equinoxes or solstices: mean values of these periods define the synodic months and tropical years of the astronomer. As time progresses, it becomes increasingly necessary to take note of the facts that the year does not contain an exact number of lunar months, and that neither of the latter periods contains an exact number of days.

In the very long term, astronomers have to take note of slight changes in the tropical year and synodic month: and values applicable to the year 1900 are 365·242199 days and 29·5305882 days, giving 12·3682670 months in the year. In the course of a century, the three values stated will all reduce by a few units of the last figure given; and these modern estimates can be in error only by still smaller amounts.

Some calendars purchase simplicity at the price of giving up one of the objectives: in Muslim countries, where seasonal variations are less noticeable, the months are kept in step with the moon, and a 12-month year causes the seasons to run through a cycle of the months about three times in every century; the Julian and Gregorian civil calendars do precisely the opposite, keeping the year correct by following the Roman procedure of having twelve calendar months each of which—on the average—includes about one day more than a lunar month. The Jewish practice is that of the Babylonians, which was adopted also in ancient Greece: both months and years are here kept astronomically significant by having seven 13-month years and twelve 12-month years in every nineteen years; for the agreement of 19 years with 235 months is much better than might perhaps be expected in a comparison which involves such relatively small numbers.

The Jewish Passover is celebrated for a week following the first full moon of spring: this therefore involves a connexion both with the seasons and with the phases of the moon; and the Jewish calendar conveniently provides for both needs. The Christian Easter involves all this—in a calendar less directly suitable for it—and more besides; for it introduces additional considerations dependent on the cycle of the seven days of the week.

Numerical orthodoxies and heresies

The special features of the ecclesiastical calendar arise because all four gospels agree in stating that the Crucifixion occurred on the day of preparation—the Friday before the Saturday of the Jewish Sabbath—

in the week of the Passover; likewise in stating that the Resurrection took place on the first day of the week—that is, on the Sunday: hence we derive Good Friday and Easter Sunday, and also the choice of Sunday as the holy day of the Christian religion. (The phrase 'on the third day' involves the older practice of including both limits when specifying an interval.) These references established a relation between the Christian holy days and the Jewish Passover; and Christian teaching wished to emphasize a connexion between the sacrifice of Christ and the Passover sacrifice.

Controversy arose in the early Church between those who wished to celebrate Easter on the day of the Passover, regardless of the day of the week, and those who preferred the Sunday following. (The alternative of a fixed Easter was not then in question.) The first day of the Jewish month was intended to coincide with the earliest visibility of the crescent of the new moon—one or two days after the true instant of astronomical new moon—and this caused the full moon to be taken as the fourteenth day of the month: fourteen here became an unlucky number, for those who wished a common day of celebration were finally stigmatized as Quartodeciman heretics; and the Council of Nicaea in A.D. 325 laid down that Easter was to be the Sunday which followed the full moon which occurred on, or next after, the day of the spring equinox.

The participants thus achieved some of the unanimity hoped for by their patron, the Emperor Constantine: but their pronouncements still left scope for argument as to when the full moon and equinox occurred— or were to be held to have occurred. National differences of practice arose, to be gradually resolved, as, for instance, at the Synod of Whitby in A.D. 664, when agreement was secured between the Latin and Celtic Churches; and in A.D. 725 the Venerable Bede wrote what became a standard work on the subject.

Rules of calculation were rightly regarded as preferable to astronomical observations, since observations might in critical cases be unable to decide whether the equinox or the full moon occurred the earlier, or whether the full moon occurred just before midnight, or just after: a month of difference in Easter could arise in the first case, and a further week in the second. Even worse difficulties arise from the dependence of time upon longitude; for an event like the instant of occurrence of an equinox or of a full moon could be indisputably before midnight in Rome, but definitely after midnight in Constantinople or Alexandria.

Where the limits are set

The rules adopted were that the date of the equinox was to be taken as 21 March (this was approximately correct for the period at which the Council took place, though leap-year variations could then take the true equinox into 22 March and back); the Julian civil calendar, with leap year every fourth year, was to be used for the year. The full moons were assumed to recur after an exact period of nineteen Julian years of 365¼ days: this was made equivalent to 235 lunar months by arranging positions for a corresponding number of new moons spaced some with 30-day gaps and others with 29-day gaps between their calendar dates—with an occasional 31-day gap owing to the extra day of a leap year, which received no special consideration; and the cycle repeated exactly, after seventy-six years.

The Easter full moon could be either *on* or *after* the assumed date of the equinox, but Easter Sunday had to be definitely *later* than the day of the full moon—being the following Sunday if the full moon was itself a Sunday. This meant that if the full-moon date was Saturday, 21 March, Easter would be Sunday, 22 March, and it could never be earlier: when the full-moon date was Saturday, 20 March, the next full moon was 29 days later, on Sunday 18 April; this then made Easter fall on Sunday, 25 April, its latest possible date. These considerations became matters of orthodox doctrine, and were promulgated—with other matters perhaps of more evident religious importance—by various authorities.

The 19-year period was called the Lunar Cycle, and the year's place in this cycle was the *Golden Number*, which ran from 1 to 19 in each cycle: associations of dates with days of the week recurred in a 28-year cycle compounded from the joint effect of leap-year changes and the cycle of seven days in the week. In a rather forced parallelism this 28-year cycle was called the Solar Cycle: concern with the year involves the sun in *both* cycles; and the week has no solar connexion or direct astronomical basis. Easter dates then recurred in a 532-year cycle—the least common multiple of the Lunar and Solar cycles.

The errors of these approximations then began to accumulate: both equinox and full moon could be observed to be occurring ever earlier than their nominal dates. Discussion continued for about 1,000 years; looking some further millennia ahead, Dante could foresee January no longer a winter month; and by the sixteenth century the error was ten days for the sun and four days for the moon.

Reformations and their problems

In 1582, Pope Gregory XIII introduced a reformation of the calendar, to correct both of the errors: ten days were omitted between Thursday, 4 October, and Friday, 15 October, at a time of year when an exceptional rearrangement of the ecclesiastical calendar was judged to produce least inconvenience; and the dates of the full moons were moved seven days on, in the new calendar—the equivalent of three days back in the old. A bias of one day was intentionally introduced to keep Easter still more clear of the Passover date, for better avoidance of religious riots.

Three century years out of four were made ordinary years instead of leap years, to correct the accumulating error of the equinox; and eight one-day shifts of the full-moon dates were to occur in each 2,500 years, in century years three apart at first, with a four-century gap at the end of the cycle: the first lunar adjustment was to take place at the assumed termination of such a cycle, in the year 1800.

The lunar information in the ecclesiastical calendar received a new definition in terms of the *epact*: this is a whole number between 1 and 30 inclusive which gives the assumed age of the moon, in days, immediately prior to the first day of January of the year concerned. (An epact of 30 is sometimes represented by an asterisk, intended to stand for 0 or 30 indifferently.) In the Julian calendar, the epact had a fixed relation to the Golden Number, and only nineteen of the thirty possible epacts could occur: in the Gregorian calendar, this relation is in effect reviewed at the start of each new century, and the Golden Numbers continue their 19-year cycle undisturbed. The two Gregorian century-year corrections can affect the epact by one day each, in different directions, at different intervals.

Three times in each four-century period, a leap-year day which was present in the Julian calendar is omitted—in the century years where the year number will not divide exactly by 400—to correct the length of the year: but this omission has to be compensated by a reduction made to the epact, from then onwards; for the epact remains elsewhere conditioned to Julian-calendar assumptions. Apart from this, a less frequent change in the other direction is required, to make a correction for the actual length of the month: because 235 lunar months very slightly fall short of the nineteen Julian years with which—in the cycle—they would otherwise be equated. At present we are in the first of three successive centuries of stable epacts: for neither change arises in the year 2000; and both occur—only to cancel each other—in the year 2100.

We should note here that in calendars we concern ourselves with a fictitious mean sun and mean moon which have uniform motions, but no accumulating discrepancies with their real astronomical counterparts. This is similar to the distinction whereby time is determined with a uniform rate suitable for a clock, rather than with the irregularities which affect the time given by a sundial: these irregularities arise because the Earth's axis is not perpendicular to the plane of its orbit, and because the orbit is an ellipse, and not a circle. Analogous considerations can cause the mean full moons to differ by a day or more from the true full moons of the heavens—or of almanacs which correctly take note of all calculable variations. Moreover, for ecclesiastical purposes the equinox and the full moons are assigned only to dates, and not to any particular times—to avoid disputes dependent on differences of local time, or arguable cases in the vicinity of date changes at midnight: and we noted earlier that the ecclesiastical full moon was purposely placed later than the mean full moon—for a wholly praiseworthy reason.

Discrepancies between ecclesiastical and astronomical data need not therefore imply any errors in either: though paradoxes can indeed arise if this consideration is not kept in mind. Owing to varying lack of exact compensation between whole numbers of leap-year days and the excesses which they are intended to correct, the almanacs can show the astronomical equinox to occur as early as 19 March: an extreme case of this will arise in 2096. The opposite limit is an equinox late in the day on 21 March, and an extreme case of this occurred in 1903: the lack of balance is greatest over the intervening 193 years, in the course of which forty-nine leap-year days will have been inserted, although the true excess—over this period—is approximately $46\frac{3}{4}$ days only; and similar extremes occur at four-century intervals from these years. Arguments involving astronomical moons or equinoxes—or both—could occasionally give scope for believing that Easter should be either four or five weeks different from the chosen date.

Other cases can suggest that the date of Easter is wrong by exactly a week: in these cases, a difference of date in different parts of the world will usually allow local astronomical defence of the accepted date of Easter—but not always. In 1845 and 1923 the true full moon fell on Easter Sunday everywhere except for localities of large easterly longitude, which then had a full moon on Easter Monday: in 1744 there was the opposite case of a full moon which most of the world would say was on a Saturday eight days before Easter Sunday, while a few places of extreme westerly longitude would place it one day earlier still, on a Friday. There may even be an eclipse, to *prove* that the moon is full on Easter Sunday, as in Europe in 1903. These cases can arise when the various sources of variation combine to make the real moon differ sufficiently from the ecclesiastical moon.

In fact there were few relevant considerations—if any—which escaped the notice of Gregory's principal adviser, the German Jesuit astronomer Clavius (after whom a crater on the Moon has been named). In his advocacy of proposals made first by his deceased Italian colleague Lilius, he emphasized the administrative advantages of arithmetical tables, and he stated quite explicitly that two distinct moons were in question: one astronomical, or real; and the other ecclesiastical, or notional. He compared ecclesiastical data with astronomical data ostensibly for the meridian of Rome (these are apparently based on astronomical data for the meridian of Venice; but this is more a matter of illustrative convenience than religious principle, in view of the day or so of lunar displacement which was inserted to avoid coincidences with the Passover): and he directed that those in the newly discovered Southern hemisphere should base their Easter on spring as in the Northern hemisphere—where Christ had lived—rather than on their own spring, with a six-month difference.

The equinox was to be assumed to occur on 21 March in all cases, and care was taken to ensure that only a 29-day gap and not a 30-day gap could take place between a full moon of 20 March and the next full moon. Easter then was confined to the same limits as in the Julian calendar: and the full moons were also arranged to have different dates in each year of any 19-year cycle. Well-known properties of the old calendar were thus maintained; and the good repute of earlier tables and authors was not irresponsibly disturbed.

This involved suitably placing some otherwise necessary exceptions at various points in a regular interweaving of 30-day and 29-day lunar months; and Clavius is himself responsible for a further improvement— a method which secures all these results with the minimum necessity of making exceptions to simple rules for Easter.

In the published explanation of the changes, it was explicitly stated that the introduction of a fixed date for Easter would not have been a contradiction of any essential consideration of fundamental doctrine; but that it had been held preferable to secure continuity with the past— so far as possible—while arranging to avoid uncertainty and lack of unanimity for the future. The need for an occasional contradiction of astronomical truth was recognized and accepted as the price to be paid for simplicity and uniformity: and—subject to these considerations— the need to minimize the discrepancies received careful attention.

The Catholic states of Europe all adopted the new calendar within a few years; but renewed confusion arose from conflict with another Reformation. Some Protestant authorities disagreed with the change, to be ridiculed for preferring to be 'wrong with the sun rather than right with the Pope'—by opponents who had chosen to be wrong with the moon rather than be right with the Jews: and Protestant preferences for astronomical observations drew from Kepler the comment that 'Easter is a feast, and not a star'. In Western Europe, the advantages of uniformity finally prevailed; and most of the Protestant states adopted the new calendar in 1700 or 1701, leaving Britain and Sweden to do the like about fifty years later.

Britain changed over in 1752 between Wednesday, 2 September, and Thursday, 14 September, amid some clamour of '*Give us back our eleven days!*' (omission of an extra day was required because the year 1700—but not 1600—had been of different length in the two calendars). Provision was made for determining Easter by methods which differed in form from those of the Roman church, but which nevertheless produced an identical result. By the same Act of 1751, the calendar year was made to begin in England with 1 January, from 1752 onwards: it had done this in Scotland since the beginning of 1600. Before 1752 the English year began on 25 March: the Act provided that financial and legal matters were not to be anticipated or postponed, but were to continue for their due terms as if there had been no change; and as a result there is now a British financial year whose first day is 5 April.

By the early twentieth century the spread of communications had brought ever-increasing adoption of the Gregorian calendar for civil purposes, even in Oriental countries. World-wide agreement on civil-calendar dates was virtually achieved by the accession of Greece in 1924 and Turkey in 1927: except that the Greek proposals were in fact for an 'improved Julian' calendar which would gain slightly in accuracy by having two century leap-years out of nine, rather than the Gregorian choice of one out of four; and failing concessions by one side or other (or more drastic reform) this would produce rival civil calendars in Europe—once again—from the year 2800 onwards. Some other Greek proposals envisaged the Orthodox churches determining Easter in terms of astronomical data for the meridian of Jerusalem: these—if adhered to—would give opportunities for religious disagreements, occasionally, even in the present century.

The tables of the law

The churches have usually employed tabular methods for determining Easter: these mostly make explicit or implicit use of a calendar in which successive days from 1 January onwards are labelled with the letters A, B, C, D, E, F, G, continuing in cyclic succession; and the cycle pays no regard to a date of 29 February, which should be considered to have the same letter as the date 1 March. (For many centuries, use continued to be made of the Roman calendar, in which the days of the months were numbered backwards from the next Kalends, Nones, or Ides. The extra day of February was then arranged differently, as the term 'bissextile' commemorates: here there was a repeat of the twenty-fourth day of February which (by inclusive reckoning) was referred to as the sixth day before the Kalends—or first day—of March.)

Relatively to any common year, one of the seven letters can then be specified as the *Dominical Letter* of the year, to identify which dates are the Sundays. In a leap year, two letters have to be provided: adjacent pairs of letters may occur in inverted alphabetical order, or we may have AG; the first-written of the two letters applies to January and February only, and the other letter is used after the extra day, in leap years. Since 365 days include one day more than an exact number of weeks, the elapse of a common year serves to displace the Dominical Letter one step backwards in the alphabet (or from A to G): so a leap year will result in a two-step displacement, overall—and in fact the original reason for the name is this leap of the Dominical Letter.

In the Julian calendar it then was necessary only to insert series of Golden Numbers in various places, to show which dates were new-moon dates in the corresponding years of every 19-year cycle; alternatively, these Golden Numbers could all be placed in positions thirteen days later—moving them to the fourteenth day of the month, instead of the first—to indicate the corresponding full-moon dates: in either event some days would thus receive no Golden Number. The Golden Number for any year could then be used to find the full moon which was on, or next after, the date of 21 March: the first subsequent appearance of the Dominical Letter of the year then identified the date of Easter Sunday for that year.

In the Julian calendar, the Dominical Letters required a cycle of twenty-eight years for their exact recurrence, since four years which include a leap year do not contain an exact number of weeks: but the new leap-year cycle of four Gregorian centuries does in fact contain a number of days which is an exact multiple of 7; and so a four-century period here serves as a cycle for the Dominical Letter as well. (One consequence is that week-days no longer are distributed to dates with absolute impartiality—in the long run—as they were before: and the thirteenth of a month is now a little more likely to be a Friday than anything else!)

The Gregorian calendar uses epacts in place of Golden Numbers, to determine the lunar months: these follow the Julian practice, except when the special corrections are made in century years. Apart from these special corrections, the epact is made to increase by 11 from one year to the next—with multiples of 30 neglected—unless the Golden Number changes from 19 to 1, when the epact is made to increase by 12: the increases represent the number of days by which a year exceeds twelve lunar months; and they secure a return to the same full-moon dates after nineteen years.

In the Julian calendar, only nineteen values of the epact were possible: in the Gregorian calendar, the century-year corrections can operate to make unit changes—in the same direction—in all the nineteen epacts of a previous cycle. This causes thirty different sets of nineteen epacts to be required as time progresses; and every number from 1 to 30 can then be an epact at some time or other. Whereas before there were some dates which received no Golden Number, there here have to be some dates which receive two epacts: because thirty possibilities have to be distributed over a range of thirty days, in some cases, and over a range of twenty-nine days, in others, for the following reasons.

The epact is the assumed age of the moon at the start of the year, and so an epact of 30 is the indication of a new moon on 1 January: epacts which diminish by units can then be associated with later dates, in similar fashion, because each unit decrease in the age of the moon at the start of the year will cause a day's postponement to the date of the first new moon; but this system cannot continue throughout the year, or all months would have thirty days.

So a particular set of three consecutive epacts is chosen, and on alternate occasions—at later sets of dates in the year—these are made to correspond sometimes to three different days, and sometimes only to two. The epacts so selected are taken to be 26, 25, 24, for a reason we shall later discuss: and 25 is used in two forms, sometimes written as 25 and 25'. When we attach epacts to dates which are to be their corresponding new-moon dates, we then arrange that alternately at later dates in the year we have 25 and 25' coinciding on a day uniquely of their own, or else being split—with 25' coinciding with 26 for one day, and 25 coinciding with 24 for the following day: in all other cases, the epacts decrease by units, or change from 1 to 30, from one day to the next; and no epact is given to the extra day of February in leap years. To preserve the feature that no two years of any 19-year cycle can have identical new-moon dates, it is then necessary to arrange that epacts 24 and 25 cannot be in use together in any such cycle—and similarly for epacts 25' and 26.

This is secured when a rule is made that the epact 25 is to be used only when years which have Golden Numbers from 1 to 11 are in question, whereas 25' is to be used as the epact for years with Golden Numbers from 12 to 19. No three consecutive epacts can be in simultaneous use, in any 19-year cycle; and two consecutive epacts can occur only eleven years apart—with the smaller occurring in one of the first eight years of the cycle, and the larger occurring in one of the last eight years—when both are present in the same cycle: so 25 is always available for use with 26, if both are needed, and similarly for 25' with 24.

No pairs of epacts which can be of equivalent effect are then required in any of the thirty sets of nineteen epacts which can become current epacts together (for single centuries, or for up to three centuries at a time): assigning the three middle years of the cycle to the earlier subdivision then ensures that every cycle includes either an epact 24—with or without 25'—or alternatively an epact 25; and 25' is required only when 24 is present in the same cycle, which happens only in eight of the thirty possible sets.

This system will be found to place an epact of 23 to indicate a new moon on 8 March, and therefore a full moon on 21 March; and a full cycle of epacts continues thereafter, until the epacts 26 and 25' indicate new moons for 4 April and full moons for 17 April, and finally the epacts 25 and 24 indicate new moons for 5 April and full moons for 18 April.

Notwithstanding the thirty possibilities which replace the previous nineteen, the Easter full moon is then restricted to a range of only twenty-nine possible dates, within the same limits as before; and no need arises to allow Easter to occur on any date which was known to be impossible—and authoritatively stated to be so—in relation to the earlier calendar. (Similar consideration for earlier authorities caused the spring equinox to be restored to a date of 21 March as at the Council of Nicaea—rather than to the later date which it had at the time of the Crucifixion.) The greatest irregularity in the months occurs when—occasionally—four consecutive months include a total of 120 days, or when three months each of twenty-nine days occur in succession, at a change from one year to the next.

Continuing relevance of earlier pronouncements could equally well be provided by treating any other epact similarly to 25; and the original proposal (by Lilius) was to do this for the epact 30. By choosing 25 for the ambiguous epact, Clavius secured that strict numerical sequence continues for as long as possible through the range of dates for the Easter full moon: for the break in serial order then applies to 25′ but not to 25—and otherwise only to 24. Simpler rules (analogous to familiar rules for the Julian calendar) are then able to cover nearly all cases; and there is a minimum need to define and make use of exceptional procedures—the replacement of one crudely calculated epact by another, or a shift of a week in the derived date of Easter—to give them universal validity.

Gaussian error and its correction

Rules for Easter have been considered by various mathematicians, including Gauss—perhaps the greatest of all—who published a rule that ignores the change from the 300-year interval to the 400-year interval, in the lunar correction: this will give 13 April, instead of the correct 20 April, for Easter in A.D. 4200; similar errors occur intermittently, with slowly increasing frequency, in later years.

A wholly correct procedure of a purely arithmetical type was first given in *Nature* in 1876 by an anonymous New York correspondent: this includes an arithmetical device which takes care of cases which more usually had caused numerical rules to be complicated by special exceptions. The rule uses all the letter-symbols from *a* to *o* inclusive, apart from *j*: it becomes tempting to speculate whether its author was a printer, or was more familiar with an Italian (or Latin) alphabet. Based on this procedure, we have developed similar methods of our own, which are now published for the first time.

There are three points of difference between our present procedures and the one given in *Nature*. We have replaced one step of the other rule by two, so that we can calculate the actual date in the month, instead of a date which has to be increased by a unit (because zero is a possible result); but we have been able to replace two steps of the other rule by one, by taking account of a manuscript note which Gauss made to correct his error, in his own copy of his published paper. Apart from this, our procedures now give a closer parallel to the use of tables, and allow the easy determination of the correct epact and correct date of the Easter full moon, in all cases without exception.

We give one set of calculation rules in Table 10*a*: the only initial information needed is the year number for a Gregorian year; and all else depends only on the quotients and remainders which are obtained by ten successive division operations, in which there are specified divisors and dividends which are formed—with no exceptional provisions—from previous results. Our earlier discussion will allow us to explain what is concerned in the different stages which are involved.

Commentary on a decalogue

In step (1) of the procedure of Table 10*a* we identify the position of the year in a 19-year cycle, to use this later in (5) to introduce the principal constituent of the change of full-moon dates from year to year: the value of *a* is one unit less than the Golden Number; for Golden Numbers run from 1 to 19 in cases where our remainders will run from 0 to 18. In (2) we prepare to take note of the special corrections which the Gregorian calendar introduces in century years: the value of *b* increases by one unit at century years only, and the value of *c* is used later in (7), to take note of the effect which the ordinary cycle of leap years has on the succession of week-days for the same date in successive years.

From (3) we derive *d*, which increases only in century leap-years, and *e*, which gives the number of century years which have *not* been leap years, subsequently to the immediately previous century leap-year. From (4) we obtain *g*, which increases only when there is an increase of the epact because of the correction of the month; and *b*−*d* has a value which increases only when a reduction of the epact is required because of the omissions which gave the Gregorian correction of the year: at (5), we can then compute a number *h* which is an equivalent of the epact.

The epact itself is in fact either 53−*h* or 23−*h*, whichever lies between 1 and 30 inclusive; and we thus ensure that the critical epacts 24 and 25 are represented by the largest values of *h*: in (6) we can then arrange to have $\mu = 1$ only when a critical case has arisen.

Step	Dividend	Divisor	Quotient	Remainder
(1)	x	19	–	a
(2)	x	100	b	c
(3)	b	4	d	e
(4)	$8b+13$	25	g	–
(5)	$19a+b-d-g+15$	30	–	h
(6)	$a+11h$	319	μ	–
(7)	c	4	i	k
(8)	$2e+2i-k-h+\mu+32$	7	–	λ
(9)	$h-\mu+\lambda+90$	25	n	–
(10)	$h-\mu+\lambda+n+19$	32	–	p

TABLE 10 *a*

Step	Dividend	Divisor	Quotient	Remainder
(1)	x	100	b	c
(2)	$5b+c$	19	–	a
(3)	$3(b+25)$	4	δ	ϵ
(4)	$8(b+11)$	25	γ	–
(5)	$19a+\delta-\gamma$	30	–	h
(6)	$a+11h$	319	μ	–
(7)	$60(5-\epsilon)+c$	4	j	k
(8)	$2j-k-h+\mu$	7	–	λ
(9)	$h-\mu+\lambda+110$	30	n	q
(10)	$q+5-n$	(32)	(0)	p

TABLE 10 *b*

Explanations are easier with the upper rules, but computation may be simpler with the lower rules. In the xth year A.D. of the Gregorian calendar, Easter Sunday is the pth day of the nth month, with both rules. The date of the Easter full moon is obtained if -1 is substituted for λ, in steps (9) and (10).

The Golden Number is $a+1$, and the epact is either $23-h$ or $53-h$, whichever lies between 1 and 30 inclusive.

To find the Dominical Letter, divide $2e+2i-k$ or $2j-k+4$ by 7—with multiples of 7 added, if need be, since we wish to have the smallest non-negative remainder. The letter is A if this remainder is zero, and it moves on in the alphabet as the remainder increases: for leap years, prefix this by the next following letter (or G by A).

We always have $\mu = 0$ except in two circumstances: when $h = 29$, we have $\mu = 1$ regardless of the value of a, and the epact then is 24; we again have $\mu = 1$ when we have $h = 28$ and $a > 10$ simultaneously, and then the epact is 25'. By suitable use of the value of μ, we then can always pass from the epact to the *correct* date of the ecclesiastical Easter full moon (which we can in fact obtain if we replace $+\lambda$ by -1, in the expressions which give the dividends for the steps (9) and (10) of our procedure).

We next have to find the day of the week for the Easter full-moon date. With (7) we arrange to take note of ordinary leap-years; and we can then derive an equivalent of the Dominical Letter: for the Dominical Letter is A when $2e + 2i - k$ leaves a zero remainder when divided by 7, and advances by one step in the alphabet for each unit increase in the remainder, in other cases. (This applies to the letter which we use in March and thereafter, in the case of leap-years: this is the one with which we are concerned in the determination of Easter.)

Ordinarily, e will not change, and there will be a single backward step in a common year, due to a unit advance in k; or a fivefold step forward—equivalent to a double backward step—because i increases by 1 and k reduces by 3, for a leap year. At century years, i will reduce by 24, and k by 3; and e will increase by 1 for a common year, but reduce by 3 for a leap year: the equivalent of a single or a double backward step is then correctly provided, as required, in the respective cases.

In (8), a full-moon date correctly derived from the epact—in terms of h and μ—is implicitly compared with a Dominical Letter derived from $2e + 2i - k$: we thus obtain λ, with $\lambda = 0$ if the full-moon date is a Saturday, but $\lambda = 6$ if it is a Sunday; in all cases, λ is one unit less than the number of days which must elapse before there is a Sunday which is strictly subsequent to the date of the ecclesiastical full moon. We then have everything necessary to enable steps (9) and (10) to produce $n = 3$ for March or $n = 4$ for April, with p giving the actual date of Easter Sunday in the month concerned.

In our explanation, we have concentrated on the cyclic features which are required if accuracy, once introduced, is to be subsequently maintained. The initial accuracy is introduced by the constants 15 and 32 in steps (5) and (8); these in effect introduce the age of the moon and the day of the week for some particular date: the constant 13 in (4) takes note that a lunar correction was made at the start of a 2,500-year lunar-correction cycle, in the year 1800. Constants have been chosen in such a way that the rules will not require division of negative numbers.

In Table 10 *b* we give an alternative procedure, in which various sophistications have been introduced to simplify the calculation of various dividends. Some readers may care to check that the two sets of rules are arithmetically equivalent.

Hard cases and bad laws

The rules we have given here are based on slight modifications of a set of equally correct rules which we have published elsewhere: in the earlier form they gave the correct date of Easter; but they did not then allow a direct calculation of the epact, or of the date of the Easter full moon—for all cases without exception—as they now do.

We shall find that we have $\mu = 1$ with the new rules more often than we have the corresponding case of $m = 1$ in the *Nature* rule (and in our earlier rule); the reason is that we now find every Easter full moon correctly. In the other rules we implicitly use an incorrect epact to find this date with an error of one day, in the cases when we would have $\mu = 1$ here: the other rules pay no regard to this except when the date of Easter would be affected because a Sunday was taken in place of a Saturday; and corrections dependent on a term $7m$ then become effective. (We have chosen the symbols in such a fashion that identical symbols are used in identical senses, in our procedures and in the earlier procedure as given in *Nature*.)

Since only minor alterations are involved—with no increase in the computational effort—we have thought it desirable to make the changes. They provide a better correspondence between the arithmetical data and equivalent tabular data: and they will make clear that the validity of the earlier limiting dates was preserved by a means somewhat more subtle—and rational—than simply having the date of Easter earlier by a week when the limit would otherwise have been exceeded.

If Easter is to have its earliest possible date—22 March—this requires the year to have an epact of 23, to give a full moon on 21 March, and a Dominical Letter D (or letters ED, if a leap-year), to make the full-moon date a Saturday: this occurs for 1818 and 2285, but not for any intervening year. If Easter is to have its latest possible date—25 April—the epact must be either 24, or a 25 which is *not* treated as 25', either of which will give a full moon on 18 April (and in the second event the Golden Number must be between 1 and 11 inclusive): in both cases, there must also be a Dominical Letter C (or letters DC), to make the full-moon date a Sunday. This happens for 1886 (with epact 25) and for 1943 (with epact 24), but not again until 2038.

The latest date comes up about once per century. It may occur twice, as in the thirty-first century, with 3002 and 3097; and it may not occur at all, as in the forty-fifth century. The earliest date occurs more rarely: during several consecutive centuries it may occur once per century (rarely twice, as in 3401 and 3496), and then for several consecutive centuries it may not occur at all; there are no examples between 3716 and 4308. The latest date is more frequent than the earliest, because—unlike the earliest—it can arise with either of two epacts.

The cases which require a value $m = 1$ in the *Nature* rule are those where the epact is either 24, or a 25 which *is* treated as 25' (and in the second event the Golden Number must then lie between 12 and 19 inclusive), provided that the Dominical Letter is given by D (or ED) in the first case, and by C (or DC) in the second. The first alternative occurred for 1609 and will occur for 1981, but not again until 2076, to give an Easter date of 19 April: the second alternative occurred in 1954 and will not occur again until 2049, giving an Easter date of 18 April.

If we have an epact of 25 and a Dominical Letter of C (or DC), the vital question therefore is whether the epact 25 is to be treated as 25', or not: for if not, we will have an Easter date of 25 April, as in 1886, and if so, we will have an Easter date of 18 April, as in 1954. (The Golden Number is 6 for 1886, but 17 for 1954: and the full-moon dates are 18 April 1886, but 17 April 1954, because the full-moon date is obtained differently from the same numerical epact, in the two cases.)

These critical cases—and the case of the year 4200—can form useful test examples for various rules for Easter. (They will show that numerical rules in earlier editions of the *Encyclopaedia Britannica* are in error for 1886 and critical cases of similar type.)

Future prospects for Easter

With the Gregorian rules, the completion of a full cycle of Easter dates would require 5,700,000 years; these would include 70,499,183 months and 2,081,882,250 days. The cycle has this duration because a period of 10,000 years is required before there is an exact repeat of the century-year epact shifts; and in any such period there are seventy-five one-day shifts in one direction, and thirty-two one-day shifts in another—giving an overall lunar displacement of forty-three days. This has to be repeated 30×19 times before the cycle closes with a repeat of the original epact and original Golden Number, when 43×19 months will have been omitted, as compared with an exact allowance of 235 months for every nineteen years.

Any astronomical relevance would, however, disappear long before the completion of the cycle: and the new rules will themselves be in error by several days, after the passage of a few tens of thousands of years. This arises from two causes. Residual imperfections of the revised rules would still accumulate even if the day, month, and year continued to have unaltered duration. Apart from this, the periods concerned, and their ratios, are not strictly constant: tidal friction makes each successive day longer, in the average, by a few millimicroseconds—equivalent to the time required for light to travel several feet; and various gravitational perturbations combine to affect the other periods also, over very long periods of time.

Puzzles and Paradoxes

At the limit of present-day accurate time-keeping, there is already a need to have two quite distinct measures of time: one—essentially for civil purposes and other matters conditioned to the Earth's rotation— has to remain in mean agreement with the progressive increase of the day; but another—more suited to measurement of unvarying repetitive physical processes such as atomic vibrations, and to consideration of the dynamics of planetary motions—is now based on an appropriate subdivision of a specially selected year. Failing this, we should have to consider that precise clocks have slightly increasing rates—and planets an unaccountable acceleration—because we choso to ignore the simpler fact that the rate of the Earth's rotation is gradually diminishing.

In concluding, we should remark that the Easter Act, 1928, makes provision that an Order in Council can fix Easter to be the first Sunday after the second Saturday in April, after regard duly paid to opinions of churches or other Christian bodies—most of whom have already pronounced that no point of religious principle need make them oppose a uniformly agreed change.

If uniformity both of date and of practice could come soon, there would be attendant advantages to holiday-makers and to statisticians, in particular: and for our part we would prefer to see our rules become mathematical or historical curiosities, rather than to have them continue as something applicable to contemporary use.

11 *Problematic Lies and Unexpected Truths*

Seeking unity in diversity

The three questions which we shall now discuss are intrinsically of very different types; but they have some common features which give us an excuse for grouping them together here. In each case we shall have to examine some assertions whose truth we must regard as doubtful—some involved in the statement of the problem, and others in statements made elsewhere about the problem. In all three cases, considerations of formal mathematics are subsidiary to other issues, or totally absent: the need is more for logical arguments and correct deductions, in the ordinary sense.

All these questions have already caused some argument and led to disagreements, both in print and in personal correspondence: time will show whether our further discussion produces less disagreement— or more!

Four doubtful statements—and a fifth

The first question is one which the late Sir Arthur Eddington used as an illustrative example in his book *New Pathways in Science*. We quote this as he gave it: 'If *A*, *B*, *C*, *D* each speak the truth once in three times (independently), and *A* affirms that *B* denies that *C* declares that *D* is a liar, what is the probability that *D* was speaking the truth?'

Eddington first heard this mentioned in an after-dinner speech by Dr. A. C. D. Crommelin, shortly before their eclipse expedition of 1919 which verified Einstein's prediction of the relativistic deflexion of light: the original source was apparently a mock examination paper in the undergraduate magazine *Granta*.

He used it in his book in 1935: later in that year he wrote that the solution which he had given had brought a considerable increase in his correspondence; and he published a further explanation which he hoped would avert a similar sequel. One sequel—stimulated, rather than averted—was a somewhat technical paper by Mr. H. W. Chapman in the *Mathematical Gazette*; this advocated a different answer, in line with the one we shall give here.

The book is still being reprinted with no changes: we know of some who are unaware that its solution has been queried; and we can imagine that an understandable deference to apparent authority may have led others to abandon a correct solution, and perhaps to doubt their own capacity needlessly. This is a possibility which we would gladly remove, if we can.

When everybody keeps to the point

Economy of words produces ambiguity in the original form of the question: and we have to decide whether we can assume that each speaker had a choice which was restricted to two mutually contradictory alternatives about an immediately preceding statement; or whether we can be allowed to assume that speakers may disregard previous events, to make irrelevant remarks (or none). We shall take both possibilities in their turn.

If we assume the presence and co-operation of an onlooker X, we can clarify the first case. We can assume that C—but not X—hears D make a statement: then X asks C, 'Was D a liar?'; and B—but not X—hears C answer either 'Yes' or 'No'. So X now asks B, 'Did C declare that D was a liar:'; and A—but not X—hears B answer either 'Yes' or 'No'. Finally X asks A, 'Did B deny that C declared that D was a liar?': and this time X hears A give an answer, 'Yes'. Knowing that each of A, B, C, D (independently) tells the truth only once in three times, X has then to assess the probability that D actually told the truth. He can argue as follows:

'Suppose that I had *not* heard what A said. I could then assume that over large numbers of cases the different possibilities would arise with the relative frequencies which are indicated in Figure 11A. If the numbers given there are taken to be numerators for a common denominator of 81, they will give fractions which will indicate the proportions of cases which satisfy various multiple conditions. A true statement causes a diversion in the direction towards the left-hand border of the table, and a lie causes branching towards the right-hand border—as viewed by a reader of the text: at each stage, one-third of the earlier cases take the first course, and two-thirds of them take the second. A left-hand alternative—whether "Yes" or "No"—is then a truthful reply, and must therefore be labelled to agree with the labelling above the fork, when I ask "Did C declare . . ." and "Did A affirm . . ."; but it must disagree with the preceding legend, in the case where I ask "Did B deny . . .".

'These would be the proportions with which various cases would arise, in general: but I have some further information to show that some of them are not in the picture here; for I did—after all—hear A give an answer which was "Yes". I should divide the *a priori* possibilities into three separate groups: 40/81 of them would not have led to *A* giving the answer "Yes", so these can here be disregarded; 13/81 of them would lead to *A* saying "Yes" after *D* told the truth, and 28/81 would lead to *A* saying "Yes" after *D* lied.

'So once I *know* that *A* has said "Yes", the relevant proportions of truths and lies for *D* become in a ratio of 13 to 28; and this implies that there is a probability of 13/41 that *D* then was telling the truth.'

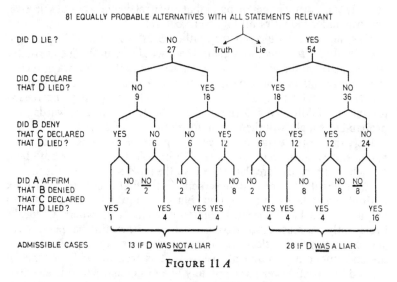

FIGURE 11 *A*

Problems raised by irrelevant talk

If instead we attempt to assume that *B* and *C* may talk irrelevantly— alleging, if we like, that there is nothing to the contrary in the statement of the problem—we shall run into difficulties. If we take this legalistic view, we ought similarly to admit that there then is nothing to prevent any of them being *selectively* irrelevant; for it is only their veracity—*not* their relevancy—which is *stated* to be independently determined in each case. Equally we must admit that we have no grounds for dismissing the possibility that each may be fully aware of all that has taken place before he speaks.

If so, *A* could then decide that he will *never* talk of *B*'s statement when *D* lies; or that he will *never* talk of *B*'s statement when *D* tells the truth: and no matter what *B* says, *A* can sometimes say what in fact he is known to say—namely, 'Yes'—possibly as a truth, and possibly as a lie. If we are aware of his policy, the probability that we are asked to find will then be 1 in the first case, and 0 in the second: if we are not, all we can do is conclude that the probability must lie between 0 and 1 inclusive—exactly as if we knew nothing about anything concerned!

This may not be much to our liking: but if we want to get round this difficulty we have no choice but to read some implicit conditions into the statement of the problem. Suppose that we still hope to allow possibly irrelevant answers. We might try to assume that no one had any superfluous information—for instance, that *A* and *B* must be quite unaware whether *D* lied or not, and that *A* must be ignorant of what *C* actually said; or we might demand that any irrelevance was not selective, and was independent of all that went before.

This, however, would not stop either *C* or *B* from deciding to talk irrelevantly *all the time*; and again there would be nothing to prohibit *A* from making his assertion—sometimes—though if *B* always speaks irrelevantly this can only happen because *A* decides to tell a *relevant* lie. If *A* is unaware of *D*'s veracity or mendacity, or pays no regard to this, no additional information can be transmitted onwards: the probability sought will then retain its *a priori* value of 1/3.

We can use the diagram to see the effects of allowing *B* and *C* to make irrelevant answers. If *D* and *C* both told the truth, or both lied, *C* could not then declare that *D* lied; so the label NO will remain correct for nine possibilities of double veracity in the first event, and thirty-six of double mendacity in the second: but we cannot label the other cases YES unless we have relevance guaranteed—in cases where *C* speaks irrelevantly we must again have a label NO. When this happens, a YES and all below it is effectively transferred across to superimpose on the corresponding NO and all below it: this transfer will interchange NO and YES at all lower levels, on any line of descent which is affected; and labels will no longer derive uniquely from the veracity patterns concerned.

Eddington's value of 25/71 for the probability could admittedly be derived by requiring artificial patterns of relevance and irrelevance; but—even so—his own derivation implies what must be considered to be a quite impossible pattern. His denominator of 71 comes from arguing that of the eighty-one alternatives originally possible, only ten (from the two cases where we have underlined the NO label) are absolutely impossible—when we know that *A* has given an affirmative answer— if relevance is optional. This is true: but both *C* and *B* must then decide for or against relevance in accordance with a *foreknowledge* of the veracity, or otherwise, of those who are yet to speak, if other replies possible when statements are relevant are not—sometimes—to become impossible in cases where Eddington has in fact assumed that they will occur.

He also maintains that if *A*, *B*, and *D* all tell the truth, *C* can be a liar if he is irrelevant, and that this veracity pattern should therefore be counted as admissible: but it is inadmissible if C's lie were to consist of saying that D was a liar; and we have no grounds to decide which choice C would make. Consideration of the veracities of A, B, C, D in this order—rather than the reverse—is putting the cart before the horse.

Varying relevance will cause arbitrary transfers of branches and frequencies to other places in the tree-diagram: so any unique answer must imply an explicit or implicit relevance pattern for the speakers. This being so, we think that unconditional relevance, with an answer 13/41, is the only sensible choice.

Exercises, examinations, and executions

For our second question, we shall discuss a paradox which has appeared—in many places—in various equivalent forms. References to fire-alarm or air-raid exercises have given topical relevance in some circles; elsewhere the context has been that of setting an examination: a more dramatic presentation is stated in terms of an execution, and a victim who will be pardoned if he can prove that he was expecting his executioners on the day of their professional visit.

The common feature is that some event is required to take place unexpectedly before a known time limit; and an argument is given which appears to show that this is a logical impossibility. For the examination, the argument takes the following form.

A teacher is supposed to be told by his headmaster to set his class an unexpected examination: he is to make all necessary preparations, and is to warn his class, one Friday, that there will be an examination—unexpectedly—on one of the days from Monday to Friday inclusive in the following week.

The teacher then argues with himself as follows: 'The examination cannot be left until the Friday. For as soon as Thursday is past, with no examination, the pupils would know to expect one on the Friday. But they can argue this as well as I can, and once they work out that the examination cannot be on the Friday, they would then expect it on the Thursday, if it had not occurred earlier: so Thursday must be ruled out, too. But once Thursday is ruled out like this, similar arguments then rule out Wednesday, then Tuesday and Monday—so there seems to be no way to set an unexpected examination at all!'

He then departs to try out this argument on his headmaster, troubled by a feeling that examinations can—and do—happen, unexpectedly, in circumstances much like his own.

How the unexpected can always happen

To resolve this paradox—or any other—it is desirable to examine the preliminary assumptions carefully, and to state them with rather more precision.

Two statements are supposed to be made: a first statement '*There will be an examination on some day from Monday to Friday inclusive, next week*' and a second statement '*Before the examination is announced, pupils will not be able to deduce that it is about to take place*'. The argument previously given then proceeds with the implicit assumption that everyone—*including the pupils*—may regard these two statements as unconditionally true.

This is similar to the usual assumptions for problems, examination questions and the like; but it is not at all a logical necessity: cases to the contrary may be undesirable, and unintentional, but they can exist. In another case, the two statements could have been 'There *will* be an examination' and 'There will *not* be an examination': we could not *then* proceed by assuming that both statements were unconditionally true.

We therefore have an assumption, which we had better put in the form of a third statement: '*The pupils may regard both the previous statements as unconditionally true.*' What the argument of the paradox then does is to assume the truth of *all three* of these statements, and to deduce logical consequences from them jointly, thereby arriving at a contradiction.

Truth of the first statement implies that if Friday arrives without any earlier examination having occurred, there must be an examination on the Friday; truth of the third statement then implies that the pupils would then know to expect it: but truth of the second statement implies that they are not to be able to expect it. A danger of contradiction arises, which is averted by concluding that Friday must not arrive with no earlier examination having occurred. So Friday is then removed from the list of possible days; but even so the emergence of a contradiction is only postponed.

Thursday, as the last day now remaining, can—and must—be removed by similar arguments, and then earlier days in their turn, also; but when we finally dispose of Monday in this fashion, we have a contradiction of the first statement; for we have then proved that the examination cannot take place within the period during which the first statement requires that it must.

There is nothing wrong with any of the reasoning so far: for in actual fact this conclusion is a logical consequence of assuming the joint truth of *all three* of our statements.

What we should now do is to apply the same type of reasoning as in a *reductio ad absurdum*—which is precisely what this argument amounts to: the correct conclusion is that one at least of the hypotheses—our three statements—must be false.

This means that if our first two statements *are* true, it becomes logically absurd to assume that the pupils—in any way whatever—could properly be *convinced* that both were true: for *this* is what leads to the contradiction. Truth of the two statements, and justification of the right of the pupils to assume their truth, are two entirely different matters; and if the first two statements are in fact true, this very fact—logically and automatically—must *prohibit* the pupils from assuming that they are true.

It is then readily checked that the first and second statements *can* be true, provided that the third is false; the examination can occur on any day at all, and can even be left until the Friday, if the teacher wishes.

What a pupil *should* say, before announcement of the examination, is: 'If I could assume—at this moment—that both statements were true, this would guarantee that one of them was in fact false, which is absurd: therefore I *cannot* in fact assume this. For all that I know, the first statement may be false, and there may perhaps be no examination at all; alternatively the second statement may be false, and if the first is true I *would* then be entitled to expect one: but since I can't tell whether the first is true or not, I can't *logically* expect one, unconditionally. So they *can* set an examination today which I *can't* logically expect; once they have done so, the first and second statements will both *become* true, and I shall be convinced of this in retrospect: but I can't logically be convinced of their truth in advance, which is what I should have to be to prove the teacher a liar.'

A pupil who simply says on the Friday 'But I *knew* it would be today!' has in fact reached a correct conclusion *by incorrect reasoning*, and this can be explained to him, as above. His arguments can be dismissed, just as if he had reached the right result by a wrong procedure in the mathematics class: for in the logical problem, as in mathematical problems, the pupils are required not merely to reach a conclusion which *is* correct, but to know that it *must* be correct, since it has been established by valid logical arguments.

In the present case we can give—and have given—*another* valid logical argument, to demonstrate that no valid logical argument can justify expectation of the examination, by the pupils, in the way which the paradox requires.

Ways of dodging the real issue

The last section is a repetition of a discussion which we originally published elsewhere: we then sought to forestall some likely correspondence by remarking that we had designedly emphasized logical impossibilities at the expense of practical impossibilities, since the former were more fundamental. We said we were aware that there were some who brought forward *practical* reasons why the pupils could not be sure of the inevitability of an examination—the master might drop dead, the school burn down, the world come to an end; but that this was not the point. Practical difficulties could be removed by further hypotheses: but with all practical difficulties thus removed, the logical impossibility would remain; and this, we claimed—as we still claim—is what truly resolves the paradox.

Hopes were in vain: the correspondent who had originally sent us this problem as a challenge wrote to argue that the pupils would require supernatural powers to be able to be sure that some catastrophe would not prevent the examination: this, of course, is true. The short answer is that they would then be no more able to make a liar of their teacher; and that this is well worth pointing out. We repeat here what we then said: the problem should not be thought of as an experimental problem involving questions of physics or biology; the paradox can be disposed of, not only for this actual world, but for all possible worlds—even hypothetical worlds where pupils indeed had supernatural powers.

Another reader objected that we had made the pupil exchange 'the reasonable assumption that he may take the two original statements at their face value and see what they are worth for the very much stronger assumption that they are necessarily compatible'. He finally pointed out what no one could dispute: if the first statement is altered to say only that the examination *may* be held, or if the second statement is altered to say that the examination will not be predictable in advance *unless it occurs on the Friday*, this will prevent the conclusion that no unexpected examination is possible.

To this we replied that the whole point is that the face value of the two statements is substantially higher than their true worth, and that taking things at face value always includes an element of risk. Here it means assuming that the statements are compatible with each other, and with a right of the pupils to assume this: which is just what they are not. For the rest, we readily agreed that all difficulty was removed; but pointed out that the paradox was then removed as well. The baby is not to be emptied out with the bath water: and the paradox has to be disposed of by dealing with it, and resolving it—not by ignoring it and substituting something else.

This problem seems to bring out the worst in some people. We have not yet lost friends by it; but we have come near to this, and so have others. We will stop here: in our imagination we hear a nightmare orchestration of axes being ground and knives being whetted—with some thorns giving a crackle under an occasional pot.

Some circular arguments

The number π is ordinarily defined as the ratio of the circumference of a circle to its diameter: but its numerical value can be determined otherwise than by measuring lengths on actual circles. Geometrical arguments led Archimedes to establish upper and lower limits of $3\frac{1}{7}$ and $3\frac{10}{71}$; the first is the familiar approximation $\pi \simeq 22/7$ which is in everyday use. Other methods involving some more advanced branches of mathematics have recently culminated in a value to 100,000 decimals which was derived by an electronic computer; and attainment of a million decimals may well come within the next few years—to test and prove the capabilities of some more advanced machine.

In our third question, our concern is not with estimates of this type, but with claims which have been made for estimates derived from other methods which employ much less expensive physical apparatus. These methods are of an experimental nature, and the calculation depends on relative frequencies of two different possible results of the experiment. This possibility arises from the following considerations.

Suppose we can perform an experiment which has two possible outcomes, where we count one as a success and one as a failure. If we can assume that the probabilities of success and failure remain constant, we can estimate the probability of a success by determining the ratio of the number of successes to the total number of trials, in some series of experiments; and this estimate will become increasingly accurate as the number of trials increases. This might, for instance, form a suitable inspection procedure before acquiring biased coins or loaded dice: actuarial science provides an analogous but more reputable application —the analysis of mortality statistics to provide survival probabilities for purposes of life assurance.

In some situations we may have other grounds for knowing the value of a probability. With a true coin and a fair tossing procedure, the chance of a head (or a tail) is $\frac{1}{2}$; similarly with a fair cubical die, it is $\frac{1}{6}$ for any particular face. We can assume this in theoretical questions: in practical cases we may make experiments to see whether the actual proportion of successes will justify our applying these theoretical values. Many technological applications of statistical theory are similar to this in principle.

In the eighteenth century the French naturalist Comte de Buffon discussed a question in geometrical probability, and showed that the number π was involved in the answer. A practical experiment based on his problem then gives a means of estimating a value of π from the results, and various series of experiments of this type have actually been performed.

The experiments involve the dropping of a needle at random on to a grid of parallel lines. To find the theoretical probability, we replace the needle by a straight-line segment of length l, and assume that the lines have zero breadth and are distant a from each other: we then assume that all orientations of the segment and all positions of its midpoint are equally probable.

The condition $l < a$ ensures that no more than one intersection is possible; and the probability we require is then the proportion of cases in which such an intersection occurs, rather than none. It turns out that this probability is $P = 2l/\pi a$: we can prove this in at least two different ways.

Suppose that instead of a needle we had a circular disc of diameter x: its centre then could equally well be anywhere, on any line perpendicular to all the grid lines, and along this line it could move a distance x equal to its own diameter, while still intersecting a line; then it could move a distance $a-x$ before a new intersection occurred at the next grid line. This gives a representative sample, and the intersections and non-intersections are then in the ratio of x to $a-x$; the proportion of intersections to total trials is x/a, and this is then the probability of an intersection. (The situation here is roughly similar to a game of shove-halfpenny.)

In other cases the only thing that matters is the maximum extension in a direction perpendicular to the grid lines. If our needle invariably fell perpendicular to the lines, its whole length l would count, and the probability would be l/a; if it always fell parallel to them, its effective length would be zero. When all orientations are equally probable, its effective length is its actual length multiplied by the average value of $\cos \theta$ for $-90° \leqslant \theta \leqslant 90°$; an early result in the calculus shows this to have a value of $2/\pi$.

Another way of proving the basic result involves assuming that the needle is divided into a very large number of small equal pieces. Each of the pieces is then equally likely to be anywhere in the plane, with any orientation, and this is equally true if these pieces are formed into any other shape. Over *all* the cases, the total variety of positions of the small segments is the same: there will be just as many intersections in the one case as in the other, in representative samples of the same size; but they will be associated differently.

If we make the small pieces into a closed regular polygon, there will be *two* intersections, or none, in every case, instead of *one* or none, as for the line segment; but the double-intersection results must occur only *half* as often as the single intersections did in the other case.

When the number of pieces increases indefinitely, the polygon tends to a circle of circumference l, with diameter l/π; this has a probability $l/\pi a$ of intersecting one of the lines, as we saw earlier. If we break the circle and start to straighten the arc, we get more and more chances of two single intersections separately, instead of one double one; and when we straighten the arc completely, we will have our straight-line segment back, with no possibility of *other* than single intersections: these then have *double* the last probability—a value of $2l/\pi a$, as before stated.

Too good to be true?

The experimental results fall into two groups. In the decade 1850–60, three determinations were made: a typical one is that of Wolf, who made 5,000 trials and found $\pi \simeq 3\cdot1596$. In the decade 1890–1900, a Captain Fox is stated to have made some 1,120 trials 'with additional precautions', finding $\pi \simeq 3\cdot1419$; and an ever-increasing variety of authorities currently credit an Italian mathematician, described as Lazzerini, with elaborate experiments which obtained $\pi \simeq 3\cdot1415929$ (the true value is $\pi \simeq 3\cdot14159265$) from the somewhat curious number of 3,408 trials.

One authority—J. L. Coolidge—does indeed cast a little doubt on this last achievement, by suggesting that the experimenter may have 'watched his step'. In the absence—he says—of information on the ratio l/a, Coolidge makes a reasonable guess; and on this basis he concludes that there was a probability only of 1 in 69 that the last result occurred under random conditions.

Once one doubt has arisen, others readily follow. We have what purports to be an experiment with an accuracy of about one part in 10 millions: this could be valid only if the constants of the apparatus were known to similar accuracy. Is it conceivable that the length of the needle and the spacing of the lines had their ratio determined to an accuracy comparable with that of a national standard of length? Was there allowance for variable spacing or finite breadth of the lines? And was theoretical randomness achievable to so high a degree?

Even granting that these questions *might* be satisfactorily answered, there is a more awkward objection still. With only 3,408 trials, the number of successes must have been still smaller—not much over 2,000 at the most. Think of what the result must have been *one trial earlier*: with one trial fewer, there was either the same number of successes, or one fewer; an estimate of π from this would have had *a different figure in the third decimal place!*

Now if there are f favourable cases out of a total of t, we estimate π from the equation

$$P = f/t = 2l/\pi a:$$

a mathematician might here have thought l/a was likely to have been a fairly simple fraction; and he might be expected to remember that there are not in fact very many ways in which π can be approximated to high accuracy by the ratio of a pair of relatively small integers.

In the region in which we are interested, π is notoriously *very* different from the general run of numbers: the remarkable approximation 355/113 is not bettered by using larger numbers until we arrive at 52163/16604. But 355/113 gives a value $3\cdot1415929$—in exact agreement with the experimental value: *and the unusual prime number 71 is a factor not only of 355, but of 3,408 as well.*

When we first began to think along these lines, we then realized that if the ratio *l/a* was a fraction which had a numerator of 5, these results could have a very simple explanation: the most likely denominator seemed to be 6 (or perhaps 8), when the number of successes in 3,408 would have to be 1,808 (or 1,356). We next took steps to obtain the original account, in the 1901 volume of *Periodico di Matematica*; and we made two very interesting discoveries.

Evil spells: and how to avoid them

The first discovery was that the author's name is not Lazzerini, but Lazzarini: so we deduced that other authors had presumably copied from one another, without consulting the original—apart from someone at the head of the list, who had been careless. The second was that the ratio *l/a* was there to be found, if anyone looked; this ratio is clearly stated to have been 5/6 in the vital experiments, and the number of successes in the 3,408 trials was in fact 1,808.

Now this makes everything obvious, and anybody can now repeat the Lazzarini experiment with very little difficulty. If the ratio *l/a* is even approximately equal to 5/6, you can assume that it *is* this, and start tossing needles: you must not count the successes unless the number of trials is a multiple of 213; and sooner or later the successes will be the same multiple of 113, and you will have an estimate $\pi \simeq 3 \cdot 1415929$.

If you proceed like Lazzarini, cumulating results, you have about one chance in three of making out at or before 3,408 trials, even if someone is watching you when you start; you may find you can do better by deleting some initial trials afterwards, to start the count at some other trial. Another way is not to cumulate, but to make separate runs of 213; you are then more likely than not to get your 113 on or before your thirteenth trial.

We suggest that it is unnecessary to have an elaborate clockwork arrangement to drop and restore the needle, and a recording apparatus to register a hit, such as our author so carefully describes. If we seem unsympathetic, we have this justification:

From what precedes, Lazzarini might be considered simply to have devoted much effort to little purpose: but in his paper he details his numbers of favourable cases for two series of trials, at 100, 200, 1,000, 2,000, 3,000, and 4,000 trials, with 3,408 given intermediately in one series; and this might perhaps be counted as a mistake.

The whole set, taken together, agrees *much too well* with theory: each run between successive counts gives a result which has a probability of the order of 1 in 10 of arising fairly by chance; more accurately, we can calculate that agreement as good as here, or better, would arise fairly by chance in about one case in ten millions. 'Watching his step' could scarcely give him this on the even thousands: one way or another, he must have had quite remarkable luck in discriminating the occasional doubtful record.

The earlier workers who just failed to get the second decimal had the sort of luck which might ordinarily be expected. To have *confidence* in the nth decimal place, we require comparable experimental accuracy, and about 10^{2n+2} trials: in other words, one million millions, for a fifth decimal—not just a few thousands.

We first published these findings in 1961: we have recently discovered that Mr. N. T. Gridgeman anticipated us by a few months, to publish similar conclusions—but not a true spelling of our hero's name—in an article in *Scripta Mathematica*. This article identifies three authorities— quite properly characterized as 'otherwise judicious'—who have written widely circulating books which quote Lazzarini's result with all undue respect; and it concludes with a description of a similar but simpler experiment of his own which Mr. Gridgeman thinks worthy of similar esteem. Concurring in this belief, we may help to give it wider currency by quoting his account here:

'Handing my pupil a needle, I explained the problem to him. An able and willing youth, he at once bared some floor space and threw the needle down. It fell clear of the edges of the floorboards. He threw again, and this time it fell athwart two boards. Then he measured the boards, which were $3\frac{1}{2}$ inches wide, and the needle, which was $2\frac{3}{4}$ inches long, fetched his slide rule, and presently announced: "I estimate $P = \frac{1}{2}$, and therefore π to be 3·143."'

It may be worth remarking that another paper in the 1901 volume of *Periodico di Matematica* will provide evidence that Lazzarini was interested and skilful in the type of mathematics which is involved in finding good fractional approximations to π. Since sixty years have elapsed since the date of his paper, we have little ground to expect that he is still alive; but we might hope he would now prefer to be rightly judged a most ingenious and plausible hoaxer who succeeded—and still succeeds—in deceiving many who should have known better: for this would place him in a much rarer category than that of the somewhat futile experimenter he might otherwise be thought to be. At least he deserves to have his name spelled correctly in future.

So too does Mr. Gridgeman, whose second initial is printed differently in two places in his article: and the same applies to the present author —should anyone want to quote *him*!

12 *A Christmas Cracker with 100 Birds*

The start of the trail

At a Christmas party in 1960, the author's elder daughter—aged 9—was collecting slips of paper from the remains of some chain-store Christmas crackers. In most cases these had simple jokes or riddles; but she found one which proposed the following problem: '*A farmer sells 100 head of cattle for £100. A cow sells for £5, a sheep for £1, a pig for 1s. How many of each were there?*'

Here we admittedly have a somewhat specialized form of literature, but one which can compare favourably with other types of publication in regard both to numbers printed and to extent of circulation. We imagine that many readers will have met this problem similarly, and may have given it little thought—other than perhaps to look with some amusement at the unrealistic livestock prices, or to dispute whether sheep and pigs can rightly be called cattle. Some may have wondered why an answer was given which ignored the obviously simplest solution 'All were sheep'. The problem nevertheless merits more attention than might at first sight appear.

Balancing cows against pigs

There is little difficulty in the solution of the problem. If we are not just to have 100 sheep, we must make a purchase of cows which is compensated by a purchase of pigs; and if we can thus arrange to spend some whole number of pounds on the same number of cows and pigs taken together, the remainder can then be made up of sheep without disturbing the balance previously obtained.

One solution—as we saw—is to spend nothing on cows and pigs, and have none of these animals: this apart, we can note that each purchase of a cow causes an excess spending of £4 beyond what will make the numbers of animals agree with the cost in pounds, whereas each purchase of a pig will similarly leave an amount of 19s. in hand. To give the required relation overall, we must purchase cows and pigs in numbers which are in inverse ratio to these associated discrepancies; and since only whole numbers are in question, we must have cows and pigs associated in balanced sets of nineteen cows and eighty pigs.

With a budget limited to £100, we can have no more than one such balanced set: we supplement this by a single sheep; and we thus obtain the solution *19 cows, 1 sheep, and 80 pigs*, which of course is the only solution if we require that every different type of animal must actually be represented in the final collection. By making such a requirement explicit, we give the problem the added attraction of a unique solution. The cracker manufacturer omitted to do this: but some others before him have shown more care in this respect.

An Arab mathematician and his problems

A little before A.D. 900, in Egypt, an Arab mathematician began a manuscript: a copy made early in the thirteenth century survives in Leyden; a Hebrew translation from the original Arabic is in Munich, and there may also be a Latin version extant in Paris. The author was probably young, and not so celebrated as he later became. His patient exasperation may evoke sympathy across the centuries (he had evidently met with what Gauss was later to call the clamour of the Boeotians): we translate from a German translation made by H. Suter.

'In the Name of God, the Compassionate, the Merciful: these are the words of Shodja ben Aslam, known as Abu Kamil. I am acquainted with a type of problem which proves to be engrossing, novel and attractive alike to high and low, to the learned and to the ignorant. But when others discuss solutions with one another, they exchange inaccuracies and conjectures, as they see no evident principle or system.

'Many—both high and low—have kept bringing me such questions; and I have given them the unique answer, when there was one: but often there were two, three, four or more answers, and often none. Once, indeed, a problem was brought to me, and I solved it, obtaining very many solutions; I went into it fully, and found that there were 2,678 valid answers. I marvelled at this, only to discover—when I spoke of it—that I was reckoned a simpleton or an incompetent, and strangers looked on me with suspicion.

'So I decided to write a book, to make the matter better understood. This is its beginning. I shall show the working for problems which have several solutions, for problems which have only one, and for problems which have none at all. And after this I shall deal with the problem for which—as I said—there are 2,678 solutions.

'This will sweep away the calumnies and conjectures. I shall justify my assertions, and truth will become evident. The book would become too long if I added everything suggested to me by the large number of solutions of this and similar problems.'

His *Book of Arithmetical Rarities* continues by giving examples of three ways in which problems in linear indeterminate equations can be

formulated—the purchase of different types of edible fowl, the distribution of sums of money with different allowances to men, women,
and children, or the purchase of different types of offensive weapons:
and he explains carefully that only whole-number solutions are in
question. After this he discusses six problems which respectively have
a unique solution, 6, 98, and 304 solutions, no solution, and finally the
promised 2,678 solutions. The first problem—with the unique solution
—is the following: '*You are given 100 drachmae to purchase 100 fowl
of three types. A duck costs 5 drachmae, 20 sparrows cost 1 drachma,
and a hen 1 drachma.*'

So a thousand years have served merely to bring a substitution of
cows, sheep, and pigs for ducks, hens, and sparrows, and the loss of
the qualification implied in the phrase 'of three types'; the only gain
is a neat exploitation of sterling currency, in our modern version.

A problematic medieval manuscript

Some evidence of what has happened in the intervening 1,000 years
is provided by a Latin manuscript which has a date after the writing
of Abu Kamil's book, but before that of the extant copies. This is
entitled *Propositiones ad acuendos juvenes*, which we may translate as
'Problems for sharpening young minds': it was written about A.D. 1000
by a monk of the celebrated monastery of Reichenau—on an off-shore
island in Lake Constance—where one of Charlemagne's successors lies
buried. These are the problems which have been included among the
Works of Alcuin, and they form the earliest collection of mathematical
recreations from a European source: there is no direct evidence that
they are as Alcuin wrote them, or even that Alcuin wrote them at all;
but if they are not the collection which Alcuin is known to have sent
to Charlemagne, there is ample probability that they derive from this
by a line of direct connexion.

In all, the manuscript has fifty-three problems of widely varying
merit. Some are simple mensuration problems, with answers which in
some cases involve crude approximations only; one question—No. 43—
is a trap, to discover those who will attempt to divide either 300 or 30
into three odd numbers. Two ferry problems are included which we
have considered elsewhere in this book: the problem of the three
husbands and their wives is No. 17, in the Reichenau text, and No. 18
is the problem of the traveller with the wolf, the goat, and the cabbages.
A problem on transporting corn in three journeys—No. 52—is followed
by an answer which requires four journeys, with neither explanation
nor apology: similar problems are nowadays made to refer to explorers,
who may or may not have motorized transport; but here the beast of
burden whose continued sustenance forms the essence of the problem
is in fact a camel.

Elsewhere in the manuscript we find another problem which involves camels; this is No. 39, which is as follows: '*Concerning an Eastern buyer. A certain man of the East wished to buy a mixed collection of 100 live-stock for 100 solidi: and he ordered his servant to pay five solidi for a camel, one solidus for an ass, and to buy sheep at a price of twenty sheep for a solidus. Say, who will—how many camels and asses and sheep were exchanged for the 100 solidi?*'

The accompanying solution takes the form: 'Take ten nine times, and five, to make 95: that is, 19 camels are bought for 95 solidi. Add to these one, that is, an ass for one solidus; this makes 96. And then take twenty times four, to make 80; that is, 80 sheep for 4 solidi. So add 19, and 1, and 80, to get 100. These are the animals. And then add 95, and 1, and 4, to get 100 solidi. So the beasts together make 100, and the solidi 100, at one and the same time.'

This problem is noteworthy for its direct reference to the Orient; but the manuscript has five other problems of similar type: in one of these—No. 47—a bishop orders a dozen loaves to be divided among a dozen clerics, at the rate of two loaves for a priest, a half-loaf for a deacon, and a quarter-loaf for a reader. Problems of similar type soon became popular in medieval times, in the German, Italian, and other arithmetic manuals which began to promote the more widespread competence in calculation necessitated by the spread of commerce: they also began to appear in recreational collections; and one or other of these lines leads onwards to our Christmas cracker.

Contacts and conflicts between East and West

Early manuals expressed their numbers in Roman numerals, not always in the classical form: in the Alcuin text, our problem has a serial number which is written as xxxviiii, and the solution involves other numbers which are written as xcv, xviiii, and iiii. (Readers were spared this distraction, in our translation.) Elsewhere in this book—where we discuss Fibonacci numbers, in relation to Wythoff's game—we mention the *Liber Abaci* of Fibonacci (otherwise Leonardo of Pisa) which did much to promote the replacement of Roman numerals by numerals of the system we now use. These so-called Arabic numerals—having a scheme of place-values, using only ten digits, with zero included—are an Indian invention which reached Europe through Arab intermediaries; and the like is true of the first beginnings of algebra, whose very name displays an Arabic connexion.

In both cases, Abu Kamil may well have played an important part. He also wrote a treatise on the pentagon and the decagon, which is extant in a Latin version and in a fifteenth-century Hebrew version which itself appears to have been translated from a prior translation into Spanish. This treatise makes a skilful application of algebraic methods to geometrical questions (a practice which school examiners thought fit to allow only a thousand years later, too late for the benefit of the present author!): many of Abu Kamil's results appear in almost identical form, in Leonardo's works; and Leonardo elsewhere deals with arithmetical problems of the type which we have earlier discussed.

Leonardo of Pisa is one link connecting European with Arab and Oriental mathematics; and the Hebrew translations are evidence of another, indicating Jewish contacts with Moorish Spain. We may recall the Spanish education of Gerbert, who became Pope as Silvester II in A.D. 999, and suffered accusations of witchcraft—not unconnected with his studies of algebra. It becomes quite possible to imagine that our cracker problem may have reached Reichenau after travelling with Charlemagne's paladins back over the Pyrenees through the Pass of Roncesvalles. Failing some such connexion, it is difficult to account for the presence of the camels; and there is some confirmation in the fact that the other camel problem shows evidence of some damage in transit: for comparative mathematical achievements—at the relevant date—make it plausible to assume that this problem originated among Arabs who could solve it, after which it was transmitted onwards by Christians who could not.

One? More? Or none?

Abu Kamil's main contention—that some of these problems have several solutions, some a unique solution, and some none—could be established by keeping prices as in the problem which we quoted, with a variation of the number of fowls and money-units. With 50 in place of 100, we could have no balanced collection: with 200 in place of 100 we could have either one, or two; and with larger numbers, as many as we liked. This would suffice to make the point: but actually he takes another course, retaining the requirement of 100 fowls for 100 pieces, and varying the prices.

However, the Christian sources have no monopoly of the errors: the Arabic texts have their errors too. The third problem has ducks at 2 *dr.*, hens at 1 *dr.*, doves two for 1 *dr.*, and sparrows ten for 1 *dr.*; and a marginal note by a commentator claims—correctly—that there are ninety-eight solutions (as we said earlier), and not ninety-six, as is stated in the main text.

In the texts in question, some preliminary algebra is made to indicate an enumerative process for deriving solutions in a systematic succession: this is illustrated in part, and finally summarized—a procedure very liable to errors, both in the original and in any copy. Additional evidence of this is the fact that in the text of Abu Kamil's *chef-d'œuvre*—

in which there are ducks at 2 *dr.*, hens at 1 *dr.*, doves two for 1 *dr.*, ring-doves three for 1 *dr.*, and larks four for 1 *dr.*—the number of solutions is stated twice as 2,696 and once as 2,676: the latter figure has apparently been accepted as correct, by Suter and others; but the true figure in fact is 2,678. (We gave our author the benefit of this correction, in our translation.)

A count of 2,678

To justify the correction, we can apply another method of argument, as follows: we can take a hint from Abu Kamil, but use geometry to help with the algebra, rather than the other way round. As in our solution for the cracker problem, we seek to find balanced collections; and here the hens can serve as final makeweights, in collections where all excess of expenditure is invariably caused by a purchase of ducks.

Ring-doves can form part of balanced collections only if they are included three at a time in sets of 5, together with two ducks. Doves will balance with ducks in sets of 3, if there are two doves and a duck; and larks will balance with ducks in sets of 7, if these have four larks and three ducks: but one each of these last two sets will give a collection which can be divided into two balanced sets of 5, each containing two ducks, one dove, and two larks.

All solutions must therefore consist of combinations of balanced sets of 3, 5, or 7, supplemented by one or more hens. We shall need at least one 5, for the ring-doves: for doves and larks, we may have sets of 3 and 7 in which they appear separately, with or without a single set of 5 in which both appear together; we here need consider only one set of 5, or none, since we can consider two such sets in the alternative form of a 3 (with all the doves) and a 7 (with all the larks).

We have then to consider how we can sum multiples of 3 and of 7 in order to obtain something less than 100, to be supplemented by one or more hens; and likewise to give something less than 95, for similar treatment after supply of a single balanced set of 5.

We can then take squared paper, to assign a square to each allowable combination—moving to the right for each additional 3 and upwards for each additional 7, as in Figures 12*A* and 12*B*. In the first case we set an upper limit of 99, and in the second we set an upper limit of 94: in both cases we require the presence of at least one set of 3, and of at least one set of 7.

We divide the squares into sets according to the smaller of the two numbers which specify how many sets of 3 and of 7 the corresponding collections contain. The diagrams indicate these sets of squares, and a first column of numbers is given at the right of each diagram, to indicate how many squares are involved in each set concerned: at each advance, as we proceed to L-shaped regions which contain increasing

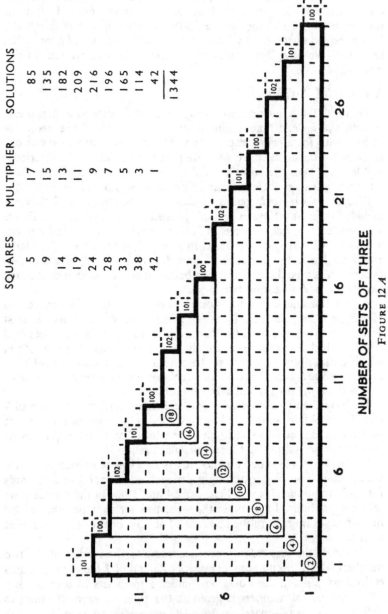

SQUARES	MULTIPLIER	SOLUTIONS
5	17	85
9	15	135
14	13	182
19	11	209
24	9	216
28	7	196
33	5	165
38	3	114
42	1	42
		1344

NUMBER OF SETS OF THREE

FIGURE 12 A

NUMBER OF SETS OF SEVEN

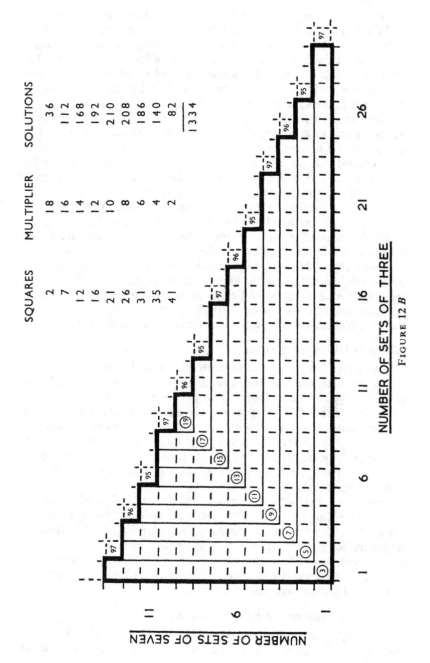

FIGURE 12 *B*

numbers of squares, the increase is two units in excess of the number of additional squares which extend beyond the previous upper and right-hand limits. We then insert numerals on a diagonal line, to indicate how many balanced sets of 5 we can form after combining identical numbers of sets of 3 and of 7, adding the odd set of 5 if there is one: this number is the same for all the cases which are represented by the individual squares in any one L-shaped region.

For each of the squares, in any region, there may be a surplus of doves, in an excess of sets of 3, or of larks, in an excess of sets of 7; but sometimes neither, and never both at once. We have to reserve at least one set of 5 for a balanced set with ring-doves, and another for a balanced set with both doves and larks; these can be secured by modification of a set of 3 and another of 7, since we have demanded the presence of at least one of each: and apart from this, any other possible sets of 5 may be assigned in either of these two ways. This will automatically provide for the inclusion of ducks; and we have already set limits which will provide for the inclusion of hens.

If $n+1$ sets of 5 are possible, we can have up to n of either type; so we have n different allowable ways of assigning them. We thus obtain multipliers n as in our second columns, to the right of our diagrams; and products of entries in our first two columns then give entries for our third columns, which we can sum to derive a total of 2,678 solutions.

Birds of China and India

It appears that no record of a problem exactly equivalent to our cracker problem survives from any earlier source; but earlier problems of similar type are to be found—always concerned with ornithological commerce. Three Chinese problems involving 100 cocks or hens or chickens date from the sixth century A.D.: with a price-list involving numbers 5, 3, $\frac{1}{3}$, Chang Chiu-Chien gives three solutions, correctly, but with scanty explanation; for prices 5, 4, $\frac{1}{4}$, Chen-Luan gives the unique solution, correctly; but for prices 4, 3, $\frac{1}{3}$ he gives only one solution, although there are two.

Similar questions were discussed in India, both before and after the time of Abu Kamil. This may connect his problems—professional and personal—with an original Chinese source. Possibly there was some return traffic: a later Indian author, Bhaskara, includes geese, cranes, and peacocks, as well as Abu Kamil's ubiquitous doves, in a problem which calls for a rajah to be presented with what we suppose are 100 ornamental (rather than edible) birds.

A contour map of bird distributions

Bhaskara's prices show some signs of artificial contrivance: five doves for 3 *dr.*, seven cranes for 5 *dr.*, and nine geese for 7 *dr.*, with peacocks priced at three for 9 *dr*. Again we have a unique species—peacocks—which alone can be used to redress a lack of balance in one of the two directions; and one peacock will balance five doves in a set of 6, seven cranes in a set of 8, or nine geese in a set of 10. We can then use squared paper to find solutions as in Figure 12C. Each new set of nine geese and a peacock causes a step upwards in the diagram, each new set of seven cranes and a peacock causes a step to the right, and each new

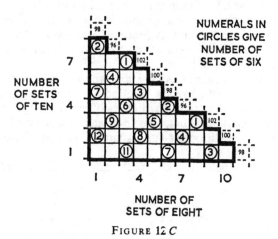

FIGURE 12 C

set of five doves and a peacock causes a step perpendicularly to the plane of the diagram, which we can show in terms of spot heights as in a contour map.

The insertion of a few solutions which we may derive empirically will display linear regularities which we can use to develop the whole set of solutions: this gives excellent security against oversights and errors. The number of peacocks is easily found as a sum of three numbers which specify the row, the column, and the spot height associated with any solution: there are sixteen ways of making the required thank-offering to the rajah, if peacocks can be bought individually; but only six ways, if peacocks are available only in lots of three—as the price might perhaps imply.

Most of the historical problems will similarly yield to an attack by simple arithmetical and geometrical methods. Later developments in mathematics have indeed brought more powerful but more elaborate algebraic procedures which could take account of mixtures of more varieties, with less simply related prices: but these are sledge-hammers which we saw no need to bring out for problems where simpler forms of nutcrackers can amply suffice.

The end of the road

Readers will now understand why we intervened to save the cracker slip from impending destruction. We have preserved it as a somewhat novel reminder of a trail which spans 1,500 years of time and stretches half-way round the world: for this trail is no narrow or insignificant path—it is a main highway in the spread of knowledge and civilization in the Western world. The advance of mathematics is a major—but sometimes overlooked—aspect of this development; and throughout its record there is abundant evidence of the ways in which many of the races of mankind have added their contributions at different times, and in different fashions.

The major factor behind mathematical progress has always been the intellectual challenge of currently unsolved problems, supplemented by stimuli arising from important possibilities of practical application: but at all times and in all localities, some mathematicians have been led to see mathematics—additionally—as a source of recreational enjoyment for themselves and others.

This is a view which we share, and would seek to promote: hence this book.

Postscript

Earlier in this book we have considered some varied topics where we could include some original contributions of our own in a fairly complete and integrated treatment. Many authors have considered other types of recreational material which we do not handle here.

Numeral references will be used to direct the reader to two lists at the end of this postscript: the numbering is serial through the two lists jointly. The first list contains a selection of general works on recreational mathematics: each of these handles a wide variety of topics, and should have much to offer to any interested reader of the present work. (We include foreign-language works, some in languages of which we personally know little or nothing: diagrams, mathematical formulae, or numerical tables can convey a welcome message across language barriers; we can vouch for this from our own experience.) The second list gives more specialized references which have direct relevance to topics dealt with in different parts of this book.

General References

The Coxeter revision of the Rouse Ball book is the most comprehensive and authoritative English-language work in this field. Many who read these words will already know this: others are recommended to confirm this for themselves. Nearly all mathematical recreations have a connexion with something which has been treated either by the original author, or by his reviser; and on many topics we need look no further to find everything that we may want. Earlier editions contain much material—later replaced—which may still be of interest to many.

Books and articles by Martin Gardner are no less authoritative, but they are written to appeal to a wider public. His world-wide circle of correspondents includes many recreational innovators, some of considerable academic eminence; he frequently gives a first publication of something quite new, handled with great charm and skill. He notices currently available commercial material, and has made notable inventions and discoveries all of his own.

Dudeney and Loyd were prolific inventors of mathematical puzzles which they presented in anecdotal settings (often with appropriate illustrations). Many of their puzzles first appeared in various periodicals. Much that they originated continues to stimulate later authors—

sometimes to praiseworthy emulation, sometimes to straightforward theft with scissors and paste.

The books by Abraham have much diverse but interesting material: they have recently been reprinted, and may especially appeal to younger readers. The books by Mott-Smith and by Graham are more modern collections which have a good measure of novelty in many places.

The Northrop book is to be recommended for its handling of paradoxes and fallacies. The Beiler book—though limited to numerical recreations—is notable for the variety of number-theory results which it can successfully explain to the interested but mathematically inexpert reader. The Hutton four-volume collection is a legacy from the more generous styles of writing of the past: it handles scientific amusements generally—not mathematical only—and is a translation (amplified) of the seventeenth-century French work of Ozanam, of similar comprehensiveness and length.

Of works in French, we first mention the seventeenth-century collection of Bachet—the first of the modern era: this has transmitted something to nearly all its successors, while being intermittently reprinted itself (the most recent version is still in print). We continue with the four-volume Lucas collection, roughly a larger and more leisured French counterpart to Rouse Ball; scarce until recently, it is now welcome as a photographic reprint, slightly reduced from the original size of page.

The third French title is a most attractive book by Sainte-Laguë, who takes a limited selection of topics—much as we did ourselves—which he handles with unobtrusive authority and with much charm of presentation, giving some of his material a fuller treatment than will be found elsewhere. (We recommend this to any who are studying both French and mathematics. It could be put into a school library, with hopes of a useful cross-fertilization!) The other work by this author has much varied material—notably on map-colouring—and a list of 348 recreational references.

As originally published in Brussels, the work by Kraïtchik had some material which was not retained in later French editions. The English translation is of the shorter version: it is a good second choice for those whose first choice would be Rouse Ball.

The Italian book by Ghersi is the reprint of a fifty-year-old work which provoked Ahrens to make some charges of plagiarism, when it first appeared. It is a small square-format volume of 700 pages of small print, which explores many by-ways of more serious mathematics—curves and linkages, for instance—as well as collecting material on purely recreational topics. In his postscript, the current reviser makes an unfortunate claim to have disproved the existence of some Latin squares whose actual discovery occurred recently—to settle a long-standing question in precisely the opposite sense!

From Brazil, in Portuguese, and in Spanish translation, from Uruguay, we have a novel volume by Malba Tahan—not so much an *alias* as a legally valid *alter ego* (by presidential decree) of Senhor Júlio César de Mello e Souza, who combined his interests as orientalist and mathematician to provide a mathematical-recreational romance of the progress from obscurity to eminence of a puzzle-solver in Baghdad of the Caliphs. Many well-known puzzles are explained, illustrated, and solved, as the plot develops; in the closing paragraphs the hero Beremis achieves marriage, conversion to Christianity, and an exit to Constantinople before the sack of Baghdad by the Mongols.

The Dutch work by Schuh contains earlier recreational inventions of a professor who still can write on similar topics as a nonagenarian: he has much original material, of which he gives an exhaustive account. The Swiss work by Sperling—we select one of several by this author—is written for younger readers: it has an avuncular presentation—by one Onkel Witzig, indeed; and has good descriptions of some puzzles involving practical topology. (This book might help a young mathematician with his German!)

In German, from Germany itself, there is a counterpart to Rouse Ball in the three-volume work of Schubert, later (and currently) available in single-volume revision; there is also the two-volume treatise—the word is inescapable—by Ahrens, a work most amply and valuably supplied with full historical references, back to medieval origins. At more popular level we have a collection of fairly standard material by Lietzmann, and a smaller but more modern collection by Gündel.

We also mention the *Anschauliche Geometrie* of Hilbert and Cohn-Vossen—some lectures of a master mathematician put into book form by a disciple—which can show that a popular presentation of really significant mathematics can be made as fascinating as any recreational diversions. An English translation—*Geometry and the Imagination*—is now available, after what seems a strange delay of about twenty years.

In scope somewhat intermediate between this and straightforward recreation, there is the originally Polish work of Steinhaus—*Kaleidoscope of Mathematics* in most of its present dozen of languages, but *Mathematical Snapshots* to the English-speaking world. We envy those who have the first English edition—printed in Poland: this had a quite fascinating collection of cardboard objects in a pocket at the end. Later editions have had to forgo this, but they include new material as some compensation. From Poland we also have a pair of works by Jeleński which deal with more standard recreational topics.

Among Russian titles we confine ourselves to directly recreational works. (Besides these there are many popular presentations of various fields of mathematics, at elementary level, in which recreational illustration is not forgotten. Their value—educational no less than recreational

—is being currently recognized by translation into English: with some titles the translation process is now a two-valued function!)

The first Perelman title is an older work, including some physics with its mathematics. Inexpensive translations—into English, and into Spanish, to our knowledge—are available for other works by this author, from the Russian foreign-language publishing organization. The Kordemsky title is a 600-page collection somewhat similar in level to the work of Lucas. It is full of diagrams which tell their tale independently of understanding of the text; this is true also of many formulae and much numerical material. This book is printed by the 100,000 in Russia, and is available at a remarkably low price. Those who will pay more for a language they understand better can have a French translation—in two volumes, separating the easy from the less easy: but not yet an English one. The Domoryad title is a more standard collection, with some novelties; an English translation is here available—a benefit to be weighed against a nearly tenfold increase in cost.

We bring this international tour to a close by mentioning that we have two Japanese works by Fujimura, in which we have found some diagrams which we know we can understand (even to the correction of an error), and some numbers which we think we understand. For the rest, we realize only that the sequence of characters on the page differs by 90° as between two otherwise somewhat similar books. We would include these in our list if we knew how to do it.

Those who seek a recurrent source of stimulation will find this each month in *Scientific American*, and annually in *Eureka*. In the former they will have Martin Gardner's work as it appears—now about three years ahead of its collection in book form: with the latter they will make contact with the lighter side of British mathematical activities at Cambridge. The American *Recreational Mathematics Magazine* had much varied material, some of considerable interest: regrettably, it has had to discontinue publication after only fourteen issues. (Among other grounds for regret, we note that claims made in respect of a quite fallacious proof of the cubic case of Fermat's Last Theorem, in the final issue, must now stand with no subsequent retraction!)

Readers who may be still unsatisfied are referred to the title at the head of the list—a bibliography of over 2,000 items comprising both books and periodical articles, classified by content. This work by Schaaf is an inexpensive paperback, now in its second revision. It will lead the reader to many specialized works omitted from our lists not because of any lack of merit.

One More River to Cross

It would have seemed improper to begin our book with anything other than difficult-journey problems (here we gladly respect a precedent set by Lucas, Ahrens, and Sainte-Laguë). Some of these puzzles are perhaps the best known of all puzzles: with many centuries of background, they now have a world-wide circulation—we can produce accounts of the three-couples problem in at least a dozen languages, from Latin to Japanese.

Anyone at all can immediately understand what is involved; and interest may be aroused all the more readily because these problems appear as questions of logic rather than of conventional mathematics. It is easy for anybody to attempt them (possibly practically, with such aids as coins, counters, court cards from a pack, or pieces from standard board games); and many will solve them—efficiently, or not, with various mixtures of insight and perseverance—before their first enthusiasm fails. At the same time they give scope for showing how trial-and-error can be replaced by methods which have more power and elegance—an objective which we keep in mind both here and elsewhere.

Solutions of similar problems which we do not discuss can be found in other works. In particular, Sainte-Laguë (19) discusses a general method whereby any number of jealous husbands can satisfy all their travel requirements, using a boat for only two persons, provided that they can make use of an island to secure acceptable three-part separations of the personnel. He also gives a more efficient procedure for the case of four couples only.

Kraïtchik (21) shows how the general case can be solved, whether or not the wives are able to row: in the latter case he is quoting Tarry, whose consideration of similar difficulties for polygamists is included in additions to the French translation of the book of Rouse Ball (1). Some applications of graph theory to these problems—and to many other problems—are discussed in a standard text by Berge (38), and at a more popular level by Ore (39).

We know no treatment other than our own which points out implications of symmetry and reversal in the three-couple problem; and we think we are the first to produce the problem of the father and his five sons—a higher analogue of the historic problem of the wolf, goat, and cabbages.

Berge and Ore give graph-theory diagrams for this last problem: we have been able to give a simpler diagram here (and feasible diagrams for other problems), by realizing that we can manage with a halved multiplicity of junction points if we make each point correspond to two situations which differ only by reversal of the banks of the river; we then require that an appropriate cyclic path must be formed from an *odd* number of steps.

Ahrens (27) is now a somewhat rare book; we take this chance to quote from it not the more traditional Latin quatrain which is also to be found in Hutton (16), Lucas (18), and other works, but a thirteenth-century couplet—less familiar—which makes ingenious use of the potentialities of gender-inflexion in Latin:

> *Binae, sola, duae, mulier, duo, vir mulierque,*
> *Bini, sola, duae, solus, vir cum muliere.*

These two hexameters give eleven successive passenger lists, alternatively to our tabular solution—at less length, and perhaps more memorably!

False Coins and Trial Balances

We have no wish to list everything which has been written—or even everything we have read—on coin-weighing problems. We shall do better if we give some references which have something of continuing interest.

In attributing the problem with light-weight counterfeits to the period of the First World War, we give credence to some who assure us of their personal recollection of its magazine publication at that time. A reference (40) indicates that the problem was a known one in 1945; there may well be earlier references of which we are unaware.

Grossman (41) suggests the generalization to counterfeits which may have errors of weight in either sense: this seems to be the first publication on the standard twelve-coin problem. Later developments suggest he was dealing with a current problem, rather than producing a new variant of his own; if so, the original inventor remains unknown. The allegations of war damage and projected retribution are made by Littlewood (42).

Dyson (43) gave a ternary-scale treatment with digits 0, 1, 2; he remarks that an earlier note by Goodstein stopped short of dealing with the true maximum number of coins. (This earlier note has since been cited in isolation.) Some results by others are noticed editorially in the same issue. C. A. B. Smith (44) followed with what probably remains the best single reference available. Observations from the information-theory aspect are made by Kellogg and Kellogg (45): our treatment of unilateral and bilateral suspects in the sequential case is similar to that of Kendall and Thomas (46).

We have reason to think that C. A. B. Smith was a large part of Blanche Descartes (47). Those who wish to subscribe to *Eureka* should contact its Business Manager (address: The Arts School, Bene't Street, Cambridge, England). Steinhaus (31) provides his Polish readers with coin selections specified by Polish words of mnemonic significance only. His English readers have a sequential solution pictorially illustrated (an error in the second edition is corrected in the third): part of this solution shows that Smith's list of useful weighing selections is not exhaustive, though it may well be sufficient.

The use of ternary-scale weights goes back to Bachet (17), who showed how weights of 1, 3, 9, 27 units could weigh up to 40 units: not all of his countless successors give him proper credit. Angle-gauges now used in engineering consist of wedges for 1°, 3°, 9° and 14°, with a 30°–60°–90° triangle: with these, combinations of three or fewer will give all angles by steps of 1° to 90° (and indeed to 96°). The triangle is an obvious convenience and economy; but if it were replaced by wedges for 40°, 70°, 103°—as in the scheme envisaged in (48)—no more than three wedges at a time would be needed, to provide unit steps as far as 120°.

Conversions to binary-scale numbers can be simpler still if we note that in our repeated divisions by 2 the unit remainders imply an odd number in the previous line and the zero remainders an even number. We can therefore start with a given number and halve successively, disregarding fractions: odd and even numbers then respectively imply unit and zero digits in the binary representation, in order of increasing significance. This is the basis for a 'Russian peasant' method of multiplication which is considered in many of our general references, and elsewhere.

New Weighs with False Coins

Smith (44) has an attractive mnemonic notation for coins of varying status: he uses A, B, C, D, E respectively to denote above-weight suspects, below-weight suspects, correct coins, doubtful coins (bilaterally suspect), and the extra (or notional) coin. He uses −1, 0, 1 as ternary digits, as does Grossman in a later note (49): two comprehensive papers by Hammersley (50, 51) have a similar basis. The reversed-sign treatment for coins labelled 1, 4, 13, 40, . . . is due to Grossman: we think our replacement of this by a single exception—when this is possible, as for four or five weighings—is new.

The problem in which the balance is supplied with its weights is posed at the end of Smith (44), but is left to the reader: apparently it is to be credited to Smith's friend, Mr. H. Wright. This problem has been handled by Sprague (52), who arranges to make many discriminating ratios give the numbers of the coins directly: but this is not possible for them all, and we have preferred a different treatment here.

The analogous problems for a spring balance (or weighing machine) seem to have had their first publication in *Recreational Mathematics Magazine*. Hunter and Fujimura (53) gave the problem for five good coins and a counterfeit, with three weighings. Fujimura (54) continued with the case of four weighings, and one counterfeit in fifteen: he has published on both problems in Japanese. In discussing these problems, we note that we need not in fact have assurance of a counterfeit—all coins can be proved good, if indeed this is the case. Both for the beam balance and for the spring balance, we have shown how to make efficient use of larger numbers of weighings.

In the problems where determination of actual weights is required, our personal preference is for methods designed to make a discriminating ratio take values which are distinct for different locations of the faulty coin. This compels us to add proved good coins, in a later weighing, in our solution for the last of these problems.

An alternative method is to make a greater number of combinations of the weighing results, and to note which combinations give true ratios in sympathy with the numbers of coins implicitly concerned. Individual coins can then be identified by distinguishing combinations which give true ratios from combinations which do not. This is what Fujimura does: we have seen similar solutions by Mr. A. W. Joseph and by Mr. Th. A. Metakides.

Some of these solutions include tables of formulae for calculating the true and false weights after the identification of the false coin has been made: but there are many alternative forms possible for these formulae. Seeing no strong grounds for preferences among them, we prefer to identify the bad coin, and then to calculate and apply corrections which remove error effects from the weighings: this gives a uniform procedure which readily provides checks against mistakes. However, all these coin problems leave scope for a great variety of equally valid solutions; readers could well be led to something which they may prefer to what we have given here.

Jug and Bottle Department

Ahrens (27) quotes a thirteenth-century reference for the problem of halving eight measures of wine, using measures for 5 units and 3 units: he assigns Tartaglia's four-container problem to a work dated 1556. (He also states—on the authority of Arago—that it was success with a problem of this type which led Poisson to find that his true vocation was mathematics, rather than either law or surgery, with which he had had little success!)

The first problem is also to be found in Bachet (17), where there is a tabular solution, and a good discussion based on a backward analysis. Similar problems have commonly introduced some measure of diversion into books on arithmetic, and more sophisticated variants have been created by Dudeney and Loyd: see, for instance, No. 365 of (5), Nos. 184 and 185 of (7), Nos. 52 and 108 of (8), and No. 23 of (9).

We may suspect that Dudeney had systematic methods which he never published: at all events, it was a remark of his which seemingly inspired the work of M. C. K. Tweedie (55) which is the basis of our own treatment here. Tweedie introduces a triangle of reference, like that of homogeneous co-ordinates in plane projective geometry: we have employed this in other types of problems, and have used the three-dimensional analogue for four-measure problems.

With isometric paper—available in pads from technical stationers —these problems can be solved with much less effort than would be involved in writing tabular lists of contents; and the geometry may give obvious demonstrations of properties which otherwise may be difficult to establish.

For instance, Ahrens (27) devotes much space to noting and extending a result of Schubert (26), to show that with measures satisfying $a > b > c$ we can make all integral two-part divisions of a units if b and c have no common factor and satisfy $b+c-2 \leqslant a \leqslant 2b+2c+1$: this becomes almost a triviality if we consider how a parallelogram of sides b and c is involved in the graphical treatment.

Some of our work will suggest a general problem which does not seem yet to have been solved: can we specify conditions—in terms of the numbers involved—to determine whether or not some desired state is impossible of attainment because lines from its representative point generate a closed path which meets no vertex of the graphical diagram? Two of our figures illustrate cases of this type: it also is the situation which we have called 'going round in circles', in relation to the emptying of a barrel. Though we should like to be able to recognize this situation in advance, we do not know how to do this: perhaps we may stimulate some reader to produce a solution.

Our 35-move problem (to produce two single-unit quantities from 22 units, using measures for 7 and 12 units) was deliberately invented to be an especially troublesome variant on a theme taken from Dudeney: the puzzle composer seeking what we may term a *pessimum*, as others seek an *optimum*!

Our final section on mixed drinks derives from one of the problems included in a still-continuing annual series set by the Swedish firm *LKB Produkter* as New Year greetings to their customers (56): this one was notable for the inclusion of a catch question which inspired a Nobel Laureate to some ingenious trickery which earned him a supply of whisky!

A Gamut of Geometry from A to Y

The game of Vish is described by J. L. Synge in (57). Within the limits of Euclid's postulates, some arguments based on inaccurate figures can prove all triangles to be equilateral, or two angles to be equal when one is a right angle and the other is not. These (and other fallacies) are instructively discussed in a book by Maxwell (58) and in a recent English translation of a Russian work (59).

Puzzles and Paradoxes

A rigorous set of postulates for geometry—due to Hilbert—is to be found in (30). These are made to include an explicit assumption that a straight line cannot pass through a triangle and intersect the perimeter only once: this can plug the loop-hole which Euclid overlooked, and can thus remove the flaw which the fallacies in fact exploit.

We first met the 25-point geometry in an unusual little book (60) by Lillian R. Lieber (illustrated in an exotic vein by her husband). Written explicitly for 'the celebrated man-in-the-street', this aims to let him run as he reads, by dividing the text in the manner of free verse. Short phrases—involving single ideas—are each given a line of their own; and implications of logical reasoning are discussed not for mathematics only. (These authors have other books of similar form.)

Geometries with a finite number of points had been considered by Veblen and Bussey (61), but predominantly from the projective viewpoint. So far as we know, the Lieber book has the earliest explicit consideration of related metrical implications—in regard to lengths, angles, and equalities between these. This extension provides closer correspondence with the elementary geometry which is familiar to many. It was this which led us to develop the rhombic-lattice diagram, and to make our enumerations of triangles and quadrilaterals (this forced us to discover the ambiguous-size quadrilateral!); and we went on to examine further correspondence in some other branches of metrical geometry which upper-form pupils may well meet at school.

Race-track Problems and Legal Fictions

A note by Walker (62) provided the basis for our treatment of the race-track problem; this led us to seek our representation of alignments and angles for the 25 points, in terms of 6 pointers moving on a dial of 25 letters and 6 numerals. There is now a monograph by Ryser (63) which considers difference-sets (along with a mass of other material concerned with number theory, arrangements of elements in sets, and statistical design).

Ryser is our authority for stating that prime and prime-power cases are now known to be the only possibilities for $N \leqslant 1600$. The first of the impossibilities (for $N = 57, n = 7, p = 6$) was established in (64) by Kirkman—the originator of a celebrated problem of arranging fifteen schoolgirls in groups by threes (considered in many of our general references).

Those who may wish to explore prime-power cases—and the related topic of Galois fields—can have the benefit of an elementary introduction by Goodstein (65), and of some numerical tables by Bussey (66). Less heroic readers may be glad to have one basic division for each of the lowest cases: so we quote results first given by Singer (67), and extend the list to cover two more cases:

$p = 2$: 0, 1, 3, 7;
$p = 3$: 0, 1, 3, 9, 13;
$p = 4$: 0, 1, 4, 14, 16, 21;
$p = 5$: 0, 1, 3, 8, 12, 18, 31;
$p = 7$: 0, 1, 3, 13, 32, 36, 43, 52, 57;
$p = 8$: 0, 1, 3, 7, 15, 31, 36, 54, 63, 73;
$p = 9$: 0, 1, 3, 9, 27, 49, 56, 61, 77, 81, 91;
$p = 11$: 0, 1, 3, 15, 46, 71, 75, 84, 94, 101, 112, 128, 133;
$p = 13$: 0, 1, 3, 24, 41, 52, 57, 66, 70, 96, 102, 149, 164, 176, 183;
$p = 16$: 0, 1, 3, 7, 15, 31, 63, 90, 116, 127, 136, 181, 194, 204, 233, 238, 255, 273;
$p = 17$: 0, 1, 3, 45, 58, 62, 73, 96, 110, 122, 142, 149, 178, 196, 267, 277, 286, 302, 307;
$p = 19$: 0, 1, 3, 13, 28, 51, 65, 82, 86, 104, 112, 145, 201, 212, 217, 241, 261, 307, 339, 375, 381.

The last number given is N, the number of units in the full circuit: multipliers less than N and prime to N will give the other divisions. Six such multipliers will produce an equivalent division, when p is a prime; the corresponding multiplicity will be 12, 18, 24, ... for squares, cubes, fourth powers ... of primes.

To obtain a full set of non-equivalent divisions, for any of these cases, the easiest way is to use the smallest possible multiplier repeatedly —removing multiples of N where possible—until the equivalent of a previous division arises: then to change to a new multiplier, continuing until the full set of non-equivalent divisions is secured. For the successive cases given, there are

$$1, 2, 1, 5, 6, 4, 6, 18, 20, 6, 51, 42$$

non-equivalent divisions to be found.

This will give readers what is needed for exploring possibilities for arrangements of feeler gauges, such as those we gave for 60 units and 61 units. Similarly they will find that with weights limited to one on each scale, they can have a set of 20 to weigh all units from 1 to 138, if they choose a set

1	15	48	49	58	79	104	107	111	119
124	130	146	148	184	198	231	232	241	262

in place of the more regular set

1	2	3	4	5	6	7	8	9	10
21	32	43	54	65	76	87	98	109	119

which has been offered as the solution for a similar problem which required weighings only up to 118 units.

From Ryser they will discover that a race-course owner whose track was 37 units in circumference could place nine cameras to divide this into sections (7, 1, 4, 6, 2, 1, 2, 4, 10): he could then count on running races over 1, 2, 3,..., 36 units even if any one of his cameras was out of action; for with this arrangement every distance is available twice over, and alternative courses never make common use of any of the cameras. A double division is possible for 11 units, in a scheme (3, 2, 1, 1, 4): but in this case the alternative courses are invariably contiguous; and *no* camera could fail here without making *some* distance unavailable.

Alignment tables for the 121-point geometry were included in the record of a lecture by Church (68): we have a copy by courtesy of Professor Lillian Lieber.

The Desargues configuration is considered in (30) in relation to space of four dimensions: the double-numeral labelling is given by Coxeter (69). Robinson (70) considers the axiomatic basis of geometry, and the implications of the Desargues configuration in this context. The other configuration of ten points aligned by threes is taken from Domoryad (37).

The yard-stick division is due to Leech (71); the quadrant division is due to Wichmann (72). We understand that J. C. P. Miller (working with the Cambridge EDSAC computer) has shown that Leech's division is optimal in the sense that the same number of points will *not* suffice for 37 units in place of 36.

We showed that the 25-point geometry could not lead to contradictions, by establishing a correspondence between this geometry and a related form of co-ordinate geometry of the ordinary type: a similar procedure can give models of non-Euclidean geometries in terms of reinterpreted concepts of Euclidean geometry. This serves to show that neither type of geometry is more logically valid than the other: it establishes that there is no hope of deriving the parallel postulate (or its equivalent) as a consequence of the other postulates; for these others apply alike to the original concepts and to the reinterpretations, whereas the parallel postulate applies in one case and not in the other. These representations of non-Euclidean geometries are discussed in (30).

Cubism and Colour Arrangements

Our treatment of the Tantalizer type of puzzle derives from an article in *Eureka*, ostensibly by one F. de Carteblanche (73). In a note in the *Mathematical Gazette*, we speculated on his relation to Blanche Descartes (of the counterfeit coins): we received a letter—in French of almost convincing perfection—in which our author purported to claim the other as his wife; but we think that this couple are one person more strictly than in the legal sense alone.

The six-cube puzzle is described in a booklet by Wyatt (74) which is still in print: the suggestion to use spots as on dice is made for another version, in a later booklet (75) which is out of print; we were indebted to his daughter for the loan of a copy.

We must take this opportunity to state that a four-cube puzzle has recently been on sale which is *not* just another form of the standard Tantalizer. This has cubes with the specifications (RR, RB, YG), (RY, RB, GB), (RY, YG, BB), (RB, YG, YB). Readers can readily use our methods to show that this puzzle has two distinct but closely related solutions.

We must also make clear that our closing remarks made reference to our elder daughter: our younger daughter must now have the credit for solving both Tantalizers—old and new—at the age of 9.

Gamesman, Spare that Tree

We have described our chosen games as 'games of perfect information with no chance moves': strictly, we should add that they have a 'stop rule' which secures that they cannot continue indefinitely. Here we use the terminology of von Neumann and Morgenstern (76) and of other works which consider a theory of games in the sense in which mathematicians now commonly use this phrase. It may be well to warn readers that most of these works will deal with very different topics from what we consider here.

We have considered some varied examples of one type of game— actually, the simplest type: and within this type we regard interesting differences of detail as a merit. The mathematical game-theorist will prefer to point out that in principle he can reduce any such game to a game of two moves only, by requiring each player in turn to state— once for all—what he proposes to do in all the possible eventualities which may arise; two such responses will specify what moves would actually take place, and what the final result would be.

Details within this last framework—and difficulties of practical application—are then of little interest to a theorist who takes this viewpoint: summarily dismissing them, he will go on to investigate games of more complicated types, which raise other questions which interest him more. His aim is to move along main roads to the frontiers; we are content to explore paths which have other attractions of their own.

Wythoff's game is the same as a Chinese national game—*tsyanshidze* —described by Domoryad (37). Coxeter (77) indicates that our proof of the general rule for safe positions was anticipated by Hyslop and by Ostrowski: the proof in (27) is more lengthy. Our consideration of the *misère* variant of this game may be new. Golden section is considered in (4), which gives other references: le Corbusier has described his *Modulor* in (78).

Wythoff's own paper (79) invites the consideration of other games with similar rules. One possibility is to retain arbitrary equal removals as one alternative, but to make the other alternative the removal *of an even number* from a single heap: there are then two distinct games, according as the total number of objects—initially, and therefore subsequently also—is even, or odd. Favourable positions are then given by rejecting fractions from even multiples of $0.7071\ldots = 1/\sqrt{2}$ and of $1.7071\ldots = 1 + 1/\sqrt{2}$, in the first case, and from the corresponding odd multiples, in the second. Most—but not all—of the higher favourable positions then carry over to the *misère* games.

The earliest—and simplest—type of impartial game goes back at least as far as Bachet (17): here there is one pile, in effect, and additions (or removals) can be chosen arbitrarily up to and including a fixed upper limit n: the winner here ensures that his move and the preceding move will together add (or remove) a total of $n+1$, once he knows that continuation of this procedure will ultimately terminate with a winning move.

Variants of this can give games (not necessarily impartial) which readers may like to explore—seeking regularities which they may try to prove generally applicable. One possibility is to take an odd number, initially, and choose the winner not in terms of who takes the last object, but in terms of who has collected an even (or odd) number at the end. Sprague (52) shows one way to treat this.

Another possibility is to prohibit successive use of the same number (by either player, or jointly by them both) or to limit the total number of times a particular number may be used.

(This latter variant is conveniently played with the use of a selection of cards from one or more packs. When the operation of the restriction is deftly concealed in initial demonstrative play, a victim can be deceived into thinking that the strategy as for unrestricted repetition is sufficient. In a known form of petty swindle, he is allowed to realize his mistake only after his false confidence—and cupidity—have led him to agree to (or propose) a raising of the stakes. Perhaps we had best give no explicit reference for this.)

Mott-Smith (12) considers a similar game where the chosen number is selected by giving a 90° turn to a cubical die whose faces are marked in the customary way: two numbers (totalling to 7) are then unavailable, at each move—those on the upper and lower faces of the die.

'Nim' you say—and 'Nim' it is

Our deepest indebtedness is to a paper by Grundy (80): this considers the game which now bears his name; it also describes the system for labelling positions which allows more complicated impartial games to be discussed in terms of the theory of Nim, if inability to move is the mark of a loser. Some similar ground is covered by Holladay (81).

Applications to many individual games of related type—specified by a compact terminology—have been made by Guy and Smith (82): there is a more popular account of some of this (concealed under a cryptic title) from the pen of our problematic Blanche Descartes (83).

Several other games are related to Nim, or explained in similar terms, by Sprague (52): we amplified a little of the theory, in our translation of his work into English; and we have given a more unified and detailed treatment to several of his games, in this present book. One of these has its basis in some quite severely mathematical work by Welter (84).

Grundy's work provides a unifying framework for many earlier discoveries. The theory of Nim was given by Bouton (85): Dudeney makes the *misère* game No. 396 of (5), without explicitly noting final-phase distinctions in his solution. In (6), Dudeney gave the name Kayles to a game which started with the second object removed from a row of thirteen: this has a form of ideal play based on symmetry considerations, with one player creating a situation where he can always continue with a symmetrical counterpart to any choice made by his opponent; the like is true if Kayles is played with a ring of objects, rather than a row.

The revised Rouse Ball (1) refers to progress made by Goldberg, who noted connexions between a more generalized Kayles and positions in Nim. Ultimately, Grundy's method was applied in (82), to provide a complete general theory for Kayles—since the heap labels are ultimately periodic, here—and for some other games where heaps may vary in number as the game proceeds.

Theory such as we have given has enabled many computers to be programmed to play games, using various input and output facilities: a Nim programme is almost a commonplace; and at least one computer has a Kayles programme.

For a computer which was our own concern, we used a game with some resemblance to Grundy's game: groups had to be divided unequally by *removing* single pieces (actually by using switches to put out lights); the piece removed had not to be at either end of a group, and not to be the middle piece of an odd-numbered group. The machine could let the player play first; for there were twenty lights in the row. (This became known as M'Ginty's game: it started life with the more classical designation *Viginti!*)

Two players could play one another with the machine as umpire: it would refuse illegitimate moves, and could indicate the conclusion and the final result. Alternatively, a single player could challenge the machine, and was given a remote (and evanescent) chance to defeat it: readers may apply the Grundy theory to this game; they should consider what can happen if a group of nine is—temporarily—assumed to have the (incorrect) label 2.

Ten Divisions Lead to Easter

Easter is considered in earlier editions of (1), in a chapter on 'Time and its Measurement' which was dropped from the 1939 revision. Rouse Ball here characterized the fundamental work of Clavius (86) as 'prolix but accurate': we are more inclined to allow that Clavius knew what had to be put on record in the circumstances of his time. He had to combat misunderstandings and objections, and did not spare his efforts— he discredits Scaliger by disposing of his circle-squaring, as well as of his views on Easter!

The paper by Gauss is reprinted—together with his manuscript correction—in his collected works (87). The paradoxical Easter of 1845 produced a discussion of the whole question of Easter by De Morgan (88), in an almanac for that year; and we have a later account from a high dignitary of the Church of Ireland (89). Those who have recourse to the *Encyclopaedia Britannica* will find a more ample discussion of the calendar in the eleventh and earlier editions. The first wholly arithmetical rule appeared anonymously, in (90).

The book by Stephen and Margaret Ionides (91) has a wealth of astronomical background material, attractively discussed; and two valuable and authoritative surveys have been included in explanatory supplements to official astronomical publications (92, 93). Fotheringham (94) discusses pre-Hellenic astronomy; Lange (95) discussed the conflicts of ecclesiastical and astronomical determinations; and Milankovitch (96) records some decisions on the calendar by the Orthodox Church.

Reference to Lange's paper provided the cases which we quote, where Easter is not astronomically justifiable at any position on the earth's surface. It is stated in (93) that such cases cannot arise; but we understand that this is now admitted as an error which is to be corrected. We also note that past issues of the *Nautical Almanac* chose to state the epact as 26 when in fact it was 25′ (as in 1916, 1935, and 1954): this, of course, makes no difference to Easter, or to the Easter full moon, but— strictly—it would locate some of the other full moons incorrectly, by one day, in the ecclesiastical calendar. We might hope for a more correct procedure in 1973 (and thereafter).

The lengths of the tropical year and of the synodic month, quoted for epoch 1900, are given in (97), deriving from work respectively by Newcomb and by Brown. Gregory's original decree—*Inter gravissimas curas*—is to be found in (86): the British Act of 1751 can be found in (98). (Displaying facsimiles of these at a lecture, we claimed a record for the first promulgation of a Papal Bull in a Scottish university since the Reformation!)

Problematic Lies and Unexpected Truths

The latest edition of Eddington's book seems to be the paperback (99): his paper in the *Mathematical Gazette* is (100). This was followed by the paper by Chapman (101).

There are several discussions of the examination paradox which we refrain from quoting, as we made nothing of them. Further explanation —in sympathy with what we have here—has been given by Martin Gardner (102). Gamow and Stern (103) give a picturesque presentation in terms of an execution: they seem to think it established that this could not take place.

Calculation of π is considered in (1), and in more detail by Hobson (104): the 100,000 decimal value is given by D. Shanks and Wrench, in (105). The 700-digit value of W. Shanks, much referred to in the past, is now known to be wrong in about 200 final digits—even as published in its third recension; see (106): but the current record for publishing wrong digits seems to be held by (107), which has the final 2,520 wrong, out of 10,000.

Lazzarini describes his methods and apparatus with loving care in (108): the discussion by Coolidge is in (109): this explains the method of determining the probability by summing expectations from segments obtained by dividing the needle. Would-be experimenters should pause before they rush to drop needles on grids of parallel lines: they should consider the possibilities of wheels with spokes, or grids of squares; and in (110) they will find how this can give them an even greater benefit than merely that of simultaneously performing several trials of the classic type. We refrain from listing the authors whom we regard as Lazzarini's victims: Mr. Gridgeman has been less sparing in the bibliography of his paper.

A Christmas Cracker with 100 Birds

When we first saw the problem which came out of the cracker, it stirred some memories of problems mentioned by Dickson in (111): this led us to the Chinese problems which we quote, and to the paper on Abu Kamil by Suter (112). We then recalled that Abu Kamil's opening remarks had been quoted by Ore in (113); and we were moved to try our hand at a translation of our own: continuing with Suter's German translation, we found the equivalent of our cracker problem among Abu Kamil's examples.

We had a photostat of *Propositiones ad acuendos juvenes*, taken from the *Works* of Alcuin (114), which we had referred to in connexion with ferry problems: we remembered that this contained other problems similar to the cracker problem; and when we investigated we again found one which was an exact counterpart. This gave us the basis for the article which we originally wrote on this topic: we remember remarking that the cracker slip had become as good as a cheque!

Some further work convinced us that the stated total of solutions for Abu Kamil's main problem was wrong; and from this we went on to consider Bhaskara's Indian problem (quoted by Suter). Our geometric methods are unlikely to be new; but we have not seen them used elsewhere.

We should finally mention that the original manuscript of the *Propositiones* is now in the Badische Landesbibliothek at Karlsruhe, where we recently had the pleasure of consulting it. The script is in a clear hand which adds no appreciable difficulty to the reading of the Latin text: photostats can readily be obtained, if desired.

REFERENCES

GENERAL RECOMMENDATIONS

0 SCHAAF, W. L., *Recreational Mathematics. A Guide to the Literature*. Third edition, Washington (National Council of Teachers of Mathematics), 1963.

1 ROUSE BALL, W. W., *Mathematical Recreations and Essays*. First edition, London (Macmillan), 1892. Eleventh edition, revised H. S. M. Coxeter, London (Macmillan), 1939. French translation, with additions, by J. Fitzpatrick, *Récréations mathématiques*, 3 vols., Paris (Hermann), 1907–9.

2 GARDNER, M., *Mathematics, Magic and Mystery*. New York (Dover), 1956.

3 GARDNER, M., *The Scientific American Book of Mathematical Puzzles and Diversions*. New York (Simon and Schuster), 1959. British edition, *Mathematical Puzzles and Diversions from Scientific American*, London (Bell), 1961.

4 GARDNER, M., *The Second Scientific American Book of Mathematical Puzzles and Diversions*. New York (Simon and Schuster), 1961. British edition, *More Mathematical Puzzles and Diversions from Scientific American*, London (Bell), 1963.

5 DUDENEY, H. E., *Amusements in Mathematics*. London (Nelson), 1917. New York (Dover), 1958.

6 DUDENEY, H. E., *The Canterbury Puzzles*. London (Nelson), 1908. New York (Dover), 1958.

7 DUDENEY, H. E., *Modern Puzzles and How to Solve Them*. London (Pearson), 1926. New York (Stokes), 1926.

8 LOYD, S., *Mathematical Puzzles of Sam Loyd* (ed. Martin Gardner). New York (Dover), 1959.

9 LOYD, S., *Mathematical Puzzles of Sam Loyd, Volume Two* (ed. Martin Gardner). New York (Dover), 1960.

10 ABRAHAM, R. M., *Winter Nights Entertainments*. London (Constable), 1932. New York (Dover), 1961, retitled *Easy-to-do Entertainments and Diversions with Cards, String, Coins, Paper and Matches*.

11 ABRAHAM, R. M., *Diversions and Pastimes. A Second Series of Winter Nights Entertainments*. London (Constable), 1933. New York (Dover), 1964, retitled *Diversions and Pastimes with Cards, String, Paper and Matches*.

12 MOTT-SMITH, G., *Mathematical Puzzles for Beginners and Enthusiasts*. Revised and corrected edition, New York (Dover), 1964.

13 GRAHAM, L. A., *Ingenious Mathematical Problems and Methods*. New York (Dover), 1959.

14 NORTHROP, E. P., *Riddles in Mathematics. A Book of Paradoxes*. New York (van Nostrand), 1944. Harmondsworth (revised Pelican Book edition), 1961.

Puzzles and Paradoxes

15 BEILER, A. H., *Recreations in the Theory of Numbers—The Queen of Mathematics Entertains.* New York (Dover), 1964.

16 HUTTON, C., *Recreations in Mathematics and Natural Philosophy.* 4 vols. London, 1803.

17 BACHET, C.-G., *Problèmes plaisants et délectables qui se font par des nombres.* Lyons, 1612. Fifth edition revised, simplified and augmented by A. Labosne, new printing with preface by J. Itard, Paris (Blanchard), 1959.

18 LUCAS, É., *Récréations mathématiques.* 4 vols. Paris (Gauthier-Villars), 1882–94. New printing, Paris (Blanchard), 1959.

19 SAINTE-LAGUË, A., *Avec des nombres et des lignes (Récréations mathématiques).* Third edition, Paris (Vuibert), 1946.

20 SAINTE-LAGUË, A., *Géométrie de situation et jeux.* Paris (Gauthier-Villars, Mem. des Sci. Math., Fasc. 41),* 1929.

21 KRAÏTCHIK, M., *La Mathématique des jeux.* Brussels (Stevens), 1930. English translation, *Mathematical Recreations,* New York (Norton), 1942. New York (Dover), 1953. Second edition, London (Allen and Unwin), 1960.

22 GHERSI, I., *Matematica dilettevole e curiosa.* Fourth edition, Milan (Hoepli), 1963.

23 TAHAN, MALBA (J. C. de Mello e Souza), *O homem que calculava.* Rio de Janeiro (Conquista), 1954. Spanish translation, *El hombre que calculaba,* Buenos Aires (Colegio) and elsewhere.

24 SCHUH, F., *Wonderlijke Problemen.* Zutphen (Thieme), 1943.

25 SPERLING, W., *Spiel und Spass fürs ganze Jahr.* Zürich (Müller), 1951.

26 SCHUBERT, H., *Mathematische Mußestunden.* Third edition, 3 vols., Leipzig (Göschen), 1907–9. Twelfth edition, one-vol. shorter version, revised J. Erlebach, Berlin (de Gruyter), 1964.

27 AHRENS, W., *Mathematische Unterhaltungen und Spiele.* 2 vols. Second enlarged and improved edition, Leipzig (Teubner), 1910–18.

28 LIETZMANN, W., *Lustiges und Merkwürdiges von Zahlen und Formen.* Breslau (Hirt), 1922. Eighth edition, Göttingen (Vandenhoeck and Ruprecht), 1955.

29 GÜNDEL, B., *Pythagoras im Urlaub.* Second edition, Frankfurt am Main (Diesterweg), 1959.

30 HILBERT, D., and COHN-VOSSEN, S., *Anschauliche Geometrie.* Berlin (Springer), 1932. English translation, *Geometry and the Imagination,* New York (Chelsea), 1952.

31 STEINHAUS, H., *Kalejdoskop matematyczny.* First Polish edition, Lwów/ Warsaw (Książnica-Atlas), 1938. English translation, *Mathematical Snapshots,* third edition, New York (O.U.P.), 1960.

32 JELEŃSKI, S., *Lilavati.* Warsaw (PZWS), 1956.

33 JELEŃSKI, S., *Śladami Pitagorasa.* Warsaw (PZWS), 1956.

34 PERELMAN, Ya. I., *Zanimatelnye zadachi i opiti.* Moscow. 1959.

35 PERELMAN, Ya. I., *Figures for Fun.* Moscow (Foreign Languages Publishing House), 1957.

36 KORDEMSKY, B. A., *Matematicheskaya smekalka.* Moscow, 1957. French translation, *Sur le sentier des mathématiques,* 2 vols., Paris (Dunod), 1963.

37 DOMORYAD, A. P., *Matematicheskiye igri i razvlecheniya.* Moscow, 1961. English translation, *Mathematical Games and Pastimes*, Oxford (Pergamon), 1964.

FURTHER REFERENCES

38 BERGE, C., *The Theory of Graphs.* London (Methuen), 1962.

39 ORE, O., *Graphs and Their Uses.* New York (Random House), 1963.

40 SCHELL, E. D., Problem *E.* 651. *Amer. Math. Monthly*, **52** (1945), 42, 397.

41 GROSSMAN, H., The Twelve-Coin Problem. *Scripta Math.*, **11** (1945), 360.

42 LITTLEWOOD, J. E., *A Mathematician's Miscellany.* London (Methuen), 1953.

43 DYSON, F. J., The Problem of the Pennies. *Math. Gazette*, **30** (1946), 231.

44 SMITH, C. A. B., The Counterfeit Coin Problem. *Math. Gazette*, **31** (1947), 31.

45 KELLOGG, P. J., and KELLOGG, D. J., Entropy of Information and the Odd Ball Problem. *J. Applied Physics*, **26** (1955), 1438.

46 KENDALL, P. M. H., and THOMAS, G. M., *Mathematical Puzzles for the Connoisseur.* London (Griffin), 1962.

47 DESCARTES, BLANCHE, The Twelve Coin Problem. *Eureka*, **13** (1950), 7, 20.

48 Brain-Teaser No. 118 (set by A. R. Legard). *Sunday Times*, 30 June and 7 July 1963.

49 GROSSMAN, H., Ternary Epitaph on Coin Problems. *Scripta Math.*, **14** (1948), 67.

50 HAMMERSLEY, J. M., A Geometrical Illustration of a Principle of Experimental Directives. *Phil. Mag.* (7), **39** (1948), 460.

51 HAMMERSLEY, J. M., Further Results for the Counterfeit Coin Problems. *Proc. Camb. Phil. Soc.*, **46** (1950), 226.

52 SPRAGUE, R. P., *Unterhaltsame Mathematik.* Brunswick (Vieweg), 1961. English translation, *Recreation in Mathematics*, London and Glasgow (Blackie), 1963.

53 HUNTER, J. A., and FUJIMURA, K., *Recreational Math. Mag.*, **6** (Dec. 1961), 47; **7** (Feb. 1962), 53.

54 FUJIMURA, K., *Recreational Math. Mag.*, **9** (June 1962), 49; **10** (Aug. 1962), 40.

55 TWEEDIE, M. C. K., A Graphical Method of solving Tartaglian Measuring Puzzles. *Math. Gazette*, **23** (1939), 278.

56 [ALVFELDT, O.], On the Mixing of Whisky and Soda in the Ratio 1:x for different small Whole-number Values of x. *Science Tools (Stockholm)*, **1** (1954), 16.

57 SYNGE, J. L., *Science: Sense and Nonsense.* London (Cape), 1951.

58 MAXWELL, E. A., *Fallacies in Mathematics.* Cambridge (C.U.P.), 1959.

59 BRADIS, V. M., MINKOVSKII, V. L., and KHARCHEVA, A. K., *Lapses in Mathematical Reasoning.* Oxford (Pergamon), 1963.

60 LIEBER, H. G., and LIEBER, L. R., *Modern Mathematics for T. C. Mits.* New York (Norton), 1944. London (Allen and Unwin), 1946.

Puzzles and Paradoxes

61 VEBLEN, O., and BUSSEY, W. H., Finite Projective Geometries. *Trans. Amer. Math. Soc.*, **7** (1906), 241.

62 WALKER, A. G., Finite Projective Geometry. *Edinburgh Math. Notes*, **36** (1947), 12.

63 RYSER, H. J., *Combinatorial Mathematics*. Mathematical Association of America, *Carus Monograph No. 14*: New York (Wiley), 1963.

64 KIRKMAN, T. P., On the perfect r-partitions of r^2-r+1. *Trans. Hist. Soc. Lancashire and Cheshire*, **9** (1857), 127.

65 GOODSTEIN, R. L., *Fundamental Concepts of Mathematics*. Oxford (Pergamon), 1962.

66 BUSSEY, W. H., Galois Field Tables for $p^n \leqslant 169$. *Bull. Amer. Math. Soc.*, **12** (1906), 22.

67 SINGER, J., A Theorem in Finite Projective Geometry and some Applications to Number Theory. *Trans. Amer. Math. Soc.*, **43** (1938), 377.

68 CHURCH, A., *A Finite Geometry*. (Multigraphed note of a lecture given at the Galois Institute of Mathematics, Long Island University.)

69 COXETER, H. S. M., *Introduction to Geometry*. New York and London (Wiley), 1961.

70 ROBINSON, G. DE B., *The Foundations of Geometry*. Second edition, Toronto (Univ. Press), 1946.

71 LEECH, J., On the Representation of 1, 2, ..., n by Differences. *J. Lond. Math. Soc.*, **31** (1956), 160.

72 WICHMANN, B., A Note on Restricted Difference Bases. *J. Lond. Math. Soc.*, **38** (1963), 465.

73 DE CARTEBLANCHE, F., The Coloured Cubes Problem. *Eureka*, **9** (1947), 9.

74 WYATT, E. M., *Puzzles in Wood*. Tenth printing, Milwaukee (Bruce), 1956.

75 WYATT, E. M., *Wonders in Wood*. Milwaukee (Bruce), 1946.

76 VON NEUMANN, J., and MORGENSTERN, O., *The Theory of Games and Economic Behaviour*. Third edition, Princeton (Univ. Press), 1953.

77 COXETER, H. S. M., The Golden Section, Phyllotaxis and Wythoff's Game. *Scripta Math.*, **19** (1953), 135.

78 LE CORBUSIER (Jeanneret, C. E.), *The Modulor*. London (Faber), 1961.

79 WYTHOFF, W. A., A Modification of the Game of Nim (1906). *Nieuw Archief voor Wiskunde* (2), **7** (1907), 199.

80 GRUNDY, P. M., Mathematics and Games. *Eureka*, **2** (1939), 6: reprinted **27** (1964), 9.

81 HOLLADAY, J. C., Cartesian Products of Termination Games. In *Contributions to the theory of games*, 3 (*Annals of Math. Studies*, **39**), ed. Dresher, M., *et al.*, Princeton (Univ. Press), 1957.

82 GUY, R. K., and SMITH, C. A. B., The G-values of Various Games. *Proc. Camb. Phil. Soc.*, **52** (1956), 514.

83 DESCARTES, BLANCHE, Why are Series Musical? *Eureka*, **16** (1953), 18.

84 WELTER, C. P., The Theory of a Class of Games on a Sequence of Squares, in Terms of the Advancing Operation in a Special Group. *Proc. Acad. Sci. Amst.* (A), **57** (1954), 194.

85 BOUTON, C. L., Nim, a Game with a Complete Mathematical Theory. *Annals of Math.* (2), **3** (1902), 35.

86 CLAVIUS, C., *Explicatio Romani Calendarii a Gregorio XIII P.M. restituti.* Rome, 1603. Reprinted in *Opera*, **5**, Mainz, 1612.

87 GAUSS, C. F., Berechnung des Osterfestes. In *Werke*, **6**, Göttingen (K. Ges. Wiss.), 1874. (Handschriftliche Bemerkung, p. 79.)

88 DE MORGAN, A., On the Ecclesiastical Calendar. *Companion to the Almanac for 1845*, London (Society for the Diffusion of Useful Knowledge).

89 BUTCHER, S., *The Ecclesiastical Calendar: its Theory and Construction.* Dublin (Hodges, Foster and Figgis), London (Macmillan), 1877.

90 [A New York correspondent], To find Easter 'for ever'. *Nature*, **13**, *338* (20 April 1876), 485.

91 IONIDES, S. A., and IONIDES, M. L., *One Day Telleth Another.* London (Arnold), 1939.

92 FOTHERINGHAM, J. K., The Calendar. In *The Nautical Almanac and Astronomical Ephemeris*, 1931–4: revised 1935–8: abridged 1939–41.

93 U.S. Naval Observatory and H.M. Nautical Almanac Office, *Explanatory Supplement to the Astronomical Ephemeris and the American Ephemeris and Nautical Almanac.* London (H.M.S.O.), 1961.

94 FOTHERINGHAM, J. K., The Indebtedness of Greek to Chaldean Astronomy. *The Observatory*, **51** (1928), 301.

95 LANGE, L., 'Paradoxe' Osterdaten im Gregorianischen Kalender und ihre Bedeutung für die moderne Kalenderreform. *SB. bayer. Akad. Wiss. (phil.-hist. Kl.)*, **9** (1928), 1.

96 MILANKOVITCH, M., Das Ende des julianischen Kalenders und der neue Kalender der orientalischen Kirchen. *Astr. Nachr.*, **220** (1924), 379.

97 ALLEN, C. W., *Astrophysical Quantities.* Second edition, London (Athlone Press), 1963.

98 Parliament of the United Kingdom, *The Statutes at Large, from Magna Charta to . . . George the Third inclusive* (in vol. 7 at p. 329). London, 1769.

99 EDDINGTON, A. S., *New Pathways in Science.* Cambridge (C.U.P.), 1935. Paperback edition, Ann Arbor (Univ. of Michigan), 1959.

100 EDDINGTON, A. S., The Problem of A, B, C and D. *Math. Gazette*, **19** (1935), 256.

101 CHAPMAN, H. W., Eddington's Probability Problem. *Math. Gazette*, **20** (1936), 298.

102 GARDNER, M., A New Paradox, and Variations on it, about a Man Condemned to be Hanged. *Scientific American*, March 1963, 144.

103 GAMOW, G., and STERN, M., *Puzzle-Math.* New York (Viking), 1958. London (Macmillan), 1958.

104 HOBSON, E., *Squaring the Circle.* Cambridge (C.U.P.), 1913. Reprint in *Squaring the Circle and other Monographs*, New York (Chelsea), 1953.

105 SHANKS, D., and WRENCH, J. W., Jr., Calculation of π to 100,000 Decimals. *Maths. of Computation*, **16** (1962), 76.

106 A[RCHIBALD], R. C., Approximations to π. *Math. Tables and other Aids to Computation*, **2** (1946), 143.

107 Oxford Mathematical Conference for Schoolteachers and Industrialists, *Abbreviated Proceedings.* London (The Times Publ. Co.), 1957.

Puzzles and Paradoxes

108 LAZZARINI, M., Un' applicazione del calcolo della probabilità alla ricerca sperimentale di un valore approssimato di π. *Periodico di Matematica* (2), **4** (1902), 140.

109 COOLIDGE, J. L., *An Introduction to Mathematical Probability.* Oxford (O.U.P.), 1925. New York (Dover), 1964.

110 GRIDGEMAN, N. T., Geometric Probability and the Number π. *Scripta Math.*, **25** (1960), 183.

111 DICKSON, L. E., *History of the Theory of Numbers,* **1.** Washington (Carnegie Instn.), 1919. Reprinted New York (Chelsea), 1961.

112 SUTER, H., Das Buch der Seltenheiten der Rechenkunst von Abu Kamil el-Misrī. *Bibliotheca Math.* (3), **11** (1910), 100.

113 ORE, O., *Number Theory and Its History.* New York (McGraw-Hill), 1948.

114 ALBINUS, F. (*otherwise* Alcuin), *Opera,* **2** (1), 440. Ratisbon, 1777.

INDEX

Puzzles and Paradoxes